FIVE
MILLION
TIDES

To Bex,

Lots of love

May 2019

FIVE MILLION TIDES

A BIOGRAPHY OF THE HELFORD RIVER

CHRISTIAN BOULTON

First published 2019

The History Press
The Mill, Brimscombe Port
Stroud, Gloucestershire, GL5 2QG
www.thehistorypress.co.uk

British Library Cataloguing in Publication Data.
A catalogue record for this book is available from the British Library.

ISBN 978 0 7509 9068 4

Typesetting and origination by The History Press
Printed and bound in Great Britain by TJ International Ltd.

CONTENTS

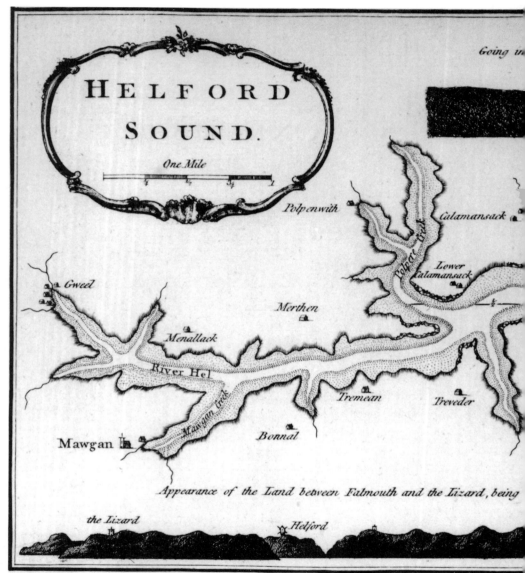

HELFORD SOUND.

One Mile

Going in

Polpenwith

Calamansack

Lower Calamansack

Gweel

Merthen

Menallack

Tolgare Creek

River Hel

Mawgan Creek

Tremean

Treveder

Mawgan

Bonnal

Appearance of the Land between Falmouth and the Lizard, being

the Lizard

Helford

London, Printed for R. Sayer & J. Bennett Map

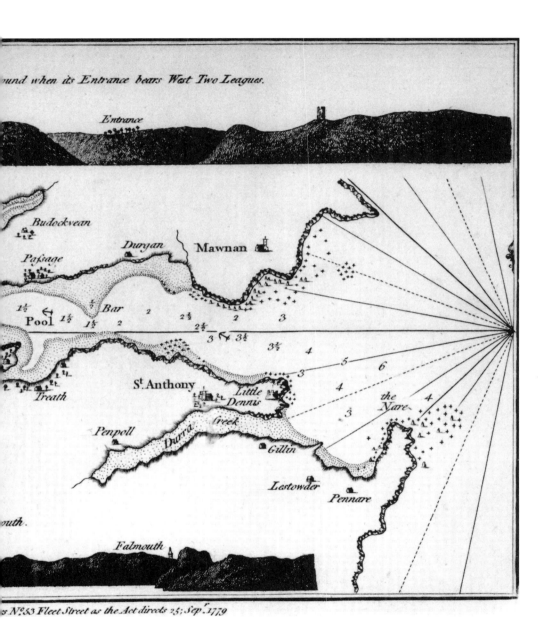

A 1779 chart of the Helford River. (Courtesy of David Barnicoat)

FOREWORD

I am phenomenally lucky in that I own a house that overlooks the Helford River estuary. For the past thirty years I have never ceased to be captivated by its ever-changing beauty. The dramatic tides, the boats, the crazy variety of weather throughout what seems like many more than four seasons, the human and animal activity (and no doubt the piscatorial action beneath the water) are never constant except in their physical and emotional impact.

And now at last Christian Boulton has come up with a book that captures the magic, history and geography of this idyllic stretch of water and its surroundings. Part of me would like to keep all this information a secret, but on balance I believe we Helford admirers have a duty to spread the word, which Christian has done with skill, panache, enthusiasm and authenticity.

Sir Tim Rice

PREFACE

In the introduction to his exhaustive *History of the Parish of Constantine in Cornwall*, the great Charles Henderson opined that 'no place in the parish has been rendered famous as the scene of some great episode in the history of Britain, and no native of Constantine has left his mark upon the history of the nation'.[1] While this work, published shortly before the outbreak of the Second World War, is an invaluable source of information without which this particular book would have been all the poorer, this sentence is to be disputed. Such an assertion could be casually applied to any of the little rural parishes around the Helford's shores, but to do so would be to apply a measure of worth in entirely the wrong way. The author thankfully went on to qualify his statement in so much as historical study 'does not need to be fed upon material of this sort', but this is not the point. In contrast to Charles Henderson's reasonable representation of a humble place, this book contests that there were times when the Helford River was actually one of the most important waterways in the British Isles. Furthermore, there are countless cities, towns and villages that are today celebrated for their historic significance that were still 1,000 years or more away from foundation when the Helford flourished.

Placing the river in the context of the wider world is central to this book, and that 'wider world' most certainly does not end in Britain or England, let alone Cornwall. Perhaps for that reason it is to be hoped that *Five Million*

Tides is welcomed as much by readers with little or no connection to the Helford as those fortunate enough to live close to its shores. As such, it is strongly recommended that those unfamiliar with the river overcome the customary urge to neglect the introduction as the detail contained therein will make that which follows far more accessible.

Admittedly, the Helford river has already been the subject of published study, both academic and popular. It has been a backdrop and inspiration for poetry and prose, biography and fiction. And yet the story is incomplete. In order to do justice to its remarkable life any account must not only rely upon hard documentary evidence, but also advocate theories where established facts are in short supply. There are too many silences to do otherwise. All that can be said in defence of this approach is that quietly contemplating a painting by Caravaggio, Gainsborough or Vermeer is far more rewarding than a cursory glance and guidebook interpretation.

However, this book does not set out to answer every question and nor could it achieve such an objective in any case. There is no great denouement at its conclusion. This is nothing to be disheartened by, not least as it would be a tragedy were all the river's mysteries accounted for. Some things are best left unexplained. As it is, we can be sure that no matter how many revelations about its history are uncovered in future, it will remain a beautiful and arcane sliver of water. Instead, *Five Million Tides* is a celebration of place, an unashamed eulogy to one of the most exquisite geographical entities in the world. It merely seeks to draw wider attention to a remarkable past that has been overlooked for too long.

It should be noted from the outset that this book seeks to place as much emphasis as possible on the Helford's ancient history. Why this should be so is due to the fundamental fact that not only did human beings interact with the river for a far greater length of time *before* written records began than they have since, but because that same interaction was so very intense compared to elsewhere in the British Isles during particular periods. Certainly, its post-medieval era was remarkably colourful and has left a great many relics, but that which preceded it was more extraordinary by far. John Burns, the early twentieth-century London MP, famously described the Thames as 'liquid history', but so too is the Helford.

Another disclosure that ought to be made in this preface is that this book is not overly concerned with the shifting fortunes of distinguished families and estates associated with the river, even though mention of notable individuals is required at times. There are several reasons for this, of which far better accounts of such matters already being in existence is the least important. Instead, the true protagonists are those who relied upon the river to survive. They are largely nameless, as the relatively poor of history always seem to be, but they have left the greater imprint upon it.

Although it is accepted that *Five Million Tides* may not pass muster with either the intractable historian or transient tourist in search of a pleasant place to take in a sea view, it is to be hoped that all in between discover something that alters their relationship with the river. It should never be taken for granted, nor assumed that it is immune from change. And to those who might wonder if the following chapters have anything to offer – to make them pause and reflect – then the author's own personal enlightenment in writing them should be of reassurance.

Lastly, I dedicate this book to my beautiful children, Alex and Kate. I sincerely hope that you treasure your future time upon the river as much as I have in the past. May you never forget our hours drifting upon the incoming tide, and warm evenings well spent crabbing from its many quays. I love you.

INTRODUCTION

The Helford has many siblings. All were born and developed during the age of rapid sea level rise that began around 11,000 years ago and which continues to this day. But as with all brothers and sisters, these drowned river valleys of Britain's far south-west are very individual in looks and character while evidently being of the same stock.

Some, like the Fal and Tamar estuaries, are larger and more imposing than the others. It is they that bear the scars of industrial activity and human endeavour more than most, although neither lacks splendour. Meanwhile, those of lesser proportions, such as the Dart and Fowey, have held on to most of their natural beauty and settled into genteel retirement after a post-medieval era of bustling maritime activity. Others, including the weather-beaten Hayle and Camel estuaries on Cornwall's north coast, seem more like distant cousins to their softer-edged south coast clan. The Helford, on the other hand, is the quiet member of the family whose story is less acknowledged and far less understood. It is the shy and enigmatic beauty overshadowed by its more celebrated kin, modest in size and one that has modestly kept its secrets.

The main body of the river lies, roughly speaking, on an east–west axis, with its broad mouth between Rosemullion Head and Nare Point opening out into the English Channel. During 'spring' tides, when the range between low and high water is at its greatest, around 30 million tonnes of water passes between these points over a six-hour-and-twelve-minute-period. Smaller 'neap' tides are more leisurely affairs, but they still provide the marine life of the river with fresh nutrients twice daily. In either case, a little under half of the volume also travels through a slender channel known as 'the narrows', which is to be found immediately downstream of the ancient ferry crossing between Helford and Helford Passage. The deepest point of the river is also at this point, a prehistoric channel scoured clean by the fast-moving currents of both ebb and flood. Even at the lowest astronomical tide the depth of 'the pool' is around 50ft, and the topographical contrasts of the river bed give rise to visible currents and eddies. The sea appears confused.

The narrows could also be said to mark the transition between the marine and the estuarine, although the relatively meagre inflow of freshwater ensures that the latter is not especially pronounced. Seaward, to the east, is effectively a large bay whose width varies between 600yd from Toll Point to The Gew, and 1½ miles between Rosemullion Head and Nare Point. Here the composition of the seabed fluctuates considerably between sand, shingle, rock and coralline maerl. It boasts some of the richest marine life anywhere around the British coast, including extensive beds of eelgrass (*Zostera marina*). This, a member of the ocean's only flowering plant family, is itself a habitat for numerous fish and invertebrates, not least the beautiful long-snouted seahorse (*Hippocampus ramulosus*). It is precious indeed.

Upstream to the west is a more secluded, sheltered realm whose defining feature is the ancient woodland that cushions it from the outside world. There are few places on Earth where large tracts of oak trees run down to the sea, but here is one of them. They are the Helford's aegis. In places their limbs not only touch the water but are sometimes submerged by it, leaving seaweed draped over ends of twigs as the tide recedes. It is a haunting sight in the faint, watery light of early morning.

These upper reaches are both permanent and temporary home to numerous species of wading bird: redshank, turnstone, and little egret among them. Here too are herons, 'the seven kings of Merthen' as C.C. Vyvyan once described them.[1] Indeed, the diversity of avian inhabitants along the course of the Helford is one of its defining characteristics: gulls, guillemots and cormorants hold dominion over the cliffs at its mouth, while oystercatchers and kingfishers lay claim to the creeks and feeder streams. All are regular visitors to the other's territory where birds of field and woodland compete with those of the sea for the attention of the listener. In the hour either side of dawn the sorrowful sound of curlew echoing between the dark wooded banks gives way to the brutal call of herring gull from above and murderous rasp of the little egret along the shoreline. To landward, the parting sounds of tawny owls are replaced by the ubiquitous dawn chorus and occasional croaks of ravens.

The shoreline of the river extends for more than 27 miles at high water, this distance including the various branches that fork out into the surrounding countryside. Each is fed by a small stream. Each has a distinctive character. Gillan Creek is the largest to be found along the southern shore, and it is also that closest to the open sea. Sometimes referred to as Carne Creek, few could possibly contest that it is one of the most glorious stretches of water in the British Isles, bordered as it is by a mix of rich woodland, centuries-old settlements and ancient fields. Over the course of little over a mile it undergoes a transformation from towering cliffs and hidden coves to a sylvan shelter from the worst of storms. The church of St Anthony, complete with its numerous architectural treasures, is its most celebrated landmark.

Travelling from east to west, the next branch along the south bank is that around which the houses of Helford village are clustered. In truth, it is more of a deep cove than a creek, and being barely halfway between open sea and tidal limit means that it has little in common with the river's other offshoots. But it is beautiful nonetheless. Meanwhile, less than a mile further upstream is the Helford's most famous branch: Frenchman's Creek. It was having spent a night anchored at its entrance aboard her yacht *Ygdrasil* in 1932 that Daphne du Maurier was inspired to write the novel of the same name. Indeed, her description of a visitor exploring it for the first time has defied the years since its publication. It surely will for a century or more to come:

Being a stranger, the yachtsman looks back over his shoulder to the safe yacht in the roadstead, and to the broad waters of the river, and he pauses, resting on his paddles, aware suddenly of the deep silence of the creek, of its narrow twisting channel, and he feels – for no reason known to him – that he is an interloper, a trespasser in time. He ventures a little way along the left bank of the creek, the sound of the blades upon the water seeming over-loud and echoing oddly amongst the trees on the farther bank, and as he creeps forward the creek narrows, the trees crowd yet more thickly to the water's edge, and he feels a spell upon him, fascinating, strange, a thing of queer excitement not fully understood.[2]

Yet further upstream, and still less disturbed, is Vallum Tremayne creek. Like Frenchman's, it runs almost directly north to south and lacks the twists and bends of most others. Excluding the nameless little pills puncturing the woods along the river's upper reaches, Vallum Tremayne is by far the smallest division. It is also the Helford's most enigmatic arm, the name suggestive of either past defensive qualities or it having once been the site of a mill.[3] Either explanation is at odds with the serenity to be found today, but that is something also true of the Helford in its entirety.

Barely the cry of an oystercatcher further upstream is Mawgan Creek. Aside from Gillan, it is the largest along the southern shore, and also that within which a sense of past human endeavour is most palpable. It is difficult to define whether it is the surrounding medieval fields, the pretty old bridges, or simply the tolling of the church bell above its upper reaches that induces this sensation, but the present surely falls behind as one navigates its channel southwards.

The final offshoot before the tidal limit is reached at Gweek is Ponsontuel Creek, the Helford's forgotten jewel. Aside from Vallum Tremayne, whose diminutive size and shallows deter most passers-by, Ponsontuel is the least frequented by waterborne traffic. Although its reclusive natural inhabitants would no doubt beg to differ, it is a great shame it is so often overlooked as its ambience is unique. To suggest that the surrounding woodland and steep banks induce an almost claustrophobic sensation would be an unflattering exaggeration, but there is certainly a sense of being enfolded and far from the modern world. It would no doubt have seemed even more isolated prior to 1922 when the ornamental Gweek Drive was opened as a public road above its western flank. And yet as its name almost certainly means 'bridge across the conduit' there is the implication of human tenure since time immemorial. Perhaps the little clapper bridge hidden from view in the woods holds the secret to its typonomic origin.

If the creeks along the south bank are greater in number, those along the north are greater in size. Heading back towards the river mouth, the first to be encountered, Polwheveral, is more than 1½ miles in length and even boasts its own subsidiary, Polpenwith. The name of the former probably means 'the lively waters'.[4] As with their counterparts to the south, these two tidal watercourses are less the haunt of people and more of wading birds skimming the water and probing the mud for nourishment. However, unlike its tree-cushioned counterparts to the south, Polwheveral feels open and spacious even if still hidden from the outside world – a paradox given that it was once a place of industry and enterprise during the early post-medieval period.

Lastly, Port Navas creek is today the gentrified branch of the Helford, although it has only taken on such an appearance in living memory. Many of the river's waterside houses are now to be found along its course, and the old quays from which granite was once shipped across the world are these days associated with pleasure rather than commerce. Helford creek is similarly enclosed by dwellings, but instead they almost all pre-date the twentieth century and were built by those who worked the sea. They are humble, and all the greater for it. As with Polwheveral, Port Navas creek meanders inland and divides into smaller offshoots with informal names such as Trenarth and Penpoll.

However, the Helford River as an entity is not merely defined by its waters and shoreline. Without the surrounding landscape by which it is enclosed it would not be the remarkable place it is. Here are to be found the communities that have contributed to its extraordinary story for more than a hundred generations. The estuary's enduring visual appeal is due to both astonishing natural beauty *and* the labours of people who once called it home.

Settlements of any appreciable size are non-existent within the river's catchment. Instead, the local population is relatively dispersed throughout a small number of villages and larger number of rural hamlets. The most 'populous' of those by the water is Gweek, today home to fewer than 700 permanent residents. Here are to be found the river's only remaining quays and wharves from which modest commercial activity is obvious, albeit only a fraction of that which would have been conducted during its zenith.

Port Navas, once an even smaller hamlet known as 'Cove', grew considerably during the early twentieth century, but still only boasts a population around 100 strong. Helford Passage saw similar development following the

Second World War, but is less peopled still save for the summer months. Also on the north bank is the tiny fishing village of Durgan, a place whose diminutive charm is only matched by the possible origin of its name – *Dowrgeun* is held by some to mean 'home of the sea dogs'. Indeed, fortunate souls may still catch a glimpse of an otter here on a calm winter's day when the leisure boats of the warmer months have forsaken their moorings. Alternatively, the more dispassionate might suggest it is the Cornish *Dowr Ganow*: the 'mouth of the river'.

Of course, the most conspicuous settlement by the water's edge is Helford itself. Indeed, it is that which is visible to approaching sailors before any other, and yet it is also sheltered from all but the most vicious of winter storms. It is unquestionably one of the prettiest villages in these islands, and still leaves those who happen across it as beguiled as the yachting correspondent of the *Daily Telegraph* in 1905:

> It is when you are cruising that you can enjoy Helford, when for days you can let your craft swing on the tide just above the bar. Helford, the little village, is simplicity itself. It drowses there in the warm sun, the air fragrant with roses, honeysuckle, and sweet-smelling creepers that hold the little white cottage walls in a clinging embrace. Fern, wild flax, and pine grow on the hillsides, and the river banks above are wonderfully carpeted with a scrub oak.[5]

However, beauty was not always the river's most defining characteristic. It had its dark side, too, even if it was a place of natural wonder. Nor was Helford village the peaceful and largely affluent community it became during the latter half of the twentieth century. Although a few still bravely harvest the sea, fishing once sustained almost all else. The people of Helford endured arduous and insecure short lives, each venture out into open water a risk that had to be taken if mouths were to be fed.

Aside from these waterside settlements (and those around the mouth of Gillan Creek), the vast majority who reside within the river's catchment area are to be found in the larger villages a short distance inland. With fewer than 2,000 residents apiece, Mawnan Smith and Constantine to the north are still by far the most significant. Despite being bordered by the sea on two sides, the former has always been predominantly an agricultural parish. In contrast, the latter grew in size not so much through the plough but more through pick and shovel, becoming a post-medieval hub of mining and granite quarrying.

The centres of population to the south are, like Mawnan, essentially built upon farming and its attendant crafts. These, from east to west, are St Anthony-in-Meneage, Manaccan, St Martin-in-Meneage and Mawgan-in-Meneage. All these villages have resident populations of fewer than 500, although their respective parishes also take in a great many smaller hamlets. The only others with any influence upon the river on account of their being the sources of feeder streams are St Keverne to the south and Wendron to the north. But the main body of the river is softer in geological terms, and thus visually, than the farthest places in which some of its tributaries rise.

Indeed, the Helford feels very different from the rest of Cornwall. It is within it, but not wholly of it. Its wooded creeks and safe anchorages are only 10 miles from the rugged cliffs of Lizard and Kynance Cove, but might as well be a 1,000. Fewer inhabited places by the sea are less alike than hamlets such as Durgan and the towns of the north coast. Nor could its immediate surroundings ever be said to even remotely resemble the uplands of Bodmin Moor or West Penwith. Moreover, the largest nearby centres of population, Falmouth to the north and Helston to the west, have no appreciable impact upon it, and the former is only visible from the headlands at the mouth. It is not 'on the road to anywhere', and for that reason has largely survived the ravages of twentieth- and twenty-first-century 'progress'.

But the river has its contrasts, too. Gazing across the gulf from north to south it is as if the wooded banks around Ponsence and Bosahan Coves exist within a different era to the more active shore between Helford Passage and Toll Point. The fields above seem more rustic and less affected by the passing of time even though their counterparts across the water are equally ancient. And while the north is the home of world-famous ornamental gardens visited by many thousands each year, the south is far less frequented. The paths are narrower, there are fewer footprints on the sand, and the woodlands are less disturbed by human voices.

Its promontories are also diverse in character. At Toll Point the backdrop is essentially agricultural, while Rosemullion Head is covered by the gorse from which it derives its name: *rhos* is Cornish for 'headland', and *melyn* means 'yellow'. And although bracken-capped Dennis Head boasts magnificent views of Falmouth Bay and beyond, nearby Nare Point slips gently into the sea as a plateau. But where the river divides at Groyne Point 3½ miles inland the landscape is wholly dominated by trees. Here, as the naturalist Oliver Rackham once observed, 'smooth wooded hillsides, subtly mottled with the different greens or browns of individual oak trees, sweep down to high water mark'.[6]

Those unfamiliar with the river are advised to view it from Mawnan Glebe, just as the antiquarian William Borlase did while sketching the view in 1736. Such a vista, from the cliffs at the mouth to calm waters in the protective embrace of woods and fields inland, helps the unacquainted understand the sense of place. After all, when viewed obliquely from elsewhere on the east coast of the Lizard Peninsula the Helford cannot even be discerned, let alone appreciated. Indeed, it is possible to gaze across to Goonhilly Downs from parts of Constantine and Mawnan parishes without observing the slightest trace of the water that lies between.

Many have attempted, with varying degrees of success, to summarise its charm – a challenging task given that there are so many features, both natural and man-made, which contribute to the whole. However, there is perhaps one often overlooked description that comes closest to being the perfect précis. Writing shortly before the outbreak of the First World War, the author and artist A.G. Folliott-Stokes described the river in the manner of someone who had stumbled across a Cornish Arcadia. It is succinct, yet difficult to surpass:

There is a peculiar charm about its wooded shores, its many secluded creeks, that wind far into the heart of the hills, its deep, clear water, and its delightful landing-places, where gnarled oak-stems are reflected in the smooth surface of the stream, and kingfishers dart like living jewels at one's approach. It is five miles from the entrance between Dennis and Rosemullion Heads to Gweek, which is as far as boats can go; and there are as many more miles of winding subsidiary creeks. And everywhere there is the charm of forest, of still water, of enfolding hills, and incomparable vistas. That evening the water was like a mirror; smoke rose straight and blue from an occasional cottage, the shores were echoing with the songs of thrushes and blackbirds, a heavy-looking cormorant flew up the river at a train's pace, and a heron stood motionless on one leg close to a spit of land crowned with some palm-shaped pines. It was a scene of great beauty.[7]

A similar picture could be painted in words more than a century later. It is to be hoped that with the determination of generations to come it will retain all of the natural wonder that inspired not only Folliott-Stokes, but Daphne du Maurier, Sir Arthur Quiller-Couch and others. The Helford has seen enough change and upheaval over the past 6,000 years and ought to be spared any more. This is its story.

1

RISE

Gilbert White was not the only 'parson naturalist' of the Georgian age. *The Natural History and Antiquities of Selborne* may be the most celebrated work of such a figure, but the musings of countless others are today confined to dusty journals in libraries and private collections throughout Britain. One such lesser-known religious polymath was the Rev. John Rogers, Rector of Mawnan for almost thirty years from 1807.

An industrious character even by nineteenth-century standards, this epitome of the country gentleman intellectual was, amongst other things, an accomplished linguist and staunch advocate of safer working practices in Cornish mines. Educated at Eton and finally at Oxford, he had even penned *On the Origins and Regulations of Queen Anne's Bounty* relating to the incomes of more impoverished members of the clergy. However, of all things, geology and botany were his principal interests, as his contributions to *Transactions of the Royal Geological Society of Cornwall* attest.

One of these papers, entitled 'Notice of Wood and Peat found below high water-mark at Mainporth in Cornwall', concerns a remarkable discovery at a beach at the northern boundary of his parish. Published in 1832, it was most likely founded upon observations made on 15 February of that same year – had he chosen to walk the mile or so from the vicarage just a day before or after, the brine-soaked timbers he encountered would likely have remained unseen below the waves:

The oak is part of a stump, standing about a foot above the level of the sand, apparently in the place where it grew. It is just one hundred yards below high water-mark. On further examination I found the root of an oak laid bare, thirty yards below the stump: and at a spade's depth below the surface of the sand. Immediately adjoining the roots of oak is the peat; I could trace the root extending about seven feet horizontally. The peat was evidently formed in marshy ground, and contains, I think, the leaves and roots of the *iris pseudacorus*-the common yellow flag which grows in the adjoining marsh.[1]

That such lost woodlands composed of oak, alder, and hazel should be under the sea begged the obvious question: why? To this conundrum he provided three possible explanations: that there had been subsidence of the soil; that the trees had once been protected from the water by an embankment; and, lastly, that the actual sea level had once been far lower. Rogers doubted the first for simple geological reasons and was even less positive about the second. As for the third, he at least resisted the obvious ecclesiastical temptation to cite Noah and the Book of Genesis.

This submerged forest still survives, uncovered very occasionally when both spring tides and suitable sand-shifting sea conditions combine. And yet its continued presence hundreds of years after the publication of his essay is unsurprising; it had, after all, already withstood the elements for around six millennia by 1832. Another couple of centuries are neither here nor there to such relics, not that John Rogers had any reasonable idea of their extraordinary age at the time. However, when a Mr F.S. Roberts reported to the Royal Geological Society of Cornwall sixty years later, the sheer antiquity of the preserved woodland had become more established. Visiting after a sequence of easterly gales had stripped the beach clean of its sand, he observed that a 'springy and spongey' mass lay beneath the surface and that it contained 'a number of trees lying in various directions and positions; some of them from twelve to twenty feet in length'. Taking the invaluable opportunity to dig, he also uncovered a jawbone that a German palaeontologist later pronounced, almost certainly incorrectly, to be of the prehistoric 'horse' *Prodremotherium elongatum*.[2]

Maenporth, just to the north of the Helford, is not the only place in the area where submerged forests have been discovered. Construction of a pier at Market Strand in Falmouth during 1871 uncovered what would once have been young oak, beech and birch trees.[3] And within the river itself, traces of 'fossilised' woodlands have been recorded in Gillan Creek.[4] These venerable remains offer us a glimpse into a lost time, the ability to touch a once-living organism from an age more than four millennia before recorded history in the British Isles began. The Great Pyramid of Giza in Egypt was still more than 1,500 years away from construction when these natural wonders flourished by the water's edge. The great cities of Europe were an even more distant spot on time's horizon. They are amongst the oldest *in situ* large organic remains in the country.

Although they are natural objects of wonderment in and of themselves, we must contemplate whether human eyes ever laid sight upon them while in leaf rather than as dark, salt-sodden, fallen hulks. Did men, women and children walk between them, through the dense undergrowth that would once have lain beneath their canopy? More importantly, just how far back in time does mankind's relationship with the Helford actually go? Unfortunately, to even begin to answer such questions it is necessary to rely as much on the theoretical as the evidential.

Like the Rev. Rogers, John Lubbock, 1st Baron Avebury, was a man of many talents. Although much of his working life revolved around matters of finance, his passion was undoubtedly for the natural world. Indeed, in 1881 he became president to both the Linnean Society of London and the British Association – the latter now known more helpfully as the British Science Association. He was close friends with Charles Darwin, too, and was thus unsurprisingly a fierce proponent of the Theory of Natural Selection. Today, however, if his name should be mentioned in academic circles it is more likely to be associated with his enthusiasm for archaeology than all else.

Victorian naturalists had a tendency to give their works overly long titles, and Lubbock was no exception to the rule. *Pre-historic Times, as Illustrated by Ancient Remains, and the Manners and Customs of Modern Savages*, published in 1865, remains one of the most influential books on prehistory ever written, and its longevity bears testament to his perspicacious mind. We still use the terms he proposed within it, the Neolithic and Palaeolithic, to describe the earlier and later stone ages. Notwithstanding that a third, the Mesolithic 'middle', would subsequently come between them as a point of reference, archaeology certainly owes a great deal to John Lubbock's original terminology.

The Palaeolithic – derived from the Greek words *palaeo* and *lithos* meaning 'old' and 'stone' – is a period of human time almost too vast to fully comprehend. Although it covers around 3 million years, very little is known of it. It does not sing loudly, but whispers from the corner of the room. It is the era in which human beings evolved in both body and mind, characterised by the use of stone, wood and bone tools and their relative increase in complexity over time. Given its enormity it has been necessary to divide the Palaeolithic into Lower, Middle and Upper divisions, each of these being divided once again based upon geography and variations in stone working imperceptible to the casual observer.

For reasons of typological convenience, the Lower Palaeolithic is generally held to have concluded around 300,000 years ago. When it might have commenced, on the other hand, will forever remain moveable depending upon what extraordinary remains might be found in the future. Here we find, amongst others, the Oldowan, which represents the earliest evidence of stone tool creation, and the Acheulean, in which the development of distinctive oval hand axes took place. These are the eras of *Homo Habilis* and *Homo Erectus*, some of our most distant hominin ancestors. It is also within the Lower Palaeolithic that the oldest surviving bone fragments of our own species, *Homo Sapiens*, have been found.

However, the hominid activity during the oldest part of the 'Old Stone Age' was not something confined to the African continent. Much as the tide had uncovered ancient remains at Maenporth for the Rev. Rogers to survey in 1828, so did it for archaeologists on the Norfolk coast in 2013.[5] When a freshly exposed sediment layer at Happisburgh was studied, it was found to contain the footprints of both adults and children who had walked together across what had then been the upper reaches of an estuary. They had made the journey around 800,000 years ago. But just as the sea had revealed these precious relics of early human activity it cruelly took them away. Within two weeks the inexorable action of the tides had destroyed the soft sediment, although not before they had been examined in detail. There were around fifty prints in total, all walking in a southerly direction, and made by beings perhaps only a little over 5ft in height. Anthropologists speculated that they might have belonged to a family searching for shellfish at low tide. Maybe they had ventured out from an island camp upon which they would have been safe from predators. Alas, as with many Palaeolithic discoveries, nothing is remotely certain.

Many other remnants of that far-off age have been found in the British Isles, and specifically from the more climatically benign phases of the Cromerian interglacial period. Flint artefacts unearthed at Pakefield in Suffolk may well be in the region of 700,000 years old that, together with the Happisburgh footprints, suggests that what is today East Anglia was a *relatively* busy place during the Pleistocene.[6]

Regrettably, no such traces of human life from that distant time have ever been discovered in Cornwall, let alone around the Helford. It is unlikely they ever will be. It seems evident that very early human activity in the British Isles was heavily weighted towards the east of present-day England. This is unsurprising. Rather than a gradual process of colonisation, the 'Old Stone Age' was a series of temporary incursions into what would *one day* become the British Isles as the climate waxed and waned. The low-lying plains now beneath the North Sea and eastern English Channel were once a Palaeolithic thoroughfare.

These ancient immigrants undertook the journey solely in pursuit of survival. It is therefore unsurprising that the majority of our nation's Palaeolithic finds have been made in the east and south-east; a relatively flat landscape where the hunter-gatherer would maximise their chances of survival. Trawlers in the North Sea often haul in prehistoric 'catches' of bones from mammoth, bison, elk and even rhinoceros. These were happy hunting grounds indeed, and it is to be expected that archaeological finds are concentrated on the fringes that have remained above the waves.

However, it would be foolish to entirely discount the possibility of human habitation as far west as the present-day Helford river area in Palaeolithic times, and especially during the 'upper' period between 50,000 and 10,000 years ago. It is entirely reasonable to suggest that sites occupied by pioneers upon a coastal plain now lie unseen beneath sea and sediment. A child collecting pebbles on a Cornish beach may yet one day rewrite the story of the south-west peninsula with a solitary piece of curious worked flint; Palaeolithic tools are notoriously difficult to identify as they often lack the definitive lines and fine working of later Stone Age crafting. Most importantly, there would have been several windows of opportunity for early humans to reach the area of land that constitutes present-day Cornwall, and not least during the warm interglacial period known as the Ipswichian which reached its peak around 125,000 years ago. This was the time when hippopotamuses were supposed to have bathed in the waters of the Thames and other British rivers, so perhaps the concept of the occasional adventurous prehistoric soul on the Lizard Peninsula should not be considered too fanciful.

If we are to believe that the west of Cornwall was too far from the overland bridge from continental Europe, the same must have been true of North and West Wales. And yet in both places relics have been found that prove otherwise. The Red Lady of Paviland – actually the skeleton of a young man – found in a cave on the Gower Peninsula in 1823 lived around 33,000 years ago.[7] More remarkable still were the remains of a young Neanderthal boy discovered at Bontnewydd in North Wales during 1981, and subsequently found to be around 230,000 years old.[8] Their forebears clearly conquered geological barriers no less challenging than those to reach Cornwall. And yet these scraps of circumstantial evidence are but an aside when one takes into account that the south-west of England possesses two revered Palaeolithic sites of its own: Gough's Cave at Cheddar in Somerset, and Kents Cavern near Torquay in Devon. Are we to dismiss the possibility that the ancestors of whoever fashioned the tools found at the latter were able to migrate a mere 70 miles further west over a period of 1,000 years or more? It is inconceivable that they did not. To do so would require that we overlook the fact that not one of the three glacial maximums to affect the British Isles in the past half a million years – the Anglian, Wolstonian, and Devensian respectively – resulted in ice sheets covering present-day Cornwall. This is not to suggest that the environment at such times was conducive to human habitation, but simply that the thaw would have set in sooner around the south-western coastline than elsewhere.

For now, though, we must content ourselves with the knowledge that the feet that trod the ground and crossed the early streams of the Helford River area between 500,000 and 12,000 years ago were less those of people, and more of deer and auroch. The wolf and bear were kings of the ancient landscape here, not man. On the basis of known finds and their relative frequency across the British Isles, it is patently more reasonable to conclude that the west of Cornwall was merely 'quieter' in Palaeolithic terms rather than being wholly devoid of human voices. After all, some flint artefacts bearing the hallmarks of being fashioned in that far-off time have indeed been pulled from the ground in the past few centuries: a Greensand chert hand axe was found on the Lizard Peninsula during the nineteenth century, while flint fragments and flakes discovered just south of the Helford near St Keverne are also of probable Palaeolithic origin.[9] Other lithics are said to be hidden from public view in private collections.

Of all stone tools of truly exceptional age known to have come to light within the realm of the Helford, the most notable is a simple hand axe from Trewardreva, Constantine. This precious implement, pale in colour and of perfect size and form for an adult palm, is more 200,000 years old and the most ancient artefact in the Royal Cornwall Museum. If only its creator could see it now. Surely only the most sceptical and sober historian would thus refuse to entertain the idea that the area was at least fleetingly visited by early man, *Homo sapiens* or otherwise, during the Old Stone Age. Regrettably, sobriety is very much required for those optimistic of definitive chance finds in future. Archaeological study is predicated upon context and, lamentably, the stratigraphic elements of surrounding rock and soil for *possible* Palaeolithic Cornish artefacts found to date are disputable. Without such compelling evidence we must accept the prospect that they came to rest in their respective locations during more recent times. We simply cannot draw firm conclusions that pass the rigorous tests required, no matter how much we might wish to. But it should not prevent us from hoping.

Unfortunately, while these deep Palaeoliths are potentially of immense significance in a wider geographical sense, they are of little relevance to the story of the river. This is not due to doubts over archaeological provenance, but for a far more fundamental reason: when they were fashioned by human hands the Helford did not yet exist. Its story – our story – was still thousands of years away from its opening lines.

For a man of science to have a crater on the moon named after him is an honour indeed, but the Swiss geologist Jean-Andre Deluc was more than worthy on several counts – not least his having been made a Fellow of the Royal Society in 1773, to which he often contributed papers for its publication, *Philosophical Transactions*.

Deluc lived to the ripe old age of 90, an almost unheard of achievement for someone born during the 1700s, and appears to have spent the vast majority of it in rude health given his propensity for extended tours around Europe. One of the last of these sojourns included Devon and Cornwall where, by 1 August 1806, he had reached the Helford River. His host during his stay, the Rev. Richard Polwhele, appears to have been rather fond of the then 79-year-old, describing him as a 'florid healthful old man – always cheerful – enthusiastically attached to the object of his pursuit'.[10] Deluc had once described himself as 'tracing the history of the Earth itself, from its own monuments', and considered what he saw before him without fear of contravening the received wisdom of the time. He had put his mind to many great matters during his life, and had even acted as reader to Queen Charlotte for more than forty years, but the complexities of rock and stone were his principal concern. The earth beneath his feet was a riddle he sought to solve.

In *Geological Travels: Travels in England,* Vol. III, Deluc recalled his couple of days in the company of Polwhele, describing the journey he took along the southern bank of the river as one 'continually ascending and descending'. Crossing 'combes which terminated at the gulph', he was particularly struck by the heavy clay soils found in the area, but most of all by the inappreciable quantities of freshwater that trickled into the creeks:

At Gweek I saw a promontory terminating a ridge of hills, from one side of which the Hel arrives, and from the other a brook that joins it; but these when united form only a small stream, though flowing in a very wide space. We were told by people on the spot that at the spring tides the water rises up to this point; that when it ebbs, it leaves uncovered a space of seven miles in length, extending on the outer side of the gulph, and consisting entirely of mud, through which the little river preserves its course; and that this ground is still continuing to be raised by the sediments of the river and of the tides. Thus it cannot certainly have been by the actions of these waters that an arm of the sea has here been formed between hills.[11]

He was correct, or at least up to a point. Then as now, the relatively modest volume of water entering the creeks seems barely adequate to cut a valley as wide as the Helford. But, in mitigation, Deluc neither had the benefit of discoveries in climatology made in recent years, nor full understanding of the vast expanse of time over which they had been flowing without abeyance. He was, however, astute enough to appreciate that the river is precisely where it is on account of a remarkable sequence of geological events.

That which lies beneath the estuary and its surrounding landscape is a melange of rock types that vary with extraordinary regularity, no matter where one begins and whichever direction one then chooses to proceed. Without these variations, and the sequence of events that bore them, it could never have been formed. The geology directly below the main body of the Helford is entirely sedimentary or metasedimentary in origin, largely being siltstones, sandstones and mudstones of the 'Portscatho Formation' – a slender band that also underlies the Carrick Roads and River Fal. These unassuming slates, sometimes referred to as Greywacke, are far more ancient than the granite for which Cornwall is so famous. Nearly 400 million years old, they were formed by the compression of earthy detritus deposited by ancient watercourses.[12] Subsequently becoming part of an abyssal plain at the bottom of a primeval ocean, these rocks existed when what would one day become the south-west of England was still south of the equator. They may appear mundane, but almost every pebble to be found upon the river's beaches has been on a truly momentous journey.

This slow, inexorable process of sedimentation continued through the late Devonian Period and into the Carboniferous; a time before the emergence of the dinosaurs when only the most primitive of vertebrates had colonised the land. However, this relatively stable geological period came to an abrupt end around 290 million years ago with a colossal mountain-building event that would ultimately result in the creation of the supercontinent Pangea. The effects on what is now the British Isles were profound. Although the Variscan Orogeny owes its name to an ancient term for a part of Saxony in modern-day Germany, few places derive as much of their actual form from this seismic event as Devon and Cornwall. Its relics are Dartmoor, Bodmin Moor, Land's End, and all other granite outcrops of the south-west peninsula. These are the observable summits of the vast Cornubian Batholith, which sits beneath these exposed tips like an iceberg hidden below the waterline. And yet there are disparities even within the granite mass itself: at Land's End the rock is almost exclusively coarse-grained, while that underlying St Austell varies between coarse, fine, and rarer medium-grained types.

Closer to the Helford's shores, the primary consequence of the Variscan Orogeny was the formation of minor faults: the Carrick Thrust along its northern edge cutting through Polwheveral and Port Navas Creeks; the Veryan Thrust below the southern shore dividing the main river from Gillan Creek; and the more distant Lizard Thrust slicing through much of the Helford's lower catchment. All are inextricably linked to the disproportionate number of tiny earthquakes that affect the area. Most are barely noticeable, but on occasions they are manifestly obvious if not at all threatening. Almost all those recorded since the beginning of the twentieth century have been centred close to Polwheveral and Polpenwith Creeks. A few have occurred beneath the lands south of the river, with one near Mawgan-in-Meneage in April 1898 resembling 'the roll of some heavy conveyance, with a distinctly felt vibration within a radius of several miles'.[13] They are the faint echoes of what occurred all those millions of years ago; the Variscan Orogeny still murmurs from time to time.

The almost circular Carnmenellis granite outcrop to the north was fundamental to the genesis of the infant Helford. Its observable legacy can be clearly seen where the strata of the sedimentary rocks along the shoreline have been lifted to rest at unnatural angles. Through these tilted beds of siltstones and coarse-grained sandstones are ancient fissures filled with once molten rock whose names could easily have been penned by a fantasy novelist – Elvan and Lamprophyre Dykes occur in several places throughout the Helford River basin. The former include the Greenstone favoured by Neolithic axe makers and medieval stonemasons alike, while the latter is a darker and more austere rock than its title might have one believe. Most importantly, it was this same granite intrusion that delivered later human inhabitants the mineral wealth upon which settlements were founded and prospered.

To the north of the river, in the parishes of Constantine and Mawnan, it is possible to sense the change from gentler metamorphic geology to the harder granitic type over a short distance. In some places one might observe the change along the length of a single field. The soil closer to the shore tends to possess a higher clay content, but the ground quickly becomes darker, coarser, and more free draining the further north one moves towards the Carnmenellis outcrop. Unsurprisingly, these localised variations influenced the vernacular architecture until the advent of brick and block, and for some length of time afterwards in places. For thousands of years the walls of houses were built exactly from what they stood upon, and it is no surprise to discover that most of the oldest buildings in parishes such as Mawnan and Manaccan are made of cob, slate killas, or a combination of both. Meanwhile, the pre-twentieth century buildings of Constantine are largely dominated by granite from the same local quarries that once directly, or indirectly, employed most of its inhabitants. These 'upland' cottages are robust in stature and hard-edged, yet still pleasing to the eye where original features have been retained. Those of 'lowland' cob are undeniably prettier – each as unique as the hands that moulded them – and were usually built immediately alongside the very finest source of clay in the parish. Most that survived demolition or decay have since been roofed with slate in the past century, but a few are blessed with the thatch they were intended to support. As Sabine Baring-Gould once opined, cob is 'the warmest, snuggest, driest material of which a *house* can be built; a material, which when used as a garden wall, ripens peaches, grapes, apricots on its warm surface. It sucks in the sun's rays as a sponge, and gives out the heat all night. Stand by a *cob* wall after a bright day, when white frost is forming on the grass, and you feel a warm exhalation streaming from the dry clay'.[14]

Although cob-built cottages are common on both sides of the river, their prevalence declines rapidly at the point at which the underlying slates give way to harder rocks. While this change is pronounced to the north, the lands to the south are a more complicated affair. Although the main body of the river lies atop Devonian siltstones, Gillan Creek cuts through what is known as the Meneage Breccia formation. This eclectic combination of rock types sees the sedimentary reinforced by the metamorphic; mudstones combine with greenstone and the quartzite formed during the Ordovician Period around 450 million years ago. But the area within which the Helford's southern tributaries rise is more remarkable still. 'A geologist approaching the solution of the question of the Lizard Rocks', wrote one nineteenth-century observer, 'ought to be armed with every possible knowledge in department of his science, in other words, an impossibility is asked of a single man.'[15] Two hundred years later they remain a source of wonderment.

Along a line between the fishing village of Porthallow in the east and Polurrian Cove in the west runs a boundary fault below which can be found a miscellany of serpentine, gneiss, gabbro, and hornblende schist. All are born of Earth's ancient furnaces, and together they represent an entirely distinct realm from not only the Helford, but Cornwall and the rest of England. This 'Ophiolite Complex' is, in layman's terms, part of the Earth's ancient oceanic crust and upper mantle that was forced upwards and laid flat upon its surface. Indeed, on the beach at Coverack, some 6 miles to the south of Helford, it is possible to walk across the actual boundary between crust and mantle; a frontier that goes by the almost unpronounceable name of the 'Mohorovičić discontinuity'.

The wonders of the Lizard Complex never cease. Mullion Island is the product of lava cooling on the ocean floor more than 350 million years ago, while at Polurrian there are rocks folded by violent tectonic forces unleashed when continents collided. And below Lizard Point itself are to be found Man of War gneisses that, at perhaps 500 million years old, are the most ancient rocks in the south-west of the British Isles.[16] Unsurprisingly, this diversity in geology leads to attendant variations in soil and the flora that takes root within it. Magnesium-rich serpentines and gabbro abound with types of slow-growing calcicoles more often associated with chalk grasslands: bloody cranesbill, dropwort, fleabane and black bog rush among them. But the presence of the Hottentot-fig, on the other hand, is evidence that the rock below is most certainly not serpentine and far more likely to be schist or gneiss.[17]

These geological variations created the blueprint for the Helford River, but it required the climate to fashion it. Flanked by hard and unforgiving rocks to the north and south, the sedimentary band that underlies the estuary was gradually worn down by rainwater gathering into little streams, sometimes torrents, over millions of years. Water is unforgiving in its pursuit of eroding the weakest first, always taking the path of least resistance. In this sense Andre De Luc was wrong, but he can be wholly forgiven on account that knowledge of glaciation events would not become fully known until more than half a century after his death.

Some 50 million years after a slow decline in global temperatures had commenced, the Earth entered the Pleistocene Epoch and a series of ice ages. These periods of rapid climate change are the primary cause of the water-eroded valleys of the Helford and almost every other river in Europe. And while the ice sheets never reached this particular part of the British Isles during the most recent freezes, there is evidence of their effect to be found close to the water's edge in many places.

When the celebrated geologist Sir Henry de la Beche studied the area around the Helford River in the late 1830s, he made note of the 'head' deposits and 'raised beaches' to be found near both Rosemullion Head and Nare Point:

> … hills of hard rocks rise behind them, showing that not only a considerable decomposition of such rocks have taken place since these beaches were elevated above the present level of the sea, but also that there has been a great movement of the decomposed surfaces of the hills downwards, covering up all inequalities that presented themselves and rendering the surface more smooth than would otherwise happen.[18]

What De la Beche had observed was a bed of angular shattered slates formed through incessant freeze-thaw action during the bitterest periods of recent ice ages. Upon these can often be seen *loess*, a slender layer of fine wind-blown material from when the climate was particularly cold, dry, and the raw prevailing winds blew from the north. Conversely, the raised beaches owe their existence to the warmer interglacial periods when the sea level was higher than today. It is true that the present-day Helford is merely a modest resurrection of a long-disappeared river of greater length and depth, but it would never have been seen by human eyes.

Some evidence of the last ice age, the Devensian, is hidden from view. Beneath the sediment of the creeks lies a band of clay deposited by an out-pouring of meltwater as global temperatures began to rise.[19] The deep water channel at 'The Narrows' may also owe its existence to this same icy exodus, or perhaps the final act of an even more distant glacial event.

If we were able to gaze out across what is today Falmouth Bay as the world emerged from the intense cold we would see a frozen, barren land-scape. Rather than ocean, there would be two rivers of meltwater flowing across a lifeless plain and joining together – one from the Helford valley system and one from that of the Fal. This combined watercourse would have proceeded south to meet the 'Channel River', the bulk of which would have been made up from sources such as the ancient Rhine and Seine. This would have raged westwards to discharge into the Atlantic and carried with it perhaps as much as half of Western Europe's drainage. Beginning as a basin in the eastern channel, by the time it had reached the Cotentin Peninsula above Normandy it would have been a colossal torrent, thundering towards its termination at the continental shelf well to the west of the present-day Isles of Scilly.[20] The *Fleuve Manche* was a natural behemoth, and would have made today's rivers such as the Thames look like trickles from a millpond.

Although the climate warmed with remarkable rapidity after the Last Glacial Maximum, the rise came to an abrupt end around 10,900 BC. Temperatures collapsed so dramatically that by circa 10,500 BC the winter chill across Britain would have been more unbearable than that experienced today in places such as Archangel in Russia or Nuuk in Greenland. If such an unusual event were replicated in modern times it would surely result in the collapse of civilisation. The cause of what is variously known as the Younger Dryas or Loch Lomond Stadial is unclear, but it was probably the consequence of vast quantities of cold meltwater entering the Atlantic Ocean and stalling the benevolent Gulf Stream. The lands now covered by the Helford would have been left biologically derelict, with further erosive outpourings through its infant valleys taking place as the climate warmed once more.

Just as with its contemporaries such as the Tamar and Fal, the Helford grew as the sea level rose with ascending global temperatures and the onset of the Holocene epoch. Their development would have been rapid at first, not least between 8000 and 5000 BC when sea level rise probably reached 22ft (7m) every millennium, before dropping to around 6ft (1m) every 1,000 years thereafter.[21] Moreover, not only were water levels increasing but the lands of the south-west were subsiding as those far to the north rose with the lifting of their ice sheet deadweight. This combination of eustatic and isostatic change would have expedited the growth of the south coast *rias*.

It is likely that the Helford became its recognisable shape around the same time that mainland Britain became an island. It has been argued that this defining 'national' event was brought about by a tsunami caused by the submarine Storegga Slide off the coast of Norway sometime around 6100 BC.[22] At that time the last remnant of Doggerland that connected Britain and Europe was merely a low-lying plain and easily swamped by the deluge. Any poor souls upon it at the time would have been drowned, with only those on the extreme fringes possessing any chance of escaping the advancing wall of water.

By 5000 BC the sea level around the coast of Cornwall would have been around 20ft lower than it is today. As such, while the Helford at this time would have existed, it would surely have been a comparatively slender entity whose limits remain uncertain. Perhaps at high tide its furthest point would have extended as far as Mawgan Creek; at low drying out to somewhere mid-channel between Frenchman's Creek and Calamansack. In other words, the young Helford's highest tides would have appeared not unlike the lowest of the present.

However, the modest sea levels of more than 7,000 years ago would have been partly offset by the river's unburdened channels. The rich sediment so attractive to curlew and oystercatcher today would have been entirely absent, the river bed a combination of clean sand and smooth gravels. Through the steep-sided main valley would have coursed a striking freshwater river, its volume swelled by the union of streams that today exist as separate entities.

Although we would not immediately identify it, the river on the cusp of the sixth and fifth millennia BC is in its adolescence. Unusually for those in the first flushes of youth, it is a quiet place whose principal sounds are of rushing water and its natural inhabitants. Its width, length and depth are increasing, and so too the extent of the little creeks that define it today.

A little more than 6 miles south of the Helford is a small farm set high above the sea upon resilient Gabbro and Serpentinite cliffs. Its name, Poldowrian, is an apt one for somewhere so close to the ocean and through which a stream cascades down to the shore: both *pol* and *dowr* have watery Cornish origins, the former denoting a source of fresh and the latter suggesting plenty of the same. It was probably known by the title long before being first recorded as such in AD 1250.[23] Perhaps those who inhabited nearby Lankidden cliff castle during the first millennium BC were responsible for the appellation and drew upon the stream for supplies. But they were not the first to call it home.

Up until a wildfire swept through the gorse and scrub in November 1967, the landowner had only been able to imagine what lay beneath the cloaking vegetation. He had long held the belief that there was something hidden from view on account of its proximity to the promontory fort, but the flames revealed far, far more than he had anticipated. Surveying the damage, he soon began to see worked flints upon the charred ground and, more tantalising still, the outline of a long-lost field system and hut circle. The cliff castle was a relic of the Iron Age, but these were of the preceding Bronze. The story, however, had only just begun.

Over the following years numerous finds would be made through both diligence and accident. When the tenant farmer attempted to bring sections of land into cultivation in 1970, the plough struck a stony mound containing dark earth and prehistoric pottery. Realising that the site may be even more significant in terms of scale, work was halted and the discovery reported to archaeologists who commenced excavation.[24] What they would uncover would make this otherwise unassuming site near Coverack one of the most important prehistoric sites not only in Cornwall, but the entire country.

More than 40,000 lithic implements have been found at Poldowrian in the intervening years. There will likely yet be 40,000 more. So too a large number of prehistoric pottery sherds, protected from damage for so long on account of their lying in soil rarely disturbed by agricultural machinery. But while these discoveries made the site a special one in themselves, realising the sheer length of time over which Poldowrian had been inhabited during prehistory proved revelatory.

Although Bronze Age remains were the most obvious signs of ancient human activity, analysis of buried charcoal fragments proved, beyond reasonable doubt, that the site was occupied during the preceding Neolithic. Yet more remarkable still, radiocarbon dating of hazelnut shell fragments suggested that they had been discarded by human hands as long ago as perhaps 5620 BC.[25] The distance in time between those who dwelt upon patches of ground just yards apart was greater than that between our modern world and the Roman occupation. The Sumerian civilisation of Mesopotamia was in its infancy when voices rang out along the Lizard clifftops.

The finds at Poldowrian reinvigorated interest in the ancient archaeology of the Lizard. As the search for signs of Mesolithic activity widened beyond the east of the peninsula, further evidence of hunter-gatherer occupation began to be unearthed at two other locations. The first, Croft Pascoe on Goonhilly Downs, was found to possess a number of small 'microlith' flint artefacts – a contrast to the more diverse assemblage discovered at Poldowrian. Meanwhile, at Windmill Farm near Ruan Major, a possible 'fire pit' containing charcoal dated from between 5300 and 4360 BC was found preserved.[26] And yet compelling evidence had already been uncovered years earlier with probable Mesolithic flint flakes at nearby Lowland Point, north east of Coverack, in 1935.[27]

Were these locations used by one single extended family on a seasonal basis, or were there several groups inhabiting the lands south of the Helford in the sixth millennium BC? Perhaps Poldowrian was a 'base camp', probably used by countless generations, while those at Croft Pascoe and Windmill Farm were more transient 'temporary' affairs. Each could have been favoured at different times of the year, as the hazelnut shells of late autumn and winter suggest.[28] Indeed, it may be that these and other as yet undiscovered locations south of the river were in regular use even earlier in the Mesolithic period. Although it has been impossible to date any human remains from the area – solely on account that no bones of such age have ever been pulled from the soil – there are comparisons from other places that give credence to this assumption. For example, a number of fragments from a similar maritime setting in South Wales have been tested and range from between 7,500 and 5,500 BC.[29] More to the point, other parts of Cornwall, most notably Trevose Head and North Cliffs on the north coast, were inhabited during both Early and Later Mesolithic periods. As such, we can be forgiven for taking the archaeological liberty of concluding that the Lizard Peninsula has been continually inhabited for 8,000 years at the very least.

Neither should the importance of the benevolent climate of that far-off time be underestimated. While it is impossible to be specific, it is likely that our pioneering inhabitants of the Helford River valley enjoyed the early stages of a 'climatic optimum' that would continue until around 3000 BC. Average annual temperatures were slightly higher than the present day, there were fewer storms, and the rain fell evenly throughout the year.[30] With so many dangers and threats to their survival, we can at least comfort ourselves with the knowledge that our distant forebears at least had the weather on their side.

We can now answer the question as to when *our* story of the Helford River, and specifically man's relationship with it, should begin. We have reached a point in time when the estuary exists in a form we would recognise, albeit narrower and slightly shorter. It is surrounded by dense vegetation and tree cover along most of its course, although the latter thins around the headlands where exposure to the elements and poorer soils inhibit growth. The oak and hazel woodlands that John Rogers would observe 'fossilised' and dead at Maenporth in 1828 are very much alive above the shoreline. But, most importantly, they have been looked upon by human eyes. It is a cool, dry morning on 1 January 4850 BC, and the first of more than 5 million tides that will be a constant through ages of stone, bronze, iron, industry and technological revolution is rising. They will take us to the beginning of the twenty-first-century-era in which we live. Much will change, but their regularity will not.

2

WAVES

On a calm, early morning in autumn along the middle reaches of the river between Frenchman's and Mawgan Creeks it is possible to sense the very ancient past. It is the time of the year and time of the clock where modern-day distractions are at their least, if not entirely absent. Rarely will the sound of machinery from a distant road or the sky above break the silence. Farms are hushed and out of sight. There are always small signs of the present to be overlooked – perhaps a small mooring buoy or beached dinghy – and the post-medieval quays at Tremayne and Merthen should be behind you. But find yourself here and you might just be afforded a few moments of being 6,000 years or more distant. To listen is all.

At times you might hear the sound of cracking twigs or crunching leaves from deep within the surrounding woodland. It will most likely be a badger, fox or even a roe deer, all ever-present through the intervening millennia. But in that far-off time it could just as easily have been a wild boar, wolf or bear. However, beware the interlopers – rabbits, pheasants and grey squirrels are latecomers whose roots in these islands do not reach prehistoric depths.

Not so the water-dwellers. They are the river's amaranthine souls, a constant from before the time human feet trod the shoreline. From the smallest invertebrates deep within the silt to the thick-lipped grey mullet shoaling just below the glossy surface, little has changed. During the climatic cycles that swept the land during the Mesolithic period, the sea was a bulwark against extremes, never becoming too warm or too cold for the species inhabiting the waters of our now temperate latitude.

The middle and later Mesolithic were times of natural plenty, but it was not always that way. In the very early years of the post-glacial period, when the world experienced rapid warming and sea levels began to rise, the landscape around the Helford would have been dominated by grassland and low-lying shrubs. Notwithstanding that the last gasp of the most recent ice age, the Loch Lomond Stadial, reversed the botanical gains for perhaps 2,000 years until its abrupt end around 9500 BC, the swift thaw ensured transition from the Preboreal to Boreal Age in the seventh millennium BC. This was the time of trees. First came the birch at lower elevations and pine at higher, then the hazel, until oak dominated the deciduous woods that covered much of Cornwall except for the rocky uplands.

The fruits of the Boreal have lingered around the Helford. While some of its beech woodlands are relatively recent, and others the product of post-medieval planting by the gentry, most are of great antiquity. Ancient woodland is formally categorised as that which has been in continuous existence since 1700, and as much as 500 acres of such is to be found around the shores of the river and its surrounding countryside. Several examples are mere copses today, remnants of greater expanses lost to the plough and industrial furnace, but larger examples have remained unchanged in terms of boundaries and constituent species since first being recorded. Those still extant include Merthen, Bonallack and Calamansack on the north bank, while the Little and Great Tremayne, Gweek and Trelowarren woods are their southern mirror images. Others are to be found further inland, shrouding the little streams making their way to the creeks: Bufton, Tolvan, Grambla, Polwheveral, Treverry and Roskymer woods among them. However, they are not merely ancient in terms of scientific classification, but also in the purest sense. They have no documented origin. Man may have harvested them, and thus been partly responsible for their present form, but they have survived from a time before the first voices were heard within.

In recent decades these woods have been less frequented by people than when they were being coppiced regularly to serve blowing houses smelting tin. They have been returned to a more primitive state. The canopy of these woodlands is almost entirely comprised of sessile oaks of various sizes that have each gained a roothold in the thin soils of the slopes. Although there are often sharp contours to the land below, the trees soften the changes as a deep snowfall softens the shape of rough ground. But do not be deceived, sessile oaks are not the only venerable entities within. While other species are less frequent in the woodlands along the northern shore (where soils are at their least fertile), a combination of oak and holly can be found close to the water where the latter often covers the floor in dense patches. Hazel is a familiar sight, too, especially on upper slopes, and most of all in Tremayne Great Wood. Ash is also to be found, although almost always with its roots in the more fruitful soils of the river's surrounding lands, including Trelowarren. In places there are limes of unfathomable age whose importance 'lies in the meaning embodied in its mysterious natural distribution' as Oliver Rackham, lover of all things arboreal, once concluded.[1]

The plants covering the woodland floors are far more diverse. Close to the water's edge along the northern shore can be found heather and bilberry, while bluebells abound in Merthen (although, admittedly, they are to be encountered in all of the Helford's ancient woodlands to a greater or lesser degree). So too is bracken and the ubiquitous bramble. In the more fertile, base-rich, southern expanses exist red campions, ferns, wild garlic and golden saxifrage, although the classic harbinger of spring, the primrose, is less fussy and takes root almost anywhere the ground drains freely.[2] Beneath and upon the trees are mosses, liverworts and lichens of innumerable varieties, including the delicate awl-leaved ditrichum whose rarity in the British Isles is, alas, known only unto bryologists.

The noble oaks are also home to countless tiny creatures, including the largest known population of the endangered ground weevil, *Anchonidium unguiculare*, which sadly lacks a common name such is its scarcity. At least it is safe here. So are the species so often found in Atlantic oak woodlands throughout the islands: the various springtails, centipedes, millipedes, shield bugs, butterflies, moths, and all. Here are thriving ecosystems both in the air and upon the ground.

These enveloping kingdoms of trees are perhaps greater in similarity to their prehistoric form today than at any other time in the past 1,000 years. To stand deep within them and look through the branches towards the water is to behold an almost identical sight to that which would have met the hunter-gatherer seven millennia or more ago. What is more, the sounds are the same, the scent of growth and decay the same, the feel of the undergrowth and ground beneath the feet the same. But can we establish beyond doubt that human beings walked through the Helford's woodland shroud more than 7,000 years ago?

If we were to rely solely upon tangible evidence to answer such a question then we might confidently conclude that they did, but only occasionally. Some stone tools of the period have indeed been found, including a microlithic blade near to Gillan Creek.[3] An even more impressive flint artefact, an adze, was found close to the head of Mawgan Creek in 1968, its ancient origins attested to by the 'broad flakes struck from the side ... forming the typical "tranchet" edge of Mesolithic core tools'.[4] But even taken together, these finds are still eclipsed by the vast number of lithic objects found at Poldowrian and elsewhere to the south of the water. And yet to infer that the Helford was somehow only on the fringes of Mesolithic life in this part of Cornwall would be unwise. In fact, it was almost certainly the most important site on the Lizard Peninsula for hunter-gatherers of the time.

Prior to the establishment of agriculture, estuaries, even small ones, were by far the most productive localities for gathering food. The river and its surroundings would have provided a rich combination of marine, freshwater, and terrestrial supplies, all within close proximity to one another.[5] Moreover, a family or small group could have easily found sustenance and shelter around the Helford throughout an entire year with little incentive to travel further afield. This contrasts with the site at Poldowrian, a location whose favourability would ostensibly have been limited to autumn on account of the hunting opportunities provided by sea birds and marine mammals. Similarly, the 'upland' sites of the Lizard plateau would probably have been better suited to occupation during late summer owing to the movement of deer and other large herbivores.

Even if we make the logical assumption that a group might have used a number of seasonal camps, and that time spent at each would have been limited, there can be no doubt that one would have been close to the waters of the Helford. We might also suggest that spring and early summer would have been the most auspicious time given that the shores of the river then, as now, would have abounded with life. Not only would the hunter-gatherers have had access to a wide variety of molluscs, but simple tackle could have been employed to catch a range of fish – the Helford is located where warm- and cold-water species overlap depending upon the season, and never more so as the water temperature increases with the lengthening of days. Alternatively, weirs and traps such as those found preserved on the River Liffey in Dublin may have been constructed to take flounder and other fish.[6] Prehistoric 'shell middens' in similar maritime settings around the British coast have shown that families were feasting upon whelks, oysters, scallops, razor-shells and limpets. All would have been plentiful around its shores. The woods, too, would have been a rich source of game, even though meat was probably a lesser part of the diet in the late Mesolithic in comparison to the early stage when herds of large herbivorous mammals roamed a more open landscape.

If the river *had* been home to Mesolithic people throughout the entire year then it is probable that the dwellings they constructed would have been not unlike that found near Howick in Northumberland. Here, the substantial size of the excavated post holes suggested a building of importance, and the discovery of hearths and hazelnut shells is redolent of the practices of their distant relations at Poldowrian. However, if the area was inhabited only seasonally, the ephemeral nature of wood and animal skin shelters would probably leave nothing for us to find today, even if they ever existed at all.

The precise location of such a camp, assuming there was such an outpost, may never be known. The likelihood is that it is lost to the sea somewhere under the sands of the wide open channel between Durgan and Dennis Head, or perhaps to woodland higher up the river's course where lack of land cultivation has left the past less disturbed. But nature may yet conspire to provide future archaeologists with another 'Poldowrian' moment. For now, however, we can only imagine what lies beneath the waves or the woodland soil somewhere around its shoreline.

If we are to accept the case for seasonal habitation around the Helford during the Mesolithic period, we must also accept that these people would have been prehistoric seafarers, too. Evidence for the use of primitive boats in the British Isles was one of the many revelations provided by the Star Carr site in North Yorkshire, where a paddle was found preserved in the peat.[7] Furthermore, that early human beings travelled around coasts, even across seas, is amply evidenced by the finding of stone tools more than 130,000 years old on the Mediterranean island of Crete.[8] There can be no other real-istic possibility than that they, or their creators, arrived there in some form of seaworthy vessel.

Indeed, it is probable that those who first populated Cornwall after the last ice age arrived by boat, although some have argued that the final inundation of productive hunting ground under the present-day eastern English Channel forced groups further west in search of new opportunities.[9] It has even been suggested that at one time the majority of the population of north-western Europe lived on the plains now submerged beneath the North Sea.[10] Meanwhile, others resolutely believe that the earliest settlers of south-west England were the descendants of the Azilian culture who had ventured north out of the glacial refuges in Iberia.[11] There is no conclusive proof to favour one scenario above the other, not least as a dateable burial from that distant time has yet to be found, but the ability to construct and pilot small craft would have been required in either case. It is likely that movement from both east and south underpinned the colonisation of the land that constitutes present-day Cornwall.

Whereas reeds would have been used in Africa and bamboo in the Far East, the first boats in the British Isles were probably made from animal hides stretched over a frame constructed of willow or other suitable wood, much as coracles continue to be today. 'Canoes' fashioned by hollowing out tree trunks were also used for travel along rivers or sheltered estuaries, rather like the 8,000-year-old Pesse Canoe – the world's oldest surviving boat – found in the Netherlands in 1955.[12] However, the discovery of worked timbers preserved underwater at the Mesolithic site at Bouldnor Cliff on the Isle of Wight strongly suggests that plank-built boats were being constructed in Britain around 6,000 BC.[13] Any and all of these boatbuilding techniques would have been available to our early Helford River inhabitants. To think that they would have never taken to the water, perhaps only using it to travel from site to site on a seasonal basis, is absurd. They might not necessarily have ventured regularly into open water, and certainly not during the winter months, but fair-weather coastal navigation by paddle is surely a skill almost as old as mankind. Be in no doubt, lying somewhere deep within the anoxic sediments of the Helford's upper reaches will be the remains of boats many thousands of years old.

There is good regional evidence to support the theory of ancient long-distance maritime travel. In 2013 at St Martin's on the Isles of Scilly, a number of microliths were uncovered by archaeologists at Old Quay. What made the discovery particularly remarkable was not that evidence for Mesolithic activity on the archipelago had previously been lacking, but the actual conclusions as to their provenance. Leaving aside that Scillonia has been separate from the mainland since the twelfth millennium BC, these particular lithics were comparable not with others from Britain, Ireland or north-west France, but examples from an area north of the River Seine and the Somme Basin, taking in much of modern-day Belgium and the Netherlands.[14] Although coincidence cannot be wholly ruled out, there are only two plausible conclusions: either people from north-east France or Belgium arrived and set up camp on the Isles of Scilly, or, early Scillonians made a return journey bringing the knowledge of their manufacture back with them. Either scenario is extraordinary, but it is not the only evidence of early coastal navigation along the English Channel.

While excavating Mesolithic pit dwellings close to Farnham in Surrey during the 1930s, the archaeologist Sir Grahame Clark found something unusual. Upon the floors of the rudimentary houses were a number of curious pebbles, clearly out of place in that they were not derived from any local bedrock or nearby source. Intrigued, he passed them on to a petrologist in the hope they might shed a little light on their origins. Following microscopic study it was concluded that one particular pebble was a 'greenish silty sandstone containing angular quartz grains up to 0.2mm diameter, with occasional grains of alkali feldspar and flakes of white mica in a matrix of chloritic and micaceous material'.[15] Remarkably, the closest match for this specific piece of unassuming rock was the Helford River. Why it should have been deemed necessary to transport it hundreds of miles is uncertain, but the implications of the discovery are significant: even before the coming of agriculture, human beings were successfully navigating the western seaways. Moreover, the popular idea that early pre-historic Cornwall was somehow far more closely linked to cultures along the Atlantic coast than others elsewhere in England is an oversimplification. Rather than seeing maritime movement as essentially a north–south phenomenon between it and north-western France and Iberia, the Helford was not so much part of a *cross*-Channel network, but more part of a *pan*-Channel one.

Even if we allow for the construction of the most seaworthy vessels of the age, it is extremely difficult to imagine any routine contact between those living in the west of Cornwall and their contemporaries in Brittany during the Mesolithic. While navigation within sight of land would have been commonplace, losing sight of the shore in even the most benign conditions would have been extremely hazardous. What is more, towering landmarks over 300ft in height would have been lost to the eye at 26 nautical miles on the clearest of days.[16] Consider, then, that the shortest distance between Lizard Point and north-west France during the middle and late Mesolithic periods would have been around 80 nautical miles at the least. Without the rudimentary navigational equipment we take for granted, any Mesolithic mariner would have had to have an exceptional reason to make such a journey, even as part of a small convoy. In contrast, routes between Britain and Ireland are less than half that distance at several points, and that between Kent and the Pas-de-Calais fewer than 20 nautical miles. Perhaps it is no coincidence that the clear majority of identified Mesolithic sites in Ireland are clustered close to the narrowest channel between it and the rest of the British Isles.

This possible bias towards coastal navigation might be the reason why the archaeological record generally shows a divergence in microlith industries on either side of the English Channel during the later Mesolithic period.[17] While movement of people and goods over distance along coastal waters would have been far easier than achieving the same on foot, 'blue water' maritime activity would have been limited until advancements were made in boat construction during the late Neolithic and Bronze Age. After all, the distance to be comfortably covered using paddles is far less than by sail. In contrast, whoever was responsible for the microliths on St Martin's could have travelled between the Low Countries and Scilly without ever losing sight of land.

Yet this is not to discount open-water voyages in the North Atlantic 7,000 years ago. They surely did happen, even if the rationale for doing so is a matter of debate. Those early seafarers would certainly have understood tidal patterns and possessed a precise knowledge of channels and submerged hazards.[18] As such, the importance of the Helford River as a safe haven in the very distant past seems assured. It lies not only at one end of an east–west coastal route, but also the middle of one connecting cultures from the south-west of France and the Atlantic facade of Britain. It would have been a pivotal point for early seafarers from all points on the (yet to be invented) compass.

However, it is unlikely that those living by the Helford River at that time had any idea that they were islanders. Perhaps their brethren living close to the coast in the south-eastern tip of the newly formed British Isles would have been the only beings with any tangible sense of their geographic severance from mainland Europe. And yet for those living in the west of Cornwall, the sea would have been the defining feature of their lives.[19] To travel any appreciable distance would have meant leaving the security of solid ground and placing oneself at the mercy of the elements. Every venture into open water would have been of importance.

The shoreline would also have been well trodden during the Mesolithic period. In many cases it would have been a far easier proposition to travel on foot around cliffs and across the beaches than through the thick forest above it. The footprints found at Formby on the Mersey estuary are perhaps evidence of this.[20] However, we must not overlook the importance of inland sites to the hunter-gatherer group, not least as their lifestyle would no doubt still have involved the pursuit of large prey as well as the seasonal collection of wild berries, nuts and fungi. Indeed, one of the most notable Mesolithic sites in Cornwall was found close to Dozmary Pool on Bodmin Moor, many miles from the sea. However, even in this regard the hinterland of the Helford would have offered much on account of its streams and their little pools. It would be here that animals would have gathered to drink, the water providing natural clearings in the woods from which hunters could ambush prey more successfully.[21] In fact, those early hunters might themselves have created clearings, all the better to attract deer and other larger mammals.

Although archaeologists and anthropologists have pondered the matter for generations, no one can be reasonably confident of knowing just how populated the British Isles would have been during the Mesolithic period. The truth is that it was probably rather variable depending not only upon changes in climate and weather (one vicious winter alone would have left many dead from starvation), but also outbreaks of disease. We can be forgiven for thinking that the period was rather like our islands' aboriginal *Dreamtime* – and in some ways it probably was – but it was also a punishing existence beset by danger and uncertainty. Some have estimated that no more than 2,000 or 3,000 souls lived between Land's End and John o' Groats at any one time between 10,000 BC and the coming of agriculture, although this is most likely a cautious view and the true figure could be twenty times greater.[22] Moreover, we must also take into account that some areas would have been able to support higher numbers than others. The Helford and Lizard Peninsula would appear to possess the attributes of one able to do just that. It was, and still is, rich in resources.

Perhaps two or three family groups, each familiar with the others, would have known the Helford in our year of 4850 BC. As Mesolithic artefacts are notoriously difficult to find north of the river, we might speculate that one of them was either permanently or primarily resident somewhere along its southern shore and thus within reach of diverse hunting grounds, both marine and terrestrial. They would probably have been darker in complexion than the average modern Briton, and a little shorter in stature. Their clothes would have been fashioned from animal skins, probably with modified sea shells as fasteners with others used as adornments.[23] But we know nothing of the language these early settlers used. We never will. Nor are we able to appreciate their unique understanding of the world around them, or their rituals and beliefs. They have left very few clues for us to find.

What we can say with a great degree of confidence is that our old preconceptions of nomadic people free from rootedness in the landscape are wrong. In reality they would have had a sense of place and belonging as strong as our own. Investigation of the famous Star Carr site in North Yorkshire show that while it was almost certainly a seasonal hunting camp, it was also in use for several hundred years during the ninth millennium BC. Here were found significant structures such as timber platforms by the edge of the lake, and even a simple dwelling house. The intergenerational aspect of this discovery is striking; people returned home each year, even if 'home' was more than one place. The Helford, too, was someone's home 7,000 years ago. We are merely newcomers.

At this time the river would have possessed a name that defined it as a geographical feature for those travelling between camps, although we will never know what that name was. People lived and thrived along its course and across its hinterlands, with the valleys, shorelines and streams conducive to survival on the most basic of levels. There is much to commend the young Helford to those living elsewhere in the fifth millennium BC: it was sheltered and bountiful, overflowing with the fish and shellfish that dominated the diet of people at the time. But there then came an abrupt end to this primitive, yet somehow beautifully simplistic, way of life. Suddenly, at least in archaeological terms, the diet of Britons changed from marine to terrestrial around 4000 BC. The maritime Garden of Eden along the Helford was, as elsewhere, lost to something else.

During the nineteenth century it would not at all have been unusual to have heard, and felt, the booming sound of explosions across the landscape north of the river. But on 9 March 1869 one detonation in particular would resonate, metaphorically, for far longer than any other. The source of the blast was to be found in a modest granite quarry 1½ miles to the north of the village of Constantine. However, far from it being solely intended to cleave rock for the broad-shouldered masons waiting below, the explosives had been placed specifically to remove an obstruction that lay in the path of the quarry's expansion. The stone to be accessed was of a superior quality, with the potential gains to be had securing the immediate futures of many workmen. The ensuing loss, however, was far greater and not of a financial nature.

The particular barrier to opening up fresh sources of granite was known locally as the Tolmen – an immense egg-shaped rock high upon the hillside and visible for many miles around. When William Borlase visited the site in the 1750s he observed that it was '97 feet in circumference, about 60 feet cross the middle' and by his calculations weighed more than 700 tons.[24] This in itself would not have been especially remarkable were it not for the fact that it was perched upon the points of two other rocks. This meant that it was possible for fully grown men to pass under it, and the stone gained something of a reputation with tourists. Many even arrived on arranged excursions to the site.

Its end was shameful and prompted outrage both locally and nationally. One particular letter to the *Royal Cornwall Gazette*, just days after the event, was indicative of the displeasure it had caused within the parish itself:

> … the rock rests at the bottom of the quarry, precisely as it stood in its former proud pre-eminence; and the sacrificial basins, lips, and channels …

may now be seen as they have probably existed for two thousand years. I saw it yesterday in deep grief and mortification, for I am a Cornishman, and have Constantine blood in my veins. I don't here mention the tradition that exists throughout this district against him who injures this Tolmen. I would rather believe that his own reflections will be sufficient punishment for the irreparable loss he has occasioned to the antiquities of Cornwall.[25]

However, blame did not initially fall on the landowner but rather the quarry's foreman, John Dunstan. Whether the proprietor of the site, Mr Hosken, was as innocent as his subsequent letter to *The Times* newspaper suggests is a matter of debate: 'I distinctly state that I have always felt too great a pride in this ancient monument to wantonly throw it down,' he wrote, 'and each member of our family, to whom the estate belongs, very deeply regrets the loss of this fine object of interest.' And yet it is still difficult to believe he failed to notice the encroachment towards its base and the threat it posed. At best he was negligent, and at worst more culpable than his employee. Perhaps the most notable of all correspondence to *The Times* was that printed on 23 March, and one that was rather more of fury than regret:

> Sir, You recorded last week the destruction of the great Tolmaen, in Constantine parish, near Penrhyn, which was blown up a few days ago for the sake of the granite by a man named Dunstan. Having been informed some weeks ago by the Rev. Mr. Winwood that the Tolmaen was in danger, I put myself in communication with the proprietor, Mr. Haskin, intending to offer some compensation for, or, if possible, to acquire it permanently for the nation; but I was assured that there was no reason for any anxiety on the subject.
>
> The mischief done is of course irreparable: but every right-minded man must condemn the wanton barbarism of him who has thus destroyed, for the mere sake of the granite on which it stood, a monument which old Borlase called the 'most astonishing of its kind'.

> I am, Sir, your obedient servant,

> John Lubbock.

The author was the very same Sir John Lubbock who had previously devised the terms Palaeolithic and Neolithic. His was an influential voice, and although the Tolmen was lost it would not be forgotten. Indeed, precisely because of the event and the outcry that followed, the Ethnological Society of London convened a meeting at which it was decided to appoint a committee. This included not only Lubbock himself, but also the renowned biologist Thomas Henry Huxley, the archaeologist Augustus Pitt-Rivers, the publisher Henry George Bohn, and Sir Augustus Wollaston Franks of the British Museum. The purpose of this committee was explicit: 'to ascertain the present state of prehistoric monuments in these islands, and the best means for their preservation'. A little over a decade later, Lubbock drove through the Ancient Monuments Protection Act 1882, with his friend Pitt-Rivers taking on the role of the nation's first Inspector of Ancient Monuments. No fewer than sixty-eight sites across Great Britain and Ireland were included in the first schedule, including Stonehenge and Silbury Hill in Wiltshire, the Plas Newydd burial chambers in Anglesea, and the Ring of Brodgar in Orkney.

The Tolmen's needless destruction was not in vain. Although Constantine can no longer boast of its remarkable landmark, other prehistoric sites of international importance owe their ongoing protection to its loss. It is therefore ironic that the Tolmen is today generally considered to have been a natural geological feature rather than the work of prehistoric people. However, it is easy to understand how antiquary and layman alike would have concluded that it was placed into position by the hands of those who had lived thousands of years before themselves. Even the pragmatic Victorian mineralogist Joseph Henry Collins noted in 1860 that 'it used to be remarked by the quarrymen that about Midsummer the rays of the rising and setting sun poured straight through the passage under the rock' and that 'it is impossible to conceive that this arrangement was altogether natural. In all probability a natural confirmation of the rocks was taken advantage of to produce a desired result.'[26] Borlase was surer still, and ascribed the hollows and cavities on top of the rock to the work of druids rather than natural weathering. And the Rev. Richard Warner of Bath added yet more gratuitous embellishments to its importance in prehistoric ritual, describing the site of the 'famous Druidical Remain in Constantine parish' with his attention being particularly drawn to 'the gloomy nature of that superstition which had such a desert for its rites, the focal point of solitude and desolation where nothing met the eye around but nature in her primaeval rudeness'.[27]

While it is easy to mock nineteenth-century overenthusiasm for mysterious ancient ceremony, it is almost certain that the Tolmen *was* a revered object by early inhabitants of the Helford River area. It matters not whether it was a purely geological anomaly or worked and moved into place by human endeavour, not least because it was located within an area where there were, and still are, authentic prehistoric stone relics. Indeed, had Sir John Lubbock been born a century earlier it would have been the desecration of another slab of Cornish granite provoking his ire rather than the Tolmen.

Just a few hundred yards away from the now disused Maen Toll quarry once stood a long-stone so huge it must have been visible for 5 miles or more. It was probably intended to be so, although for what purpose we will never know for certain. In fact, in the British Isles only the surviving Rudston Monolith in north-east Yorkshire would have surpassed in size the Maen Pearn. William Borlase reckoned it stood more than 20ft high, 10ft wide, and was somewhat pyramidal in form with straight sides tapering to a point from halfway. Unfortunately, by the time he wrote of the 'Men-Perhen' in 1754 it had already been destroyed. It was an ignominious end for such a behemoth, cut into gateposts by the same farmer who blithely described the act to Borlase. Its name, quite aptly, was thought by some to have meant the 'Stone of Sorrow'.[28]

The precise spot upon which the Maen Pearn once stood is not recorded, but it is likely to have been close to the present-day farm house. Here is to be found a small plateau, more than 500ft above sea level, and clearly visible for great distances from west, east and south. It is littered with large granite boulders. Menhirs (derived from *maen* meaning 'stone', and *hir* for 'long' in both Cornish and Breton) were not created to be hidden away in the landscape, and this giant would have been no exception.

Across the country many more prehistoric monuments met a similar end to both the Maen Pearn and Tolmen. Not only were unfortunate megaliths broken up through post-medieval industrial and agricultural insensitivity, but many would have been convenient for use in building. Countless long-stones must today be incorporated into the fabric of farmhouses and cottages constructed hundreds of years ago, while others would have suffered the indignity of being cast to the ground and buried by religious zealots. In West Penwith, for example, there was once a second stone circle near the still-extant Merry Maidens, but all was lost by the end of the nineteenth century.[29] Likewise, the Tregaseal East circle near St Just was once one of three adjacent monuments. If such megaliths as these were considered fit for pillage, what of the more modest single stones? However, not all have been lost from the lands around the river, even if they have been scarred. One prehistoric monument of note is neither complete nor in its original position. It too was once considered fit only for the production of gateposts but, unlike the Maen Pearn, it survived the ordeal.

At one time the holed Tolvan Stone near Gweek was a foot wider and a foot taller than it is today, but following its brutal cropping it is now a 'mere' 7½ft in height and width. Moreover, its situation in a cottage garden is misleading, for it probably once formed part of a nearby burial chamber – one side of an imposing *dolmen*, perhaps covered in earth, and through which access to the tomb could be gained. Close to its original position was found a trough-shaped stone known locally as 'The Cradle', and also a pit lined with stones within which fragments of pottery were said to have been recovered. Regrettably these objects have long disappeared, and with them the chance to definitively apportion even the most approximate date to the Tolvan. However, the traces of what is considered a Bronze Age barrow still exist in a field opposite the present site of the stone. But this may be misleading. It is quite possible that the original dolmen was constructed during the Neolithic, just as many megaliths of its type were.

Such holed stones are rare indeed, and no others as large as the Tolvan exist in the British Isles. It would surely have been of great spiritual importance to those who constructed it, with the hole perhaps signifying a portal to the realm of the ancestors. But here we are relying wholly upon speculation. What is known, however, is that its 'powers' were revered by local residents as recently as the nineteenth century, as the Cornish archaeologist John Thomas Blight once observed:

I was told that some remarkable cures had been effected there only a few weeks since. The ceremony consists of passing the child nine times through the hole, alternately from one side to the other; and it is essential to success that the operation should finish on that side where there is a little grassy mound, recently made, on which the patient must sleep, with a six-pence under his head.[30]

Similar practices in pursuit of improved health took place at other holed stones such as the Men-an-Tol in West Penwith, and as far away as Minchinhampton in Gloucestershire where infants were passed through the 'Longstone' in the hope of curing rickets.[31] These were hallowed places indeed, with customs and local lore seemingly unaffected by the establishment of Christianity. It remains the same to this day; we are still drawn to them in search of their meaning and, in some cases, our own.

Such was the importance of monuments such as the Tolvan that they even gave their names to the settlements that developed around them. Moreover, other long stones and burial sites influenced the titles of fields listed on various tithe maps for parishes around the river. Charles Henderson noted several in Constantine, including one close to the Tolvan under the name of 'Grambla Close'. This, a corruption of the Cornish *An-Gromlech* meaning 'Cromlech', is an old term that has been used to describe both dolmens such as the Tolvan and stone circles alike. Given the proximity of these two otherwise separate sites we might at least speculate that there were once many such monuments in this quiet corner of the Helford River valley. After all, the Bronze Age chamber tombs on the Isles of Scilly are to be found clustered together, and so it may be that here was once a funerary landscape, a place of the dead.

Henderson also noted that a 'Longstone Close' near the farm at Nanjarrow had been recorded in 1649 although, just as at Maen Pearn, there was nothing resembling the efforts of prehistoric people to be found. And yet there was one place the antiquary noted from records that proved more fruitful. The field had once been known as 'Park Menheer', and upon visiting the site Henderson did indeed find a longstone 'standing in a field near the road at the lane gate that appears to be a Menhir. It is a massive piece of granite 5 feet high, 2ft 4in. Wide and 1ft 4in. thick at the base, but tapering to a sharp point. As the stone stands at the side of the field and has no marks of recent tooling it can hardly be a mere rubbing post'.[32]

The location of this particular standing stone was at Treworval, an ancient farm settlement located between the villages of Constantine and Mawnan. The situation is amongst the most elevated to be found anywhere in the immediate vicinity of the Helford, with the river itself nestled out of sight as one gazes south over open countryside to the Lizard Peninsula. Nor is there any geographic feature to break either view or wild winter winds between Treworval and the former locations of the Maen Pearn and Tolmen giants. This is a place from which to see and be seen.

Regrettably, if there was a standing stone present at the gateway to the lane as Henderson reported, no such megalith is present today. However, located within the hedgerow of an adjacent field there *is* a curious lump of granite. It is covered in gorse for much of the year and easily overlooked, not least as it initially appears to simply be part of the boundary between two fields, put into position hundreds of years ago rather than thousands. And yet it is somehow out of place. It seems to lack the characteristics of a purely natural boulder and, although there are no others similar in size or form along the rest of the hedge, it is not alone in the immediate area.

A little over 300yd away to the north is another stone set on end into the earth, although it too cannot be that which Henderson described on account of its dimensions. Of course, it could merely be a rubbing post for cattle, or perhaps the remnants of a long-disappeared medieval field gateway, but it does have the appearance of an ancient megalith – almost 4ft in height above the ground, 2ft in width, and tapering to a point from the shoulders. With yet another intriguing chunk of stone lying half-buried in the next field, it is tempting, rather naively, to entertain thoughts of a lost Neolithic or Bronze Age ceremonial site. Unfortunately, to begin to do so would require that each of these lumps of stone are indeed the work of a prehistoric community. All of them, including Charles Henderson's missing menhir, may well be so, but in the absence of detailed archaeological study we must accept that they might simply be an unrelated cluster of varied provenances. They might not even be in their original positions. But there is something about the land at Treworval. The longer one spends there the deeper in time its origins seem. There is good reason to think this so.

In recent times a number of fascinating artefacts have been pulled from the soil. The fields surrounding the farmhouse are rich in discarded historic material, and this is never more obvious than following a heavy downpour that washes clean the stones and other hard objects. The rocks here are largely granite, quartz and slate, and so it is that anything *not* composed of such material becomes more observable; pottery, bone, brick fragments, and rusting chunks of long-thrown horseshoes among them. On occasions, however, those that catch the eye are tiny pieces of worked flint whose subtle shine marks them out as alien to the coarser natural pebbles around them.

The first to be found was a tiny arrowhead, its point missing, which was subsequently identified as of the 'British oblique' type and dated to between 2800 BC and 1600 BC.[33] Such a find appeared to confirm the opinions of archaeologists who had suspected the area of being inhabited during the Bronze Age. Studies of aerial photographs had already revealed a number of features in the landscape visible as cropmarks, including a possible enclosure and a number of barrows. This one tiny arrowhead appeared to validate the experts' conclusions, but it was not to be the only ancient artefact to be found in the area.

Soon after, a second piece of worked flint was found. This time it was a flake, possibly lost by its creator while being fashioned into another projectile point.[34] Similar examples found elsewhere had been considered to have been created at some time between 3000 BC and 2200 BC and, as such, were made by people of the late Neolithic, not of the Bronze Age. As indeed did a third artefact, another arrowhead, but this time of the 'transverse' variety whose cutting edge is much wider than that hafted on to the shaft.[35] Such weapons would have inflicted devastating wounds on their target, and it is thought that they were made specifically for hunting large animals. But, most importantly, transverse arrowheads are almost always associated with Neolithic activity.

There can be little doubt that human beings were settled in the area around the present-day Treworval – and thus the Helford River area – as far back as 3000 BC. These gently rolling fields, not at all dissimilar in that respect to those in the famous prehistoric landscape of Wiltshire, owe much of their shape to Neolithic people. When man farmed the soil here more than 5,000 years ago, Egypt had only just become united as a kingdom. This high ground was the territory of families who cleared the earth of both stones and trees, planted cereal crops and raised livestock. We cannot be certain of how their primitive settlement might have appeared, nor exactly where it was situated, but it was probably comprised of a several small houses within close proximity to one another. Whether these were square or round is not known given that both types were common during the Neolithic, with no obvious geographical pattern to their occurrence. But it is moving to think that some of the men and women who trod the ground here would have occasionally left the security of their community to make epic journeys, perhaps even to Stonehenge.[36]

How they might have appeared is similarly a matter of conjecture. However, as good a picture as any was provided by the archaeologist Lady Aileen Fox in her popular work *Ancient Peoples and Places, South West England*. No discoveries made since its publication in 1964 have suggested that she was wholly inaccurate:

> The people who formed the basis of the primary Neolithic population in the south west are known as yet only from their settlements and from chance finds of their possessions. Their physical appearance, however, can be established from the skeletons of their contemporaries inhumed under long barrows in southern England. They were of small stature, lightly boned and neatly built, with delicately fashioned hands and feet, indicating good powers of movement and skill; they had long thin faces, and probably a swarthy complexion, not unlike the North American Indian.[37]

Treworval, as with other sites of similar prehistoric origins, was suited to early agriculture on account of its relative height above sea level where the underlying granitic geology would have made clearance far easier than more densely covered, less acidic land. Early farmers would surely have avoided the heavy clay soils closer to the shore, these being beyond bone and flint ards. But this might not be the sole reason for its colonisation thousands of years ago. Those who settled here were as intelligent as us, shared the same raw emotions as us, but did not grow old like us. Disease, malnutrition and congenital disorders such as arthritis prevailed. Those who reached their late 30s or 40s were the venerable elders of their groups. So, given the burdens, dangers and physical demands endured by Neolithic people, it is clear that those living within the New Stone Age sought a connection to their departed ancestors and, perhaps, a life beyond. In fact, the geography of Treworval does much to encourage a theory of ceremonial use as well as agriculture and settlement.

It is increasingly accepted that proximity to water, and especially the sources of streams and rivers, was of immense importance to prehistoric societies both in the British Isles and beyond.[38] Many of the nation's most notable Neolithic sites are to be found in such locations, including Silbury Hill in Wiltshire which lies close to the source of the River Kennet. The reason why this should be so is a matter of speculation, although it seems most likely that the birthplaces of waterways represented the beginning of life and their discharge to the sea the end. The departed were, in effect, being taken to a place of renewal. Moreover, votive offerings were made at wetland sites throughout prehistory, the water becoming a metaphysical interface between the world of the living and the realm of the dead. Perhaps this is why the Tolvan stone, once part of a burial chamber, is to be found not only between two streams that converge nearby before feeding into the river at Gweek, but also a spring. Indeed, the estuary itself might have been venerated, lying as it does such that the sun rises at its mouth and sets at its head.

However, Treworval is unusual on account that it possesses a collection of small ponds which discharge into a stream that bends around, horseshoe-shaped, before turning south towards Trenarth and Port Navas. It forms a natural boundary to the ground upon which the extant menhir stands, almost, but not quite, at the centre. That said, the freshwater stream would not have been used for symbolic purposes alone, even assuming this was the case at all. It may well have been important to the memory of the dead, but it was even more crucial to the well-being of the living. Access to clean drinking water, for man and beast alike, was undoubtedly as important a factor in Treworval being settled as its elevated position. What is more, we must not overlook the high probability that the stream, as with others, was used as a geographical marker for both territory and navigation. The latter may well be the most significant.

It is tempting to believe that this stream acted as an enduring guide down to the creeks and shores of the Helford where a plentiful supply of food could be found. It is a theory supported by the finds of Neolithic axe heads at Trenarth and Penpoll, which suggest regular movement between the uplands and the waterside.[39, 40] Indeed, while the development of agriculture is essentially the defining characteristic of the Neolithic, it would seem foolish to assume that natives of the area were hunter-gatherers one year and successful farmers the next. Bronze Age shell middens from on the Isles of Scilly suggest that those close to the sea were still harvesting it hundreds of generations after their Mesolithic predecessors.[41] And yet they would have been a minority.

Analysis of ancient bone fragments has revealed a notable difference between those on either side of the Mesolithic–Neolithic transition. For some reason, fish and shellfish essentially disappear from the diet of Britons in a very short space of time.[42] This dramatic change in dietary habits was observed not only on inland sites close to freshwater fish resources, but also near to the coast. However, it is important to be cautious given the abject lack of human remains for analysis from either period in Cornwall as a whole, let alone the Helford River region. But the evidence for an abrupt shift to agriculture seems compelling, and there is no reason to assume that the people living around the estuary were immune from the change.

Something yet more intriguing is *how* agriculture arrived in the area. What cannot be denied is the link between megalithic culture and farming, perhaps even more specifically the cultivation of cereal crops. Whether the propensity to construct stone monuments and agriculture arrived simultaneously and were part of the same 'package' is more difficult to ascertain, but the culture that erected the menhirs overlooking the Helford and elsewhere in Cornwall was the very same that flourished and built the vast number of stone structures not only in Wales, Ireland, and Brittany, but also Cumbria, Derbyshire and Devon. The difficulty faced by archaeologists, however, is in determining whether this occurred because of the movement of people or the movement of ideas. These theories, referred to in academic contexts as 'demic diffusion' and 'trait adopted diffusion' respectively, have been championed at different times in the past. However, cultural practices and migration would matter little if the conditions for growing crops successfully were lacking.

One thing is certain, the shift from the Mesolithic way of life to one based on farming and territoriality occurred during a time of profound climatic change. The establishment of agriculture across the British Isles coincided with the same phenomenon occurring in southern Scandinavia between 4100 and 3800 BC, 1,000 years later than evidence of early Neolithic life-styles in northern France just a couple of hundred miles away across the sea.[43] Its timing corresponded almost perfectly with the peak of the climatic optimum that had been building over the preceding 2,000 years.

Pioneering agriculturalists would not only have required benevolent weather conditions to help them establish their communities, but also the most suitable soils available. Alas, more than half of the types across main-land Britain suffer from seasonal, or even year-round, waterlogging and are therefore not particularly conducive to modern farming techniques let alone primitive ones. Of course, drier conditions would no doubt have increased the growing season and made significant tracts of hitherto inadequate land better able to support crops, but a low population would have made such expansion largely unnecessary anyway. It should be noted, however, that despite the comparatively free-draining nature of the soil north of the Helford around Constantine, it would not have been especially fertile even if the land was easy to clear. To the south of the river, on the other hand, lies particularly base-rich loamy soil favourable for cereal crops. As such, it is possible to tentatively suggest that the early farmers of the area continued a fundamentally nomadic lifestyle, employing the ground to the south for arable production, and that to the north as grassland for livestock.

Some have logically concluded that singular standing stones in Cornwall are generally of Bronze Age foundation. This is on account that cremated human remains dateable to that particular period have been found close to some. Yet this assumption overlooks that they might have been set into the ground far earlier and came to represent sacred places to generations entirely unconnected to those who first raised them. Although we cannot be cer-tain of when any were set upright, the Maen Pearn and Treworval menhirs were *possibly* territorial or cultural markers for farming communities during the Neolithic–Bronze Age cusp. Perhaps they were statements of belonging around which families or groups could coalesce, offering some reassurance in an otherwise threatening world. So too the Eathorne and Prospidnick stones on the northern fringes of the Helford's catchment, or the Dry Tree menhir and giant Tremenheere longstone to the south. There may have been stone circles, too, although the closest extant example, much deteriorated, is the 'Nine Maidens' 6 miles to the north near Carnmenellis. There were more of these noble monuments once, and we can now only imagine a landscape around the river, gradually being cleared of trees and other vegetation, in which upright stones were commonplace.

The few megaliths around the periphery of the Helford's catchment are not the only possible relics of the Neolithic period. Other traces of occupation do exist but are almost invisible after thousands of years of weathering and the grind of modern agriculture. When archaeologists conducted a geophysical survey of a known Iron Age settlement at Gear near Mawgan-in-Meneage, they were surprised to reveal faint traces of what appeared to be a far older Neolithic field system.[44] If only it were possible to see what lies beneath all the other undeveloped land bordering the estuary. It would no doubt appear as a patchwork of ancient wonders.

However, there is one particularly perplexing question relating to those who farmed the land 5,000 years ago: where are their funerary monuments? With regret, we are left with mere shadows of what might have been. It was said that a boulder 'reminiscent of a quoit capstone' was found at Trevaney, near Constantine, and that its location was considered 'appropriate for a monument of this type'.[45] Alas, such evidence is speculative at best. As such, aside from the aforementioned field name of Grambla (within which a cromlech might have existed in the distant past), there are only three other possibilities. All are to be found on the periphery of the Helford River's catchment.

By far the most likely Neolithic memorial to the dead is the Three Brothers of Grugwith. Comprised of two supporting stones and a capstone, it is to be found on the fringes of Goonhilly Downs and close to the source of the stream that ultimately reaches the sea at Gillan Creek. Writing in the eighteenth century, William Copeland Borlase correctly described it as a 'half natural, half artificial dolmen' within which he found nothing but a small flint chip.[46] Another, but far less likely, candidate for a burial site was identified within the same parish of St Keverne by archaeologists in the early twentieth century. Unfortunately, a subsequent search by the Ordnance Survey of the land at Kilter revealed nothing that resembled the chambered tomb described, but rather a landscape full of naturally occurring boulders.[47] Lastly, it was reported in 1851 that in Mabe parish 'about 70 fathoms NW of Antron Village, in a field called Rocky Close, was a cromlech fifteen years ago, with its top stone thrown off; but since that time it has altogether been destroyed by the stone cutters'.[48]

Such a question does not arise with regard to the deceased of the subsequent Bronze Age. The markers of its dead are numerous, and not least on Goonhilly Downs where more than sixty mounds, some standing 4 or 5ft high after thousands of years, can still be seen. They are, without doubt, the most conspicuous relics of pre-Iron Age activity south of the river. Many others exist, or once existed, closer to the water. One such lost site was uncovered in the late 1700s at Treath, and described by Richard Polwhele with his usual combination of ebullience and attention to detail:

> On the removal of a part of a garden-terrace, there appeared, about forty feet distant from the house, and about five feet deep, some rude moor-stones, which, as they were laid open, had evidently the shape and size of a modern coffin. They were put together without cement, forming sides and ends, and a covering: but the bottom was the fast or *the country*, as we term it; on which lay a black unctuous substance, like that contained in urns, about two or three inches deep. There was no appearance of bones. The moorstone was black, and the earth around it red as if burnt: the former was almost in a decomposed state. Six or seven feet from this coffin was found another, of nearly the same form and dimensions: its contents, too, the ashes of the dead. A third was also discovered; and a fourth, and a fifth – all resembling the first in every point.[49]

Something very similar to that at Treath was uncovered at Meudon in Mawnan shortly before the outbreak of the Second World War. Here a *cist* – usually a small stone 'box', but in this case a simple slab – covered the remnants of an urn within which were cremated remains.[50] Nearby cropmarks almost certainly indicate the vestigial presence of another burial mound.[51] Indeed, there are several other possible lost barrows within the parish, including three upon the higher ground of Boskensoe Downs. A similar number were recorded by Charles Henderson at Carlidnack, but they have all long since been ploughed to nothing.[52, 53]

The same agricultural fate befell a number of possible burial mounds around Constantine, most notably in the north of the parish at Nancrossa and in the south at Merthen. Further west there is an extant tumulus at Lower Carwythenack near Gweek, although only one 'bowl barrow' remains at Boskenwyn of those denoted on a late nineteenth-century Ordnance Survey map. An impressive, albeit assumed, example still exists south of the river upon high ground at Roskruge, but those closest to the water are located upon 'the Herra' on the south bank of Gillan Creek. Upon this fascinating little promontory of rock there are two mounds, although only the eastern one is plainly visible to the untrained eye. Others obliterated by farming and now only ghostly outlines in fields can be found at Higher Roskorwell, Trewarnevas and Lannarth, while sherds of a late Bronze Age cinerary urn were uncovered near Trewothack in the mid-twentieth century.[54]

In truth, some of these prehistoric tumuli might not have been for burial of the dead at all. Some could be territorial markers, religious sites, or the remains of ceremonial backfilling of dwellings. Few have ever been excavated anywhere in Cornwall, and those that have been have provided radiocarbon dates suggesting use during the mid- to late second millennium BC. Analysis of cremated bone fragments recovered from Godrevy headland near Hayle were dated to between 1616 and 1493 BC, while charred remains found within a *cist* at Harlyn Bay in North Cornwall were found to date from between 2120 and 1880 BC.[55 56]

The differences between burial practices in the Neolithic and Bronze Ages are important because they provide evidence of the remarkable change to society that took place 4,000 years ago. The Neolithic was characterised by collective burials within noticeable megalithic monuments, of which Lanyon Quoit near Penzance is an outstanding example. Although anything similar has yet to be found in the vicinity of the Helford, curious 'entrance graves' are also common in Penwith and the Isles of Scilly, and most likely date from the Neolithic to Bronze Age transition period.

Human remains extracted from Neolithic funerary monuments across England and Ireland frequently show signs of excarnation. In effect, the bodies of the dead were left open to the elements before the remaining bones were placed with others into a specially constructed tomb or long barrow. It is probable that only those at the upper end of the increasingly hierarchical society were afforded such imposing resting places, something that might partly explain the far lower incidence of such megalithic sites. In contrast, the Bronze Age was far more about the individual, hence the pro-liferation of circular burial mounds. Moreover, it was a time when cremation was prevalent, especially during the middle period from around 1500 BC.

Although these hallmarks of burial practice within each age are blunt gen-eralisations, there can be little doubt that there was an extraordinary cultural shift between the two. Was this, as many anthropologists have argued, simply the result of assimilating new ideas from elsewhere? Were the people who erected The Three Brothers of Grugwith the forefathers of those who built the round barrows on nearby Goonhilly and around the Helford? Were the Treworval arrowheads found just a few steps apart yet separated by 1,000 years fashioned by distantly related individuals or familial strangers?

No human remains from the Mesolithic period have ever been unearthed in Cornwall and probably never will on account of its acidic soils. Moreover, only a few charred fragments of cremated bones from two Neolithic tombs have been uncovered.[57] However, despite a paucity of material for analysis, our ever-expanding knowledge of DNA means that we now know there were several great migrations into the British Isles during prehistory. The Helford River would not have been immune from these waves of colonisa-tion, and Cornwall as a whole was profoundly changed by the third.

The first was that of the hunter-gatherer families and groups whose ances-tors had moved incrementally further away from their ice age refugia with every generation. The second was that of primitive farmers and, just like the hunter-gatherers before them, settlement was by both men and women. Although there must surely have been some friction between the groups of Neolithic agriculturalists and the indigenous people they encountered, there is no evidence to suggest that they did not co-exist relatively peace-fully. Indeed, the genetic testimony for 'intermarriage' suggests exactly that. It is just that those women who married into farming families survived for longer and had many more children than those who did not.

Very few men can trace their direct paternal lineage to either of these Mesolithic or Neolithic pioneers. However, there will still be some whose male ancestors ate hazelnuts at Poldowrian or fished the calm waters of the estuary more than 7,000 years ago. Today they might as easily live by the Humber, Hudson or Sydney Harbour as by the Helford. Ancient female Mesolithic DNA is in slightly more plentiful supply and, as such, there could be tens of thousands of people who share a common ancestor in whomever it was who lost the finely crafted adze at Mawgan Creek.

Those who raised the first stones, perhaps the giant Maen Pearn menhir amongst them, would have been genetically distinct from the hunter-gatherers. Their forebears had originated neither in Iberia nor along the western Atlantic coast of Europe, but in Anatolia to the east.[58] We can also speculate with some confidence that the chisel-type arrowhead found at Treworval was the work of one whose direct paternal ancestor had arrived during this second wave of migration. It is fashioned from a pale, brown-coloured piece of flint that was probably collected from one of the coves around the Helford. Such pebbles can be found today among the prevailing slate stones, quartz gravels and maerl sand on its shores, and especially along the south bank at places such as Penarvon, Ponsence and Gillan Coves.

The oblique arrowhead, on the other hand, is very different. It is smaller and more finely worked. It is also made from a darker and more translucent type of flint, and one that has no known source in the area. The origin of the raw material was most probably around Beer Head in Devon, where can be found vast quantities of the pure unpatinated variety far superior than any Lizard chert churned by the sea. It is believed that such was the demand for this particular stone that it was being transported all across the south-west of England during the Neolithic.[59]

It is most probable, although not entirely impossible, that the two people who fashioned these arrowheads around 1,000 years apart were entirely unrelated in paternal terms. That is, the individual who knapped the transverse during the Neolithic had entirely different male ancestors to the man who fashioned the oblique. The reason is that somewhere between 2200 BC and 2000 BC a new wave of colonisation occurred across Britain and Ireland. These people had originated as cattle herders in the Pontic Steppe and had effectively overwhelmed the earlier Neolithic farmers across Europe. Ancient remains of three men from Rathlin Island in Northern Ireland who lived during the late second millennium BC proved *not* to contain DNA indicative of Neolithic people, but something entirely different. In fact, theirs was almost identical to that found amongst individuals belonging to the Unetice Culture of Central Europe that flourished at the same time.[60]

This migration was the most significant in the history of Britain. No other left such an enduring genetic footprint. Detailed analysis of the DNA of more than 100 people who lived during the Neolithic and Bronze Ages strongly indicates that almost all of the male Neolithic gene pool in the British Isles was replaced by those of the so-called Beaker people in just a couple of hundred years.[61] The overwhelming majority of men in Cornwall (and by extension one assumes the Helford River region) trace their direct paternal lineage to these migrants. So do most males throughout the country, most notably in Wales.

It was these people who probably brought with them the proto-Indo–European language that would subsequently evolve into almost all the tongues spoken across the Continent in the past 3,000 years, including English and 'Celtic'.[62] Had we been able to walk amongst those inhabitants of the river *before* this migration event in, say, 2600 BC, we would have heard them speak a language completely unrelated to Cornish or English. In fact, there is good reason to propose that it might have been a precursor of present-day Basque, an unusual language 'isolate' with no known connection to any other.

However, the Bronze Age migration event was different to those preceding it in one fundamental respect: the genetic record suggests that those who arrived in the British Isles were almost exclusively male. The question is, were the Neolithic men 'peacefully' outcompeted for indigenous females, or was there a male genocide lasting perhaps 100 years or more? While the latter suggestion is disagreeable, there is increasing evidence to suggest that those who swept into Europe around 3000 BC were horsemen who brought with them metallurgical skills.[63] In prehistoric terms, this Yamnaya culture was far more 'weaponised' than that of the agriculturalists. Or it could simply be that the new arrivals brought with them a pestilence to which the indigenous farmers possessed little natural immunity.

It has been suggested that some elements of local folklore common during the eighteenth and nineteenth centuries had been perpetuated since prehistoric times. The eminent Cornish historian Charles Thomas proposed that these might well have originated in the centuries following the establishment of Bronze Age culture in the far west of the British Isles:

To the Bronze Age immigrants, seeping into Cornwall in search of metal, or perhaps *lebensraum*, the smaller fur-clad natives with their untidy secretive lives and their strange tongue must have been objects of contempt. These surely became the 'small people' of Penwith, the 'inferior race' of the Lizard Peninsula, and the 'men of the hills' of the Wendron region.[64]

Indeed, there may never have been any significant conflict at all or, at worst, merely occasional friction between the groups. Instead, the clear dominance of the Bronze Age arrivals in the genetic record might solely be due to the weight of numbers arriving in a relatively short space of time. In any case, while Aileen Fox had been charitable in her description of Neolithic Folk, she was less so when it came to her interpretation of the physical attributes of the newcomers, describing them as 'a race of powerfully built, short, ugly men and women, with round heads and prominent brow-ridges'.

Yet it matters little what they might have looked like. Not only did their coming lay the foundations of modern British, English and Cornish culture, but Bronze Age people transformed the landscape of the river. Many of the Helford's surrounding fields were first laid out during that time and they have changed little since. Many of its villages were probably founded then, too. Curiously, some settlements appear to have been abandoned throughout Cornwall during the latter half of the second millennium BC, but it is not known why. Was the process hastened by an outbreak of disease, conflict or climate-induced famine? Or perhaps the desertion was 'planned' and part of a cultural process we cannot hope to fully understand.[65]

Unfortunately, while the memorials to the Bronze Age dead are as profuse around the river as anywhere else in Cornwall, it is deficient in established sites of occupation. Cropmarks suggestive of curvilinear enclosures of the period are evident at Bonallack in Constantine parish, although only the foolhardy would wager on their date of origin. A similar story is told by numerous other faint outlines of long-lost human enterprise to be found in fields around its shores, and it may be that many of unknown foundation situated close to burial mounds *are* of Bronze Age provenance. Nor should we overlook the sheer length of time that has passed and the deleterious effects of the elements. Alternatively, several settlements of second millennium BC might have been incorporated into, or covered by, later Iron Age earthworks.

Indeed, the only notable archaeological study of an Iron Age site in the Helford River area, namely that at Boden near Manaccan, has uncovered compelling evidence of it having been occupied as early as 1400 BC. Here were found fragments of an unusually large ceramic vessel of 'Trevisker Ware' type (a style associated with the middle Bronze Age) and the perimeter of what might once have been a domestic building from the same period.[66]

Further indication that the wider area flourished between 2000 and 1000 BC was uncovered just outside the river's catchment near Penryn. Excavations at Tremough revealed a circular structure replete with post holes, stone moulds for metalworking, a probable round house, Bronze Age pottery, and curvilinear enclosing ditch.[67] Meanwhile, to the south of the river, quantities of broken 'Beaker' pottery and a round house were found close to the earlier Mesolithic site at Poldowrian indicating probable habitation sometime between 1500 BC and 1000 BC.[68] A possible settlement site is also to be found just to the east of the famous gardens of Trebah, where a slight curve to a field boundary and recovered flint scraper provide encouraging clues.

Yet while extant remains of actual dwellings close to the river have so far proved elusive, the products of Bronze Age industry have given themselves up in modestly greater number. A slate axe was discovered close to Frenchman's Creek in the early 1950s, and another fashioned from Limestone was found at nearby Tremayne a decade later. A bronze 'palstave' axe of circa 1300 BC was revealed by ground works close to Porthallow in the late twentieth century, while another example from the later Bronze Age had previously been found close to Gillan Creek.[69]

Flint artefacts of both Neolithic and Bronze Age origin such as those found at Treworval have turned up regularly for archaeologists and unsuspecting layman alike. Lithic scatters have been encountered in every single parish surrounding the Helford, from Penpoll in Mawnan to Tregiddris in St Martin-in-Meneage. They will continue to be so. It is rich in such diminutive remains.

While we might consider the tiny pieces of worked flint to be the most enduring relics of the prehistoric era, we overlook something far greater: the very roads along which we travel. Both the lanes close to the river and the ridgeways of the higher ground were first established by Neolithic and

Bronze Age inhabitants. We might sometimes wonder why one will bend for no understandable reason, yet we can no longer see the round house it once curved around or the sacred megalith it was intended to approach. The easiest routes across the landscape were first observed, traversed and established by those who made it their home more than 5,000 years ago. G.K. Chesterton believed that 'before the Roman came to Rye or out to Severn strode, the rolling English drunkard made the rolling English road', but not here. Neither England nor Cornwall existed as geographical entities when the routes between Constantine and Mawnan, Manaccan and St Keverne, or Mawgan-in-Meneage and Helston were first established by farmers and traders.

However, while overland travel was important to those living at the turn of the tenth century BC, that undertaken by sea was far more so. It was not the highways that had brought waves of new arrivals, but the water. An even greater number of ships would soon appear on the horizon, and they would further change the landscape and culture of the Helford – a river whose importance would soon eclipse every other south-western estuary.

3

ANCIENT MARINERS

In 1999, two illegal treasure hunters deep within Germany's Ziegelroda Forest uncovered a collection of extraordinary artefacts including swords, hatchets, and fragments of jewellery. But of all the items they unearthed that night it was an unusual disc decorated with golden stars and crescents that proved to be by far the most breathtaking.

The 'Nebra Sky Disc' is the oldest depiction of the visible universe ever discovered. While its symbolic, religious and astronomical importance remains a matter of conjecture, the physical properties of this remarkable *objet d'art* are now far better understood. Although some historians were initially sceptical of its provenance, it was later demonstrated to have been fashioned during the Bronze Age, perhaps around 1600 BC. The copper was found to have been sourced from prehistoric mines near Bischofshofen in Austria, but the gold of its decoration had come from two very separate sites: the Carpathian Mountains and, surprisingly, the Carnon Valley in Cornwall.[1] It is astonishing to think that both the expertise to extract this precious metal and the sophisticated trade network required to distribute it were well established in south-west Britain during the mid-second millennium BC.

Cornwall's association with gold is well documented. Traces were often found by miners seeking tin and, in 1702, a patent was granted to a gentleman in Truro who intended to separate the two metals by 'precipitation in a reverberatory furnace'. Alas, the general eighteenth-century consensus was that chance findings amounted to little in terms of profitability, even though there was cause for optimism on occasions, as William Borlase recorded:

> … in 1753, some persons of the parish of St Stephen's Branel, streaming for tin in the parish of Creed, near the borough of Granpont [Grampound], and perceiving some grains of a yellow colour, very small, but yet so heavy as to resist the water, culled out some of the largest grains and carried the tin to a melting-house near Truro. The gold was in such plenty in this tin, that the melter, Mr Walter Roswarne, taking the gold at first for mundic or copper, 'blamed them for bringing it for sale without having first burnt it; but, upon assaying the ore, found it to make a very great produce, and exceedingly fine metal: the miners then took out of their pockets several pieces of pure gold, and one stone as large as a walnut, with a pure vein of gold in the middle of the stone, about the bigness of a goose quill; the clear bits of gold, and that in the stone, were then assayed, and produced just an ounce of pure gold'.[2]

Other singular examples were said to have been found with values of 17 and 15s, although the largest by far was 'in the possession of Mr William Lemon, Esq. Of Carclew, which weighs in gold-coin three pounds three shillings'. Earlier still, Richard Carew had observed in his *Survey of Cornwall* of 1602 that 'tynners doe also often find little hoppes of gold amongst their owre, which they keep in quils, and sell to the goldsmiths'. Such practices were certainly continuing 200 years later when small pieces of jewellery were still being fashioned by local dealers.[3]

Aside from veins of gold-quartz found in the Treore Mine near Port Issac, the occurrence of recoverable Cornish gold has always been limited to alluvial deposits in rivers and streams.[4] These are most often found where the flow dwindles to such a degree that fine grains are deposited in the sediment, something known to prospectors ancient and modern alike. During the early nineteenth century gold was recorded as having been found at several locations throughout the county, most notably in 'the black titaniferous sands of the *Manaccan* valley' to the south of the Helford.[5] Late nineteenth-century reports also mention tiny grains being found in the streams around Nare

Point and at Mudgeon Vean near St Martin.[6] Indeed, notwithstanding the verifiable proof of extraction in the Carnon Valley, it could be argued that one of the richest areas for gold extraction in prehistoric Cornwall would have been around the Helford River. Why this should be so is due to the same geological peculiarity that accounted for those finds cited by Borlase in places such as St Ewe, Creed and Kenwyn.

The Carrick Thrust is a minor shear in the Earth's surface that runs between Mevagissey in the east and Loe Pool, near Helston, in the west. As it passes the Helford River it cuts through the tips of Port Navas and Polwheveral Creeks, with Lamprophyre Dykes associated with it being found in several locations around the estuary. Such sites include Men-Aver Beach near Nare Point, the Gew by Ponsence Cove, and the cliffs below Mawnan Church, each once a fissure where mineral-rich molten rock accumulated and hardened 350 million years or more ago. Lamprophyre might well look austere, but it is inextricably linked to the occurrence of the most precious metal known to man.

It was once said that an amateur enthusiast of gold panning had found enough in one unspecified stream along the upper reaches of the river to afford a week's board and lodgings. Although such a report may be a little spurious, there can be little doubt that sites all along the Carrick Thrust – and thus the Helford – were being similarly worked in antiquity. Many Bronze Age artefacts found in Ireland were fashioned from gold sourced in south-west Britain rather than in Ireland itself, the inference being that material gained from a distant 'esoteric' source was imbued with more value than domestic produce.[7] Some have gone as far as to claim that Cornwall and west Devon were once a 'Klondike' in miniature, with one estimate claiming that as much as 200kg of gold were extracted between the twenty-second and seventeenth centuries BC.[8]

Although jewellery made from gold has occasionally been found in Neolithic contexts, such as at the Varna Necropolis in Bulgaria, the prehistoric manufacture and trade in the metal is largely limited to the Bronze Age. Indeed, it is almost entirely absent from the archaeological record of the following Iron Age, with those artefacts found in Cornwall, such as the Rillaton Gold Cup and Harlyn Bay lunulae, all dating from the second millennium BC. There will probably be such aurous relics lying in the soil of the

Lizard Peninsula that, if ever found, will surely accompany the remains of a once-important member of Bronze Age society.

The truth is that gold was merely a by-product of extracting something far more important to trade: tin. The rich mineralogy of the south-west peninsula of the British Isles has been understood for fifty centuries or more and by a great many peoples. Although the present-day counties of Devon and Cornwall have been an important source of metals such as copper, arsenic, and silver over the years, tin has been the principal element around which their combined mining histories have been woven. It is a metal with which modern humans are extremely familiar, yet it is also vanishingly rare.

The primary ore in which it is found is cassiterite, an oxide associated with quartz veins in igneous rocks such as granite. Although the abandoned mine houses are the most manifest symbols of the eighteenth- and nineteenth-century mining peak, for the vast majority of history the production of smelted tin focused upon sources found within the sediments of streams and rivers. Being significantly heavier than other constituent parts of granite, the ore was extracted much in the same way as 'panning' for gold. Once purified, its inclusion with copper – the principal constituent of bronze – meant that robust and durable artefacts could be cast, ranging from spear heads and axes to finger rings and awls. The ancient world craved sources of tin, and even mythical heroes such as Achilles were associated with the metal.

There were a select number of places from which this most coveted of elements could be obtained during prehistoric times. In Asia they were confined to Uzbekistan, Afghanistan and Tajikistan, while in Europe the border between present-day Germany and the Czech Republic, the north-west of the Iberian Peninsula, and Brittany were the most exploited. All were worked from the Bronze Age onwards. However, despite little evidence of significant industrial endeavours in the third millennium BC, it is clear from both the Nebra Sky Disc and a tin 'rod' found in Sweden that Cornwall was an important source 4,000 years ago.[9]

Writing in the fifth century BC, it was the Greek historian Herodotus who first documented a trade in the metal, although he admitted to having no knowledge of the place from whence it came. Four hundred years later in the first century BC, the Greek geographer Strabo introduced the concept of a group of islands off the coast of Britain called the *Cassiterides*. Tin, he says in his *Geography* is 'produced both in the country of the barbarians who live beyond Lusitania, and in the Cassiterides Islands; and tin is brought to Massilia [Marseilles] from the British Islands also'.

The identity of this mysterious archipelago has been debated for centuries, it supposedly being where Phoenician traders who sailed across the Mediterranean Sea and Western Atlantic around 1500 BC to 600 BC acquired their tin. Strabo declared that they were ten in number, being located 'near each other in the high sea to the north of the port of the Artabrians', their whereabouts coveted by Rome.[10] It is tempting to conclude that the Cassiterides were the Isles of Scilly, although they were far more likely a fictional construct from an age where stories were famously embellished for effect. However, we cannot immediately dismiss the legend that adventurous Phoenicians frequented the North Atlantic, far from their home along the coasts of Lebanon, Israel and Syria. The belief that they travelled to southern Britain has long been held in Cornwall, even though there is scant archaeological evidence to support the theory. The hypothesis which holds that their ships frequented the haven of Helford has yet to be reinforced by the discovery of any artefact, but such oral tradition is difficult to repudiate. Perhaps a trade in perishable goods might account for a lack of definitive relics.

Arguably the most important ancient document that confirms the existence of an export of tin prior to the Roman invasion is the *Bibliotecha historica* of Diodorus Siculus. Although written at some point between 60 and 30 BC, Diodorus is supposed to have based his account on a long-lost description of a voyage made by the geographer Pytheas 300 years earlier. This describes the 'inhabitants of Britain who dwell about the promontory known as Belerium' as particularly welcoming towards foreign merchants, and also being those who worked the tin into ingots. These castings were then transported across the sea to Gaul, where they were carried on horseback for a month until reaching the mouth of the River Rhone.

The 'Belerium', or 'Belerion', that Diodorus described is generally accepted to have been Cornwall or the wider south-west peninsula, although some have suggested that it specifically relates to Land's End. The name is thought to mean 'shining land'. More contentious, however, is the identity of an island referred to as 'Ictis' where the merchants acquired their tin from the natives. Although it may have been a geographic myth based on distorted second-hand accounts, many locations along the south coast of England have been proposed as its site. These include the Isle of Wight, Burgh Island (a topographical near match), Looe Island, and Mount Batten near Plymouth.[11] However, the most popular theory is that which advances St Michael's Mount in west Cornwall – a causeway submerged twice a day by incoming tides gives it more than just a passing resemblance to the island described by Diodorus. But the search for Ictis is a distraction. In truth, there are several places supported by geological and archaeological evidence that are far more likely to have been important prehistoric trading sites. The fact that none of them correspond to poetic details within *Bibliothecha historica* is completely irrelevant.

It is important to acknowledge that St Michael's Mount *is* perfectly placed to act as an outlet for the tin-rich grounds between Marazion and St Erth. However, the Hayle Estuary – bounded by the present-day town of St Ives to the west – would surely have been a safer place for the loading of merchant ships than Mount's Bay. Why would prehistoric seafarers prefer to navigate and beach their vessels in waters frequently exposed to harsh Atlantic winds rather than a sheltered estuary? Perhaps their visits from the Continent were seasonal, or maybe the route around Land's End too perilous. It is possible that they utilised both, but there were better alternatives to either.

Another obvious location for the dispatch of prehistoric tin across the English Channel is the River Fowey. Close to both the St Austell and Bodmin Moor granite outcrops, its estuary is a small natural harbour offering great protection to vessels in all but the worst southerly gales. The ground to both north and west is rich in cassiterite, especially across the large area of upland terrain it drains (once known more appropriately as Fowey Moor rather than Bodmin). However, the River Camel also rises on the same ground from which it flows north to Padstow Bay and the open sea. It is perhaps no coincidence that some of the Camel's tributaries still contain exceedingly rich accumulations of tin.

However, there are two locations far more suited to the export of tin than all others. One of these is the western side of the Fal Estuary, which provides access to the abundant grounds of the Carnon Valley. The other, of course, is the Helford River. But why should this sea inlet of middling proportions stand out among so many other auspicious places from which to conduct trade 2,000 or more years ago?

It is thought by some that the intermediaries in the export of tin from the south-west of the British Isles were the Veneti, a Celtic tribe of present-day north-west France. These maritime people of the south coast of Brittany were described in detail by Julius Caesar in *Commentarii de Bello Gallico* first published in the mid-first century BC:

> The influence of this state is by far the most considerable of any of the countries on the whole sea coast, because the Veneti both have a very great number of ships, with which they have been accustomed to sail to Britain, and [thus] excel the rest in their knowledge and experience of nautical affairs; and as only a few ports lie scattered along that stormy and open sea, of which they are in possession, they hold as tributaries almost all those who are accustomed to traffic in that sea.

Prior to their defeat at the hands of Caesar, the Veneti were clearly the most important middle-men of prehistoric trade between Britain and the rest of Europe. Tin extracted from Cornwall and Devon would have made its way to the coast, where these accomplished sailors would have loaded it on to their ships before setting sail for home along the Armorican coast. When Diodorus Siculus wrote of those in 'Belerium' who were 'especially hospitable to strangers' he was attesting to this very interaction. And it was those same Veneti merchants who would begin the process of transporting the tin to the shores of the Mediterranean Sea at places such as Marseilles.

The Veneti would have known the Helford intimately, being both well-equipped to sail across turbulent seas and then successfully navigate its creeks. Caesar's observations on their impressive ships proves it, these being described as robustly constructed of oak, flat-bottomed, and using sails made of hides or thin leather that would better withstand the conditions experienced in the Atlantic.[12] Admittedly, most of Cornwall would have been within reach of sturdy vessels such as these but, as most modern mariners will attest, while sailing through a storm is one thing, deliberately steering into one is quite another. In effect, the Helford *was* the best option from both a geographic and meteorological standpoint. Trade seeks out the easiest and most profitable possibilities, and those were to be found in the calm waters guarded by Nare Point and Rosemullion Head.

First, the Helford River is the most southerly haven in the British Isles. Of course, the Fal and Fowey are both just a few miles further north, but all others would have involved a significantly longer journey across perilous and unpredictable seas for those approaching from the south. Today's sailors know full well the dangers of crossing the Channel and, as such, it is manifestly obvious that their prehistoric and Roman counterparts would have faced great adversity even under conditions we might consider relatively benign today. Although there is no doubt that European seafaring merchants from the Bronze Age onwards sailed into the estuaries along Cornwall's north coast, their preference must surely have been those on the south, assuming equal gains were to be had.

Second, the Helford would have offered the safest of anchorages to those ancient mariners, just as it does for small vessels in the twenty-first century. Once past the dangers posed by the Manacles to the south, any ship entering the roadstead would have been protected from all but the worst of storms. Only malevolent winds from the east or south-east make the river perilous, and such weather is the exception to the south-westerly rule. It is, without doubt, one of the finest natural harbours in the North Atlantic for vessels of modest size.

However, the navigational benefits it offered would have meant nothing without practical access to sources of tin and, in this crucial respect, the Helford is peerless. Although there is little in the streams to the south, the prehistoric trader would have well known the rich sources of the metal in those to the north-west. Indeed, within the present-day parish of Wendron are to be found some of the highest concentrations of alluvial tin anywhere in Cornwall.[13] That these should have been exploited in prehistory is best evidenced by the Trenear Mortar Stone, now a Scheduled Ancient Monument, which is to be found in the Cober Valley. This enigmatic granite slab is the only known prehistoric ore-grinding mortar in Britain.[14] Covered in smooth oval hollows created by those crushing rocks by hand, it is almost certainly a relic of Bronze Age industry. It is profoundly moving to think that the hard labours of those at the mortar stone more than 2,000 ago contributed to some of the bronze treasures found throughout Europe.

From this tin-rich area the producers and merchants would have had several potential options for export across the English Channel, including the Hayle Estuary and Mount's Bay. However, the Helford would have surely been the preferred choice on account of its proximity and relative safety. Yet even if this were not the case, the streams that flow directly into the river at Gweek and Polwheveral Creek would have been valuable sources in themselves. Indeed, close to the head of the latter is a curious stone embankment known locally as The Ramshire. Although neither its true function or age are known, one of the reasons suggested for its existence is that it once acted as a dam for tin streaming. If this is true it becomes irrelevant that it is *probably* of post-medieval date rather than prehistoric, as even this would prove that the extraction of tin by such means was once a practical proposition. Alternatively, it may simply have been a structure for holding timber, or perhaps a swan pool.[15]

Whether they hailed from Brittany, the Mediterranean or elsewhere, the early traders who came to the Helford River would have been sailing up a body of water not unlike the one we see today. Much of the ancient woodland that once shrouded it would have already been cleared during the Neolithic period, and many of the present-day field boundaries already established for 1,000 years. Although sea levels were perhaps 3 or 4ft lower in the first millennium BC than they are today, the Helford would have possessed deeper channels allowing access to the head of the river on all but the lowest of tides.

However, do not imagine for one moment that overseas merchants would have anchored in a quiet backwater where only a few primitive native inhabitants would have been on hand to meet them. The truth is precisely the opposite. Indeed, during the latter part of the Iron Age the Helford River area would have boasted one of the highest population densities in the British Isles. This is not a fanciful exaggeration intended to overstate its importance, but rather one that is wholly supported by observable evidence. In fact, for a time at least, the river might have been as important and vibrant a place per square mile as the Thames. That time was the century before the Roman invasion, and its legacy is a remarkable collection of settlements and defended sites that are still visible today. The Helford was once Cornwall's Iron Age 'metropolis'.

In 1833 a gentleman cutting a new road through part of his estate near St Keverne made an unusual discovery. There, 2 or 3ft below the surface, lay a number of stone graves, each formed by six stones placed on edge: two on either side and one at each end with each aligned in an east–west direction. Within some were found an array of artefacts including glass beads, bangles, and a brass ring, but the most impressive object to be pulled out of the ground was a decorated mirror, about 6in in diameter and surprisingly well polished given its having lain under the soil.[16] Not that he was aware at the time, the finder, Mr Samuel James, had stumbled upon a significant Iron Age cemetery. Unfortunately, the graves no longer exist, but the Trelan Bahow mirror itself does, protected in perpetuity by the British Museum.

This beautiful bronze object has since been dated to some point during the early first century BC. However, it is not entirely unique, with a number of other similar artefacts having been recovered over the past 200 years, including the lavishly decorated Holcombe Mirror from Devon. But the one found at Trelan, 4 miles south of the Helford, most closely resembles that known as the Mayer Mirror, whose provenance is thought to be somewhere in the south-east of England. The 'Aston Mirror' found in Hertfordshire also bears similarities but, unlike the Trelan Bahow item, lacks its handle. In all surviving cases, this particular element features a loop from which the mirror might have been hung from a wall. Interestingly, the mirrors found in Britain are significantly different to their continental counterparts of comparable age.[17]

The initial assessment of the Trelan Bahow looking glass was that it must have belonged to a woman, and an important woman at that. This may be true, although we will never know given that all identifiable human remains had decomposed long before it was discovered. But it might equally be a lazy assumption, based on the behaviour and culture of modern males rather than their Iron Age forebears. However, on the basis that a similar artefact found at Birdlip in Gloucestershire *was* interred with a young woman, the likelihood is that the individual buried at Trelan was also female.

Arguably of greater archaeological interest are the details of the burial itself. Formal Iron Age cemeteries are rare, and the practice of crouched inhumation within cists largely confined to the south-west of England and Wales. Of course, we cannot be certain that the body at Trelan *was* buried in such a foetal arrangement, but based on contemporary examples from elsewhere in Cornwall, most notably at Harlyn Bay on the north coast, it seems most likely. In most cases the dead were laid on their left rather than right sides and, when present, grave goods often feature items 'imported' from elsewhere in southern England and also from south-west Europe. Such burial practices appear to have reached their zenith between the second century BC and the early Roman period.[18]

It is probable that many Iron Age cist graves around the river were inadvertently destroyed by increasingly mechanised agricultural practice during the nineteenth and twentieth centuries. A deep plough under power would easily mutilate such sites, leaving them unrecognisable as something of archaeological importance. Moreover, unlike their Neolithic and Bronze Age counterparts, Iron Age society was seemingly less concerned by creating conspicuous mounds or stone markers, thus making them more prone to accidental damage. However, there must surely be hundreds, perhaps thousands, still lying deep enough below the topsoil to have avoided ruination. And if this seems to be an unfeasibly optimistic estimate, consider the extraordinary number of domestic settlement sites to be found close to the river's shores. Hundreds of thousands would have lived and died within its catchment over thirty generations or more between 800 BC and the Roman conquest.

How large the Iron Age population of Cornwall became during the period is unknowable, but some have estimated that at its height it may have been as high as 100,000.[19] However, recorded rounds and other enclosed settlements indicate several areas of particularly dense population for the time. Chief amongst these is West Penwith, whose less disturbed uplands have ensured the survival of many sites, not least the villages of Chysauster and Carn Euny. But there is also a significant cluster to be found by the Helford, and especially around upper reaches. In fact, both the Fal and Fowey estuaries appear sparsely populated in comparison, although it is entirely possible that many archaeological sites have yet to be identified in both cases. Still, that so many have survived in an agricultural area such as the Helford is indicative enough: it was a place of exceptional importance in the first millennium BC. Even before aerial photography had made the profusion of Iron Age sites in the area all the more notable, the naturalist Oliver Rackham had come to the same conclusion:

There can be no doubt of the Iron Age landscape. Around the Helford River there is perhaps the greatest concentration in Great Britain of rounds, hillforts and similar structures … Whatever the reason for this concentration of earthworks, they imply a large population, and their siting demands good views of the sea.[20]

Broadly speaking, the transition between the late Bronze Age and the early Iron Age is thought to have taken place around 800 BC. Of course, this date does not represent a distinct horizon, but suffices in terms of compartmentalising archaeological and cultural differences between the two. However, evidence suggests that, in Cornwall, it was not until the seventh century BC that iron began to dominate bronze for use in tools. As such, other diagnostic features such as the construction of early hill forts and changes in ceramic design have instead been used to mark the transition.[21]

Archaeological remains from the early Iron Age before 400 BC are not especially common in Cornwall. The pottery from this period is generally simple in form, and only a few sites have produced ceramic sherds that can be confidently ascribed to it. Two of these are cliff castles: Trevelgue Head near Newquay, and Maen Castle close to Land's End. It should be noted, however, that very few cliff castles have been the subject of detailed excavation, and those of Dennis Head and Rosemullion Head could both yet prove to have been founded in the early first millennium. This seems to be particularly likely in the case of the latter given that Bronze Age barrows supposedly once stood within.[22] However, evidence for settlement during the latter part of the early Iron Age has been uncovered at the multi-period archaeological site at Boden Vean, near St Anthony-in-Meneage.[23]

Precisely why the period should be so archaeologically mute is almost certainly due to the population collapse that took place at the end of the preceding Bronze Age. There is little doubt that climate change played a significant role in this decline, as the abandoned settlements, field systems and stone circles of Dartmoor imply. Having flourished during the middle Bronze Age when the prevailing weather was kindlier, the onset of cooler, wetter, conditions from circa 1400 BC dramatically reduced the agricultural prospects of its inhabitants.[24] The people of other upland areas such as Bodmin Moor soon joined in the exodus.

A second, more marked, climatic downturn commenced around 900 BC in which wetter and stormier conditions affected the British Isles, most notably in the north and west. But while human activity across Europe seems to have declined most conspicuously from 800 BC onwards, the most observable episode of climatic deterioration did not take place until half a century later. Clearly, something else other than climate change was responsible for the dramatic slump in population.[25]

It seems increasingly likely that the transition between the ages of Bronze and Iron was one of extreme economic and social upheaval. Across Europe old trading networks would have broken down as demand for different raw materials grew, and tribal conflict would have been widespread. As forced migration of cultures took place, the transmission of disease would have become a far greater threat. Indeed, archaeological study may yet one day reveal a catastrophic pandemic that swept the entire continent from the Mediterranean to Scandinavia. The twin threats of war and disease might well underpin the growth in numbers of hill forts and cliff castles both in Cornwall and beyond. They were refuges for all eventualities.

Those living around the Helford during that time would not have been entirely insulated from the unrest occurring across the sea and elsewhere in the islands. Given that the river was undoubtedly a primary site of tin export, the changes in demand for that particular constituent of bronze would have affected the local economy to some degree. However, tin remained necessary for many artefacts in a great many places, so the change was probably more of a temporary setback than a comprehensive collapse in the industry.

In any case, the Helford would have better weathered the storm than almost anywhere else in the south-west of Britain. The cooler climate and its attendant problem of reduced agricultural productivity would have been partly offset by the superior nature of the ground. The land within the river's catchment is more conducive to farming than the majority of that to be found within Cornwall, with most of the county covered by poor or moderate soils.[26] It follows, therefore, that significantly greater populations could be sustained by the relatively rudimentary farming practices of the Iron Age around estuaries than in upland sites. The sheltered river would also have provided abundant food for the pressured Iron Age population just as it had done for the local Mesolithic communities 4,000 years earlier. While most of Cornwall's ancient woodland had already been cleared, the last vestiges around the upper shores would have been sustainably coppiced for fuel and building materials. This invaluable resource would have been fiercely protected by those communities living around them and may even have become a source of violent conflict at times.

High population densities, however, require something above and beyond the simple ability of the land to support increasing numbers of human beings through agriculture. In earlier cultures such as the Neolithic, settlement clusters were often formed because of a ceremonial or 'religious' focus. The Iron Age, on the other hand, was less dominated by spiritual riches and more by the material variety. Unusually, the Helford was pivotal in the export of not one, but two significant sources of wealth. It was, without any doubt whatsoever, an extremely important Iron Age 'point of interaction' within a network of trading points along the English Channel.[27] If the Helford's importance to the ancient tin trade has been overlooked, so too has the gabbroic clay ceramic industry which took place just a few miles to the south and which flourished for thousands of years.[28] The prosperity of the river's inhabitants really was underpinned by the very geology beneath their feet.

Gabbro is a dark, igneous rock formed when magma trapped deep beneath the Earth's surface cooled to form a crystalline mass. Named by an early nineteenth-century geologist after a small village in Tuscany, it is to be found in numerous places all over the world, but in the British Isles is limited to only a few places – invariably very beautiful – including the Isle of Skye and Carrock Fell in Cumbria. The most famous outcrop, however, is that to be found on the Lizard Peninsula, where it weathers to form clay 'most suitable for the variable temperature and thermal shocks likely to be experienced by bonfire-fired ware'.[29] Such characteristics would have been prized indeed.

It was in 1969 that the celebrated archaeologist Dr David Peacock concluded that almost all the early Neolithic pottery found in Cornwall had been made from material derived from one particular source. This, he said, was 'an area of somewhat altered basic or intermediate plutonic rocks and the only possible source in south-west England is the gabbro that outcrops over about 7 square miles of the Lizard Head in Cornwall'.[30] Here, close to the present-day village of St Keverne, would have lived a thriving 'industrial' community employed in extracting the clay and, perhaps, fashioning it into exportable wares. Ceramics created from gabbroic clay, both wholly and in part, have been found on Neolithic sites as far away as Hembury in Devon and Windmill Hill in Wiltshire. At Hambledon Hill in Dorset were found almost complete pots within an area seemingly reserved for the deposition of the dead, implying that this simple product of the earth was imbued with a mystical property well beyond its practical nature.

However, the largest collection of gabbroic ceramic fragments comes from excavations undertaken at Carn Brea some 20 miles to the north. Here, in a settlement dating to around 3700 BC, were uncovered around 500 vessels almost all made from clay containing gabbroic temper. So too were the pottery sherds found in early Neolithic pits near Portscatho on the Roseland Peninsula and at the defensive enclosure at Helman Tor on Bodmin Moor.[31] It is therefore not an overstatement to say that this relatively small area of ground to the south of the Helford dominated the production of pottery in the south-west for thousands of years. Moreover, given the certain existence of trading networks operating at that time, the river must surely have been one of its primary locations for dispatch.

The greatest mystery, however, is how such a significant endeavour taking in so great a period of history – from the lithic age to that of iron, some 4,000 years – should have left no trace of its centre of production. Neither professional historian nor layman archaeologist have so far found the 'ground zero' of gabbroic clay pottery manufacture. Perhaps it is mute, lying somewhere beneath the thin soils of the Lizard Peninsula waiting to be discovered. Or it may be because production was undertaken at a number of sites as small-scale 'cottage industries' and are thus less likely to be visible today.[32] Alternatively, it could simply be that so great a time has elapsed that small sherds have been destroyed by repeated ploughing and other agricultural activity.[33] More likely, however, is that it was the raw clay rather than finished wares being exported; a theory supported by the simple observation that the proportion of gabbroic clay within pottery decreases with distance from St Keverne.

Although the trade had its roots in the Neolithic, the production of gabbroic pottery reached a climax during the Iron Age and Romano–British period. This distinctive feldspar-flecked clay has been found in Trevisker

Ware from the Bronze Age; Glastonbury Ware of the early Iron Age; almost all South Western Decorated Ware of the middle Iron Age; and Cordoned Ware of the late Iron Age. Interestingly, those sites beyond Cornwall that have produced ceramics containing gabbroic clay are disproportionately located towards the south coast.[34] One such location is the famous Maiden Castle in Dorset, where many ceramic sherds have been found to contain clay derived from the Lizard Peninsula.[35] This further endorses the theory that movement of materials was predominantly via water, and quite probably from the shelter of the Helford. Those controlling the resource would no doubt have been wealthy by any prehistoric standard, and it just might be that the individual who was once buried with the mirror and adornments at Trelan derived their apparent riches, directly or indirectly, from Gabbroic clay pottery.

This is not to say that everyone living close to the estuary in the first millennium BC was personally involved in either industry. In fact, a relatively modest proportion of the local population would have concerned itself with the acquisition or movement of clay, pottery, or tin ingots. Instead, most would have supplied the population with the products required to sustain the trades and the wider community. No doubt a great many exotic things were exchanged with foreign merchants, but the bulk of the material needed on a day-to-day basis would have been locally produced: grain, meat, vegetables, drink, wood and clothing among them. Just as many of England's medieval towns were built upon products such as wool or salt, so the lost settlements of the Helford were founded upon earth and metal 1,000 years earlier.

Unlike preceding periods, the most conspicuous relics of Iron Age activity around the river relate not to the dead but to the living. The most obvious of these are the numerous 'rounds' for which archaeological excavations throughout Cornwall have suggested late Iron Age origins, and occupation until the sixth century AD in some cases. The majority, however, flourished during the Romano-British period.[36] Most were surrounded by single ditches whose invariably shallow depths imply a reduced defensive capacity in comparison to hill forts and cliff castles. A great many are small and would have enclosed a solitary dwelling, while others were clearly capable of accommodating numerous families in many separate houses.

The limited excavations of Cornish rounds have indicated that the houses within were also of circular plan. Usually a central ring of posts would have borne the weight of the roof, with the outer wall made of various materials depending upon the location; timber in some, granite or other locally available stone in others. Most possessed a central hearth, the smoke from which would have risen through the thatch above. It is possible that some of those that did not have any 'fireplace' within were used for storage rather than human habitation.

Around the river there are vestiges of numerous Iron Age rounds still to be seen and touched, and the previous existence of a great many more are given away by tell-tale crop marks visible from above. One of the most impressive is surely that at Carlidnack in the parish of Mawnan, although it now lies entirely within inaccessible private land. The tree-capped earth ramparts to the north are breathtaking, being over 14ft in height in places and in a remarkable state of preservation given that they have withstood the elements and human interference for 2,000 years or more. Here too are the remnants of what would once have been an impressive defensive ditch, now shallow but formerly of considerable depth. Walking around them on a still winter's day is to lose the sense of passing time.

The centre of the Carlidnack round has long since been levelled through agricultural labour, and also partly through the construction of a dwelling. When the previous building was demolished in the late twentieth century to make way for a larger house, the digging of foundation trenches allowed archaeologists to observe, retrieve and record that which lay beneath the soil. There were no signs of structures within the limited excavations, but over seventy pottery fragments were recovered, most coming from two broken jars. Many showed signs of having been burnt after breakage.[37] Although most of these fragments were attributed to the first and second centuries AD and subsequently used as evidence for dating the round to that period, a small number of pieces belonged to earlier South Western Decorated Ware suggestive of pre-Roman settlement.[38] Indeed, that the foundation of the round should have been ascribed to the Romano–British period was an act of undue caution based upon very limited observation. After all, Bronze Age barrows once stood just outside its perimeter suggesting possible continuous use for 3,000 years or more.

Carlidnack is well over 300ft across and covers an area of more than 1½ acres. And yet an almost circular outer enclosure containing what was probably a contemporary field system is also evident. This outer perimeter is more than 800ft in diameter in places and falls steeply to valleys that run down towards Maenporth. It may be that traces of ancient dwellings lie hidden beneath the earth of this peripheral domain, with the inner, more fortified element, a defended place of refuge in turbulent times. Curiously, there appears to be an annexe to the west, although for what purpose it was constructed is a matter of pure speculation. Recorded variously as 'Kaerluniek' and 'Carlunyck' in 1327 and 1397 respectively, possible origins of the name include 'Fort of the Flax Land' and – less likely albeit of great appeal – 'Fortress of the Moon'. Of all possibilities, however, the 'Homestead above the Anchorage' seems the most credible, overlooking Maenporth as it does.[39, 40]

Carlidnack is not the only extant round in Mawnan. A much-degraded, although potentially important, settlement site is to be found amid farmland between the main village and the outlying settlement of Meudon. Indeed, it is from this Iron Age relic that the latter gains its name, probably being derived from the old Brittonic 'Mawidunon' meaning 'fort of the youth' or similar.[41] The remains visible from the adjacent footpath are limited to a terrace on the slope of the hill and part of the curving boundary 'fossilised' in the hedge to the east.

A little more is evident to the untrained eye at Carwinion, ¼ mile to the south-west. It too is accessible via footpath, although few who walk it are aware they are striding past where a small Iron Age village once flourished. As with that at Meudon, the extent of its boundary has been partly preserved by the hedgerow on its western side. But far more becomes apparent from the slope below from which a central depression encircled by ploughed-down ramparts can be seen. Traces of its ditch can also be made out in places, especially after heavy snowfall, although not to the same extent as that at Carlidnack. The adjacent house and its estate undoubtedly take their names from this prehistoric settlement, which roughly translates as the 'white fort'. The suffix is the same in sound and meaning as that of the River Wnion in North Wales. The Carwinion round is a little more than 200ft in diameter, large enough for perhaps three houses, while the more oval example at Meudon is fractionally larger. Whether their ramparts were once topped with a wooden palisade is not known, and nor is the period in which they were founded. Alas, there is even less diagnostic evidence available for other potential defended settlements within the same parish, including those at Penpoll, Tregarne, Trerose and Mawnan church. Doubtless many more have vanished without trace.

The rounds of Constantine parish were well covered by the illustrious Charles Henderson. Of those he recorded, the small example at Goongillings was of particular interest on account of its position 'on a lofty promontory between the branches of Polwheveral Creek'. He also noted that it was situated below the summit of the hill rather than on top of it, just as most Cornish rounds appear to be. Perhaps choosing to build them in such locations combined the defensive benefits of high ground with the practical avoidance of exposure to the worst of the elements to be endured at the crown. Whatever the reason, the entrances to these rounds were invariably positioned downslope, perhaps to aid drainage.

Also in Constantine are probable Iron Age or Romano–British settlements at Treviades, Trebarvah, Merthen Downs and Trevassack amongst others, although in most cases all that remains are faint outlines in ripening barley or curves in hedgerows. However, the most spectacular cropmarks must surely be those located above Roskymmer Wood near Gweek – the presence of a round more than 200ft in diameter and surrounded by several defensive ditches is breathtaking when viewed from high above. Associated field systems, pits and enclosures can also be discerned from the sky but not the ground. It must have been a far more important and populated place than the presumably contemporary settlement at nearby Gweek Wood, an otherwise better-preserved round.

However, of all the corners of the Helford River catchment none are more notable for their Iron Age relics than St Martin-in-Meneage. That in the poorest state of preservation is to be found above the eastern bank of Vallum Tremayne creek, although of those rounds yet discovered it is closest to the Helford's waters. Less than an acre in size, it is also one of the smallest examples in the area, but whoever built it clearly had lives intimately intertwined with the river.

A far more impressive ancient site in every respect is to be found close to the source of the stream that falls into the same creek above which the

Tremayne settlement stands. In fact, Caer Vallack is a prehistoric puzzle that is likely to continue to confound until comprehensive excavations are made. First, it is of an unusual oval shape with a more traditionally circular annexe of inferior size located to the west. Limited excavations have revealed a small number of fascinating artefacts which include the tip of a Neolithic polished axe and a fragment of South Western Decorated Ware pottery of the middle Iron Age. Caer Vallack was clearly a place of great importance for thousands of years.[42]

Alas, the theory that it might have once been the residence of a local chieftain is at odds with geophysical evidence that revealed a tantalising, but confusing, glimpse of what lies below. The western enclosure lacks any tangible evidence for human habitation except for possible pits that form no recognisable trend or pattern. The eastern enclosure, on the other hand, features signs of possible small-scale industrial activity and, more curiously, a rectilinear anomaly along the northern perimeter.[43] If this *was* a prehistoric building, it certainly bore no resemblance to the familiar round house so often encountered elsewhere.

However, the largest and most important prehistoric enclosure around the river is to be found at Gear, just a few hundred yards away from Caer Vallack. Attempts have been made to find a connection between the two, but Gear Camp is entirely different in almost every way. It is vast, covering almost 15 acres of ground, and possesses ramparts that remain more than 5ft high in places despite the weathering of 2,000 years or more. Polwhele had 'little doubt' that this impressive enclosure was a 'Roman camp of the Saxon class'.[44] So often judicious on matters of antiquity, in this case he was very wrong. Human activity at Gear predates the Roman invasion of Britain by millennia.

Notwithstanding its ancient foundation, the extant boundaries are definitely of Iron Age origin. Gear is a 'Slight Univallate Hillfort', a type whose rarity on a national scale makes it all the more important. It probably took on its present shape at some time between the eighth and sixth centuries BC before being abandoned at an unknown time. And unlike the ambiguous subterranean images revealed at Caer Vallack, those from Gear suggest a thriving community. There are numerous circular anomalies suggestive of dwellings, and evidence of divisions between areas for livestock and human residents.[45] There was also a sizeable gateway in the west side of the enclosure, access through which allowed inhabitants – and presumably visiting traders – passage to Mawgan Creek. If the Helford River had a capital during the Iron Age, it was at Gear.

Although the undulating hills around the river often interrupt lines-of-sight over great distances, there would have been a degree of interconnectivity between its rounds and Gear in particular. That communication between hill forts was possible – and probably desirable – during the Iron Age has been demonstrated in experiments elsewhere, and it seems likely that contact between groups around the Helford could have been easily achieved by beacons or other visual methods.[46] As such, we might speculate that despite the first millennium BC being otherwise notorious for its warfare, conflict and violence, those living around the estuary were interdependent. The river needed to be protected for the benefit of all.

Cliff castles, or at least the limited remains thereof, are common along the coastline of south-west England and South Wales. Such promontory forts are also plentiful in number in Brittany, and especially Finistère, which boasts sizeable examples in Castel-Coz and Pointe de Lostmarc'h. As such, many have tried to establish a connection between the Veneti traders who flourished during the Iron Age and the establishment of such defences in Cornwall. Although there are clear similarities, the idea that powerful chiefs and tribal warlords from the other side of the Channel were responsible for their introduction is unlikely. Their existence in both places owes more to geological affinities than cultural connections, even if we know the latter was well established by that time.

In truth, constructing a cliff castle would have required less manpower and fewer resources than a hill fort. They are simple but effective defensive enclosures defined by the existence of a rampart across the neck of land between the mainland and the headland, invariably across the narrowest point. Some are univallate, a few multivallate. Only a small number have been the subject of detailed excavation, with the Rumps at St Minver and Penhale near Perranzabuloe on the north coast being notable examples. Finds at the former included numerous sherds of decorated ware pottery and part of the skull of an infant.[47] Both sites were found to have held one or more round houses, indicative of long-term human occupation, with radiocarbon dates for charcoal at Penhale clearly showing activity during the first century BC.[48]

The Helford possesses two such promontory forts: Rosemullion Head and Dennis Head. Nothing is yet known of what lies deep beneath the soil and undergrowth at either, and the construction of a Second World War anti-aircraft battery upon the former does little to help make sense of a confusing topographical picture. But the lack of extant remains should not cast doubt upon their importance, as anyone gazing out to sea from Rosemullion will appreciate. From here it is possible to see land over 25 miles away on the horizon when the air is at its clearest, with the implication that such distant places were part of the known world for those gazing from the same spot thousands of years ago.

Rosemullion and Dennis Head cliff castles were surely statements of power. And yet while they faced one another across the mouth of the river, it seems far more likely that they were complementary rather than being the strongholds of adversarial groups. Together they symbolically guarded its entrance, implying that those who ventured within did so as supplicant not belligerent. It has been suggested that promontory forts might have been maritime trading points, but while such an arrangement would have been feasible at Dennis Head on account of sheltered anchorage within Gillan Creek, the rocky reefs of Prisk Cove below Rosemullion makes such a theory redundant. Only slightly more credible is that they played a religious or ceremonial role, this on account of earlier Bronze Age funerary relics having been found at some.

Although the rounds and forts provoke discussion and conjecture, the most enigmatic structures of the Cornish Iron Age are underground chambers known as fogous. The word is Brittonic in origin and means 'cave'. The closest parallels to be found elsewhere are the souterrains of Scotland, Brittany and Ireland, although those in the Emerald Isle are generally thought to be of later date. Those in Cornwall, however, are most assuredly prehistoric, and surviving examples are concentrated in two areas: West Penwith and around the Helford. Why this should be so is unclear, although it ostensibly suggests cultural connections between the two, set within a wider distribution across the Atlantic facade of Europe in the first millennium BC. They are almost always associated with settlements, invariably rounds or hillforts, and were constructed by the topping of dry stone walls with flat slabs followed by burial beneath the earth (except in rare circumstances with 'above-ground' construction where adverse geology is present). That, however, is where the structural similarity ends. Each is unique in size and plan.

The most well-known of all is that to be found close to the top of a hill slope near Trelowarren in the parish of Mawgan-in-Meneage. The Halliggye Fogou has long perplexed archaeologists and antiquarians alike, and probably always will – fogous do not give up their secrets easily. One of the earliest detailed written accounts made of this subterranean enigma was provided by the Rev. William Jago in 1885. Aside from the precise point of his entry to the passage, since altered, the same description could be made by any present-day explorer:

> Having descended by the steps to this black hole, I thrust myself in – legs first, backward and downward – and was soon standing on a pile of large, loose debris in a low, narrow, stony corridor, extending in a curve to my right and left. It was pitchy-dark in each direction. The dead stillness of the place was broken only by the constant drip, drip of water soaking down from the deep earth overhead. It has been said that in consequence of the prevailing atmosphere being so heavy, and the Fogou so deeply imbedded, no sound made within the dungeon-like walls can be heard by anyone outside.[49]

As the author Geoffrey Grigson once suggested, 'blow out your candle in the Halliggye *fogou*, and you can feel in another way, more acutely, all the chancy existence of those who once crouched there in the blackness waiting for the ill-disposed to stop searching for them or for their goods'.[50] But were these curious man-made caves really places of refuge or something more otherworldly? Various hypotheses have been proffered to explain their existence, but no definitive answer has ever been found in the dark, dank passages of Halliggye or any other 'fuggy-hole'.

There are only three obvious explanations for why Iron Age groups should have expended so much energy and time constructing fogous. The first, that they were for the storage of food, seems unlikely on account of the inherently damp atmosphere to be found below ground in Cornwall. Although most known examples possess two entrances and are aligned roughly on a south-west to north-east axis to supposedly aid ventilation, the reality is that cereal crops, root vegetables and meat all require drier conditions than any found at Halliggye or elsewhere. Only dairy products and beer could have been successfully stored under such conditions.[51] Perhaps they were.

That they served a ritual function was championed by many old antiquaries, and it is easy to understand the attraction to such an explanation. Not only has the colourful image of an Iron Age religious landscape dominated by druids and sacrifice long been in the public consciousness, but the practice of depositing human remains in underground chambers during the Neolithic unduly influences consideration. No signs of interment, cremation or otherwise, have ever been confirmed except for possible burnt fragments at Carn Euny fogou in West Penwith. However, we should not overlook the reports of deer bones, a 'Celtic' cup, and a vase of ashes reputed to have been found at Halliggye by the then landowner, Sir James Vyvyan. The theory of cultural or religious use is further encouraged by the simple fact that many fogous were deliberately made to be difficult to access. It is as if entry to the underworld was being made as challenging as possible, so we cannot entirely discount a ceremony that our modern worldview leaves us unable to comprehend. Rites that took place below ground would not necessarily permanently endow the space with ritualistic paraphernalia.

The third explanation is that they were temporary refuges in times of conflict. The theory is that inhabitants of the settlements within which fogous were situated could use them for protection from projectiles such as slingshot or arrows, and especially from hit-and-run attacks that were supposedly common in Iron Age Celtic Britain.[52] It is also possible that the curving passageways evident at Halliggye, Carn Euny and Pendeen Vau would have afforded protection from any successful breach of outer defences, much as the zigzag of First World War trenches achieved. The hidden second entrance could also have provided an emergency means of escape in such circumstances. Alternatively, we might turn the refuge idea around and hypothesize that fogous were Iron Age prisons where captives from other groups could be retained pending ransom or something far worse.[53]

That at Halliggye is not the only perplexing underground chamber in the vicinity of the Helford. Another celebrated example, known locally as

Piskey Hall is to be found north of the village of Constantine at Bosahan. Fortunately, the Rev. Polwhele left us with a detailed picture of its internal appearance before accelerated decay befell it during subsequent decades:

> It is thirty feet long and five feet wide. It consists of rough stone walls – six feet four inches high, and is covered with rocks, of various dimensions. The whole lies under the surface of the earth; with an aperture at each end. In this vault, also, at one end, is a *round pit*, cut out in the rocky floor; two feet and three inches in diameter, and nine inches deep. This pit was found full of ashes.[54]

If only the 'pit of ashes' had been discovered when scientific analysis could have thrown greater light upon their composition and, perhaps, the function of a fogou. However, Iron Age slag and pottery fragments *were* later recovered, suggestive of a possible connection to the production of metals. Indeed, many fogous are curiously close to alluvial sources of tin and other valuable elements, and none more so than Piskey Hall, whose proximity to ancient tin works is remarkable.[55] Regrettably, nothing remains of the enclosing round which was said to have been faintly discernible until the middle of the twentieth century.[56]

Given the unintended despoilment of archaeological evidence by over-enthusiastic antiquaries at both Halliggye and Constantine, it is a matter of great fortune that a third example should have been 'rediscovered' in the parish of St Anthony-in-Meneage. A fogou had been documented at Boden Vean during the early nineteenth century, but it remained lost until being accidentally uncovered more than a century later. Excavations revealed that this particular souterrain had probably been constructed during the latter part of the early Iron Age, with dating evidence from carbonised pottery suggesting foundation between 420 and 350 BC. Furthermore, the site itself had been previously inhabited during the Bronze Age, and continued to be so until the seventh century AD.[57]

Just like Boden, many places around the Helford River were occupied for thousands of years, probably without interruption. That this should have been so is not necessarily because of a defining advantage to their position, but because some places were important for reasons we cannot necessarily appreciate. Perhaps we should accept that the same is true of the perplexing fogou. As with menhirs and stone circles, we vainly attempt to find a simple primary reason when the answer might be far more complicated, encompassing a wide range of practical and spiritual needs relevant to those living more than 2,000 years ago.[58]

For whatever reasons fogous and cliff castles might have been constructed, their very existence around the Helford River is further evidence of a heavily populated and culturally developed region of the British Isles during late prehistory. If we were afforded the opportunity to travel back in time and walk across the landscape in the first century BC, we would find ourselves in a place both at once wholly recognisable and entirely alien. The river would abound with boats, but nothing like the pleasure craft of today. Instead there would be a multitude of small utilitarian vessels connecting the various settlements around its shores, while large leather-sailed trading ships from all along the south coast of England and northern France would be beached along its upper reaches. Look out to sea and many more of the latter, 40ft or more in length with side-hung rudders and a square sail upon a midships mast, would be seen approaching on the horizon.

The lanes we travel would be no more than rough tracks pounded by beasts of burden, but they would still seem strangely familiar in their corners and curves, the same then as they are today. Nor would we need to walk too far to find ourselves met with the local inhabitants given that settlements exist every mile or so. Some would be home to twenty or more. As a stranger we would probably be greeted with indifference, even goodwill, by those closer to the shoreline whose familiarity with 'foreigners' is greatest. Those further inland, however, might be less inclined to offer a cordial welcome – antipathy boils under the surface, the thin veneer of civilisation that binds the people of the area maintained only by brutal ruling families and those who speak on behalf of the gods.

If we are fortunate we might find ourselves in the company of those willing to offer us temporary shelter and sustenance. The latter would be in the form of coarse breads and hearty stews made of fish or wild game, and perhaps a few cups of weak beer. They might even allow us to rest for the night within the protection of their guarded settlement. And as the light gives way to darkness we would be able to fully appreciate just how well populated the Helford River is – the flicker of twenty or more fires are evident between Dennis Head and the furthest reaches of the tidal river where Gweek now lies. Listen carefully and there are voices whose words could only be vaguely understood by scholars of Celtic tongues. But soon new languages will drift in on the waves of the open sea and those who speak them will represent a force too great to resist. The Helford's status as a haven of free trade and independence is about to come to an end with the arrival of new overlords.

There is little more than 5½ miles between open sea and tidal limit, but the Helford influences, and is influenced by, around 50 square miles of country-side. Its catchment includes Goonhilly Downs on the Lizard Peninsula to the south, and the granite quarries and mining areas of Halvasso and Wendron to the north. To the west lies the second oldest town in Cornwall, Helston, although most of the rain that falls upon its ancient streets finds its way into the River Cober.

More than thirty streams feed into the Helford, but many of these are little more than humble rivulets at times. They are generally short in length and of meagre flow, born of tiny springs amid farmland and destined to mature under the protection of slivers of ancient woodland rarely visited by people. The longest of all is that which a few refer to as the Lestraines river, although a 'river' in any geographical sense it is not, being far better known to resi-dents of Constantine as the Ponjeravah stream. This particular watercourse usually trickles, but sometimes rages, southwards for 6½ miles before com-bining with the smaller Carvedras stream and tumbling into Polwheveral Creek. The Manaccan river, or the Durra, is only fractionally shorter and drains a similar area of sparsely populated land to the south. Some of its water is drawn from lush pastures closer to the sea, but most of the flow is derived from rainfall upon the hard stones of the Lizard.

At Gweek there are two tributaries. That which enters the estuary to the south is sometimes called the River Helford, but it would never have been known as such in antiquity. It most likely came by its title in an act of toponymic boredom and is far better described as the Mellangoose stream. Meanwhile, through the centre of the village runs the more aptly-named Gweek river – also occasionally referred to as the River Helford, just to add to the confusion – which also happens to be the most voluminous of all in terms of flow. Most of its course runs through ancient woodlands growing upon acidic soils and rocky ground, winding around, over and in between granite behemoths. After a storm it is heard before seen, although even a short-lived summer drought will render it barely ankle deep. In places it disappears into dense undergrowth, where fallen trees and decaying boughs prevent access to all but the smallest of creatures. Then it will reappear within a clearing where the flow is briefly arrested by levelling geology. An entire day can be spent following its wandering route without ever encountering a soul or completing its course.

The Gweek river is, as ever, the product of several smaller subsidiaries. That which begins life above Trebarvah Woon is almost as long as its parent, but the little feeder stream that rises from a spring near the hamlet of Manhay near Helston is more remarkable by far. This is not due to a notable visual appeal or defining feature, but simply because its sediment contains far higher concentrations of alluvial tin than any other that discharges into the Helford. And close to where it meets the main stream under the cover of trees south-east of Grambla Woods is to be found a most unusual earthwork whose location close to this confluence might be more than mere coincidence.

Although now in a state of decay, covered by trees and undergrowth, this almost perfectly rectangular enclosure is a little-known site of immense significance to the story of the Helford and Cornwall as a whole. Mid-twentieth century archaeologists were cautious in ascribing it any particular date or provenance; it *may* have been Roman, they thought, but given the paucity of evidence for Roman occupation in Cornwall at that time, quite probably not. An older record, however, had been more certain. Perhaps influenced by local legend passed down through the generations, when the Ordnance Survey revised the area for its 25in series in 1906 it confidently designated the site as a 'Roman Camp'. An excavation in 1972 proved them to have been *close* to the truth.

The main entrance to Grambla was found to have been in the centre of the southern side, where the surrounding ditch had ended with a 'causeway of undug rock'. Moreover, the investigation also uncovered traces of what would have been a structure of considerable defensive strength:

The rampart terminals were also square ended and had been revetted by drystone walls of granite blocks. The gate structure was represented by a quadrilateral setting of four stone-lined postholes forming an entrance passage 2.6 metres wide, with a stone-packed slot, or threshold, joining the two outer postholes. Such an arrangement could have supported a timber tower over a gate.[59]

With potential structures in the north of the enclosure left undisturbed, the archaeologists concentrated on two 'boat-shaped' buildings to the south that had been joined by a rubble-stone yard. In one they discovered a central hearth, and in the other several pits that contained traces of slag – a relic of metal smelting. They also found pottery sherds made of a coarse fabric similar to those uncovered at other sites in Cornwall, something that suggested that Grambla had been occupied long after Rome had ceased to exert power over the British Isles. But there were two finds of particular importance. The first was a fragment of a Samian Ware bowl dating from the second century – a reddish ceramic associated with Roman Gaul – and the second a coin of Faustina II, Roman Empress and wife of Marcus Aurelius, dating from around AD 149. The coin had been minted less than ten years after the construction of the Antonine Wall in Scotland, when Roman Britain was in its ascendancy.

It will never be possible to know the ethnicity of those who lived at Grambla Camp during that period, whether they were of Cornish stock or had hailed from somewhere across the Empire. That said, Roman coins and pottery do not appear within square encampments by sheer good fortune. At the very least, those who once owned them must have been 'Romanised' to some degree. In any case, it is folly to dwell too long on an identity we could never ascertain. Instead, ask why such a structure – one rather alien to the far south-west – should be found where it is.

That Cornwall had a different relationship with the Roman Empire than elsewhere in England is not in doubt. But the fashionable narrative that it was somehow a place apart from more 'subjugated' areas is erroneous. If places such as Bath were the gentrified settlements and Chester the barracks, then Cornwall was the place of industry; somewhere the well-heeled third-century patrician would have had little desire to visit let alone settle. There is no villa complex like Chedworth or Fishbourne to be found here, no obvious monuments to Roman civic pride, nor well-trodden thoroughfares like Watling Street. But, then again, we must not forget it was a similar story for the overwhelming majority of provincial Britain at the time, with life continuing much as it had through the Iron Age. Cornwall was not especially unusual in this regard.

The Helford River, however, *is* unusual. Grambla is but one of many square or rectangular enclosures to be found within its catchment. And while the absence of forensic archaeological study leaves us only able to speculate on their purpose, there is something remarkable about the relative number of these straight-sided earthworks.

The closest example to that at Grambla is less than 1½ miles to the east at Carwythenack. The same Ordnance Survey map of 1906 that denoted Grambla to be a Roman camp did the same with this outpost overlooking Naphene Downs. Alas, there is little left of the structure that would have given its name to the ancient manor of *Caerwethenek*: 'the castle in the wooded place'.[60] An earlier map of 1888 still shows a few trees on the site but these, along with the ramparts and ditches, are now long gone. Only from the air is it possible to trace out its lines and curved corners as crop marks. It is a tragedy.

Yet another possible example has since suffered an even more inglorious fate in the Parish of Mawnan. Aerial photographs from the 1960s suggested a square enclosure of uncertain date or function at Glendurgan but, alas, any remaining archaeology now lies hidden beneath a twentieth-century car park. There are those who remember being told by their grandparents, as they were told by theirs, that the nearby track leading from Durgan towards Trebah was used by Roman traders. It was supposedly a safe anchorage offering easy access northwards to the tin grounds. But this is pure conjecture, even if colourful and tempting. In all probability, what was seen was nothing more than the remnants of a medieval enclosure for livestock.

Other similar long-disappeared enclosures whose existences are now but ghostly traces in maturing crops include two examples at Mawgan-in-Meneage. One of these is situated close to the church at Gwarth-an-Drea and would have provided its inhabitants with fine views over Mawgan Creek to the south-east. The other at Carleen is significantly smaller, but still more than 100ft in length and breadth. Another larger example is to be found at Trewince, close to the source of one of the streams that feeds into Gillan Creek. Their origins are uncertain, but we may at least speculate that if only one is subsequently found to possess Roman influence then our understanding of the area in the centuries following the birth of Christ moves further and further away from one of insularity.

However, there is one such rectilinear enclosure that is far beyond all others both in terms of preservation and potential archaeological importance. A Scheduled Ancient Monument about which very little is known, Merthen Camp commands high ground above Groyne Point where the river divides between the main channel to Gweek and Polwheveral Creek towards Constantine. Its strategic importance cannot be lost on even the most naive observer. Aside from the very entrance to the estuary, no other place is better suited to monitoring inland access than this very point. It is unsurprising, therefore, to discover that its name is probably derived from 'Merdhyn', meaning 'fort by the sea', although whether that particular title derives from these earthworks or the nearby medieval manor we cannot be absolutely certain. Situated as it is within private farmland, few are ever afforded the opportunity to see it up close, nor take in the commanding views out towards the open sea. On a warm summer evening it is a peaceful place where the present and its distractions are lost. Only the crickets in the undergrowth seem busy while all else is languid.

It cannot always have been so restful. Its scale and the obvious amount of manpower required to construct it attests to that. Walking around the perimeter of these two conjoined structures, one is immediately struck by the height of the ramparts and depth of ditches that, even though softened by centuries of weathering, would still represent a formidable obstacle today. The banks are as much as 5ft in height in some places, and the trenches of similar scale. The Merthen enclosures are large by prehistoric standards, covering around 2½ acres of ground. A third possible example is to the north of the eastern enclosure, although nothing now exists above the surface of the earth.[61, 62]

It is tempting to conclude that these structures were built specifically for defensive purposes. This, however, seems an unlikely explanation when the lie-of-the-land is considered. First, they are too far from the shore to be solely concerned with the explicit protection of the Helford's upper reaches, although this does not discount the possibility that people could have been sent forth down to the waterline when required. Second, aside from the ditches and banks of the earthworks themselves, there are no other obvious defensive structures, such as a vallum, to be found in the gently sloping surrounding countryside. In this sense, the Merthen earthworks are far removed in character from almost every classic Cornish cliff castle if, of course, we are to make the assumption that they are contemporary in date. This, though, does not alter the fact that the 'camp' would have been an extremely secure enclosure, and eminently defendable even if its inhabitants could not necessarily have prevented potentially hostile forces from landing on the shore.

If we are to begin to answer the question as to Merthen's purpose then it is the obvious we must first consider. Indeed, the most singularly remarkable thing about the place must surely be its position. Although it might not be obvious to approaching sailors today, Merthen was originally built to be seen. It was a statement, landmark, and warning. But are we able to reasonably speculate as to who was responsible for its creation in the absence of detailed archaeological study?

There are many native Cornish examples of sub-rectangular enclosures, and caution has been urged against considering origins based on shape alone.[63] However, if the Merthen earthworks supposedly have no connection to Rome then they are a remarkably good imitation of one that does. It would be the most astonishing coincidence.

Roman forts are almost always rectangular and invariably possess rounded corners.[64] Few examples diverge from this plan. Medieval enclosures, on the other hand, tend to have sharper angles, while most defended settlements of Iron Age Cornish tribes are rounded or curvilinear. In this sense, the supposedly 'Roman Camp' at Carwythenack is far more likely to be a purely local structure and can almost be discounted as having any connection to Empire. Not so Merthen.

If we overlook the possible example of Roman earthworks at nearby Grambla and the large Iron Age to Romano–British enclosure at Carvossa, near Truro, we are left with only one certain Cornish site where legionaries were stationed. Nanstallon, near Bodmin, was probably constructed during the early years of Roman rule between AD 55 and 60, and situated to take advantage of the overland trade route between the Fowey and Camel estuaries. It has been suggested that it briefly housed a detachment tasked with administering the extraction of lead and silver in the locality.[65] If so, the parallels with Merthen and its access to tin grounds become even more distinct.

However, any historian would no doubt point out a number of weaknesses in an argument advocating Roman influence. First, they would contest that the camp at Merthen may well be rectilinear, but it is both imprecise and squarer than the classic 'playing card' shape associated with legionary camps. Second, the double earthwork is not a feature with obvious equivalents elsewhere. And, third, almost every other camp and fort dating from the Roman period is located on, or close to, a road. Indeed, most earthworks of modest size are 'marching camps' along the network. The Romans were not especially comfortable with travelling by sea, and less still across the turbulent North Atlantic. It would therefore be reasonable to assume that the example at Merthen is probably something other than a Roman fortification. Until archaeological study provides a definitive answer we cannot be certain and ought to err on the side of caution. Yet there is evidence enough to rebuff even these reservations.

Temporary camps of similar size are actually not at all uncommon. In the once militarised zone of Wales, Scotland and North West England there are some that enclose areas of ground not unlike that at Merthen. More importantly, the eastern enclosure – considered to be the first of the pair to have been constructed – is effectively identical in length and breadth to the fort at Nanstallon. Merthen East measures approximately 330ft by 280ft, Nanstallon 330ft by 290ft. This could be merely be chance, but it is a most extraordinary correlation nonetheless. Both these 'squarer' fortifications are typical of those constructed by Roman auxiliaries rather than legionaries. In other words, Nanstallon, and perhaps Merthen, were made by those who had joined the Empire's military from conquered territories in present-day France and Germany. These would have been the men given the task of exploring and securing land west of the main fortress at Exeter, and it is not too outlandish to suggest that the Merthen camp was built by a small detachment of the Nanstallon garrison. The conquest of Cornwall was probably short-lived and the far south-west effectively secured by AD 70.[66] If this was a place for an advance military detachment then the close proximity to several freshwater streams would have been important to sustaining 100 soldiers or more and, perhaps, their horses.

The 'double earthwork' is also not without precedent, even if it is not an especially common occurrence. A number of forts and camps do indeed have annexes, including examples at Gelligaer in South Wales, Rough Castle on the Antonine Wall in Scotland, and Metchley in the West Midlands. In some these additions were probably 'practice camps' constructed by fresh auxiliaries being trained in the art of building defensive structures.[67] This is not something we can even begin to assume to be the case at Merthen, but neither can it be entirely ruled out. The imprecise rectangle could be due to conscripted locals unfamiliar in Roman building techniques being employed during an expeditious manufacture.

Neither should the fact that Merthen lacks access to any well-known thoroughfare such as Watling Street or the Fosse Way prejudice an argument in favour of Roman origins. Although their existence is rarely acknowledged, there are several Roman milestones to be found in Cornwall, each thought to have been erected to mark the completion or repair of a road section. Some, such as that found during ploughing at a farm at St Day near Redruth, still bear legible inscriptions.[68] So too the early fourth-century example within St Hilary church near Marazion dedicated to Emperor Caesar Flavius Valerius Constantinus. Furthermore, we should not overlook the fact that there was already a rudimentary, but practical, road network in place throughout Cornwall at the time of the Claudian invasion of AD 43. It had likely existed for 2,000 years or more previous, and the routes would have been the most perspicacious given the variable and often rugged terrain. There would have been little for the Roman administrators to improve upon in this regard. In any case, auxiliaries from Gaul would have been far more comfortable with conquest by sea than their landlubber legionary counterparts from Rome itself. In fact, they probably accounted for most of the marines of the *Classis Britannica*, the British Fleet. As such, a metalled road would not necessarily have been a prerequisite at all.

However, it may be that any idea of a connection to the early Roman incursion into the south-west peninsula is incorrect. It is just as reasonable to theorise that it is a product of the third or fourth centuries when Iberian sources of tin were dwindling and those of Cornwall were in the ascendancy. Indeed, it has been suggested that Merthen Camp was once a customs post with one enclosure dedicated to processing tin exports, and the other to housing officials.[69] There is much to commend this hypothesis, not least the clear views of the river's approaches that would deter any trader from attempting to avoid paying dues by coming ashore elsewhere. It might also explain the existence of the rock-cut track leading from the water's edge to the perimeter of the western earthwork and beyond, as Charles Henderson recorded. The 'ancient road' he observed to the north is easily overlooked from the ground today, but it remains faintly visible from above as it follows field boundaries before joining the existing lane into Constantine. Access to the tin-rich grounds between Wendron and Rame would thus have been relatively straightforward.

There is also the underwater topography of the river at Merthen which lends support to the theory of a customs post or trading station. Indeed, just to the east of its quay is a deep pool; a curious anomaly within an ever-shallowing watercourse. It was here that larger vessels of the eighteenth and nineteenth centuries would wait for the rising tide to take them on their way to Gweek, guaranteed to never bottom-out even on the lowest of waters. So it would also have been 2,000 years or more ago. Merthen has long been the finest anchorage in the Helford.

One other rectilinear enigma exists in the river's hinterland. A particularly square earthwork is to be found at Trenower, near Newtown St Martin, close to the highest point in the locality. To the west rainfall trickles into Frenchman's Creek, to the east into Gillan. The plot in which it is situated was once known as 'Windmill Field' on account that one had stood in the corner of the enclosure during the eighteenth century.[71] However, this curious feature was surely constructed a long time before corn was milled upon it. The consensus suggests that its origins are Iron Age, and that it is merely an atypical defended settlement amongst the 'rounder' rounds. But there is another plausible explanation.

Close to the acknowledged Nanstallon Roman camp is what many believe to have been a contemporary 'signal station' or 'fortlet' that would have offered communication benefits to the main garrison. Like the Trenower anomaly, the intriguing structure at Lostwithiel covers an area of just over an acre. What is more, both have entrances in their southern sides. Perhaps here was built a simple wooden structure from which contact via smoke or fire was achieved, commanding as it does fine views down across the Gillan Creek valley and north across the river itself. Indeed, is it not possible that it was one of a small number of such outposts connecting a lookout at Lizard Point from which advance warning to both Helford and Mounts Bay could be transferred?

If we are to seek out other possible stations between Trenower and mainland England's most southerly point we are met with several possibilities. One rectilinear enclosure formerly denoted as a 'Roman Camp' on Ordnance Survey maps is to be found near Croft Pascoe pool on Goonhilly Downs. Alas, recent archaeological opinion has swayed more towards medieval origins, and its relative elevation to the surrounding landscape would probably preclude it from communication anyway. A more practical site would have been at Predannack where, coincidentally, a small rectilinear earthwork was identified from aerial photography.[72]

One final and entirely speculative piece of evidence for Romano–British activity at Trenower came to light in the mid-nineteenth century after being unearthed in a nearby field. There, it is said, was found a crude mass of tin, sometimes known locally as 'Jew's House tin' weighing a little over a pound, 'some miles from any now-known habitat of tin ore, and far beyond the confines of this region'.[73] Alas, as its age will probably never be known it offers little in the way of substantiation.

Regrettably, the case for Roman influence on these mysterious 'camps' can never be argued safely without extensive archaeological study. There remains the possibility that the example at Merthen was merely part of the medieval deer park known to have existed there, although this would be surprising and disappointing in equal measure. Similarly, they may pre-date the first century AD by some time. If so, the profusion of these rectilinear enclosures within the Helford's catchment begs the question as to whether there was a particularly distinct culture within the area during the Iron Age. But of one thing we can be certain: Merthen, and the Helford as a whole, was a focal point of a prehistoric trade in tin.

If Ictis was real and not merely the product of ancient fiction, the Helford would have been its equal. As the author of *Gulliver's Travels*, Daniel Defoe, observed, it was at this 'small but good harbour' that 'many times tinn ships go in to load for London'.[74] It follows that if such a trade was so notable in the profit-driven early eighteenth century, it would have been even more so 2,000 years earlier when the nearby cassiterite-rich streams would have been conducive to lucrative exploitation.

However, should Grambla, Merthen, and Trenower ultimately be found to possess nothing more than a negligible association with the Roman occupation of Britain, it most assuredly does not mean that the Helford as a whole did not. In fact, the river stands out for another reason when it comes to that particular time of conquest.

There are a great many documents, letters and books that have cruelly changed the course of history without as much as a grain of truth within them. Forgeries and fakes have been responsible for loss of reputation and, worse, loss of life. Most hoaxes, however, merely result in acute embarrassment for those taken in by the deceit, and especially if they have otherwise enjoyed a blemish-free academic life.

Some, like Samuel and Daniel Lysons, did not live long enough to see the deception exposed. These two antiquarian brothers collaborated on several volumes of *Magna Britannia, Being a Concise Topographical Account of the Several Counties in Great Britain* during the early nineteenth century, including an edition on Cornwall. Unfortunately, the series ended abruptly in 1819 following Samuel's death, and no further books were produced in the alphabetical sequence after Devonshire. It should be stressed that, aside from the use of one particular source, each edition of *Magna Britannia* is an otherwise admirable endeavour. They remain invaluable sources of information and are as easy to absorb today as they were for those reading two centuries ago.

Although they would never have known at the time, the authors occasionally used bogus 'evidence' from a document called *De Situ Britanniae* (*The Description of Britain*), which was believed to have been a late-medieval manuscript by the monk, Richard of Cirencester. This in itself was reputed to have been created from a long-lost account of the islands by an unnamed Roman general, providing numerous new names of places never before encountered in any other work. Unsurprisingly, it was considered revelatory following its publication in 1757, almost ten years after the forger, Charles Bertram, had made its existence known to the respected historian and Fellow of the Royal Society, William Stukeley. Indeed, for almost eighty years scholars and academics cited *De Situ Britanniae* with impunity until various experts began to cast doubts on its validity.

In truth, Daniel and Samuel Lysons can be wholly forgiven for their relatively infrequent referral to *The Description of Britain* in their works. In fact, the occasional mentions are still enlightening, such as the section concerned with Roman roads and stations in *Vol. 3, Cornwall*:

> The rude monuments of the early inhabitants of this island, indeed, already described, are found in abundance; yet, in the walk of Roman antiquity, we are perplexed with the same obscure and broken lines of roads, and the same meagre and hypothetical list of towns, which we meet with in all our other counties. We cannot bring a stronger proof of this than by observing that, of the places mentioned by Richard of Cirencester, either in his map or his 16th *iter*, as situated in this part of the country, *Halangium*, *Tamara*, and *Cenen* have been fixed at Helston, Tamerton, and Tregony, from the resemblance of names only, the weakest foundation on which an antiquarian system can be raised ... *Ceneum* from resemblance of name chiefly, has been fixed at Tregony; but, from the situation of Condora, and the discovery of coins ... there seems to be better reason for placing it there.

The 'Condora' referred to is today known as Condurrow, a quiet hamlet close to St Anthony-in-Meneage. It is a tiny agricultural settlement situated amongst beautiful and fertile countryside, and nothing would appear to validate the suggestion in *Magna Britannia* that it may have once been a notable Roman location – not even a fictional one invented by an eighteenth-century con man. And yet there is evidence that, if presented in relation to almost anywhere else in the British Isles rather than Cornwall (which has lately attempted to disavow any notion of Roman control), would suggest that there *was* something of importance nearby. Indeed, it is not the fact that there was a discovery of coins in this apparently inconspicuous corner of Cornwall, but the astounding number of them.

According to contemporary reports '24 gallons of the Roman Brass Money' were unearthed, a volume that would equate to around 180lb in weight.[75] The whereabouts of these coins today is unknown, and without detailed study it is impossible to confirm either authenticity or age. However, we can reasonably assume that they were deposited at some point in the latter half of the fourth century AD. The precise spot at which they were exposed is also guesswork, but according to the Rev. Richard Polwhele was within 'the enclosure of a small garden [which has] since been levelled with the field'.[76]

Of course, a hoard of coins does not mean that the site at which they were found was once 'Roman'. However, it was not specifically Condurrow attracting the interest of old antiquaries, but more the nearby promontory at the mouth of the river. As far as William Borlase was concerned, the case for Roman control of Dennis Head was compelling:

> This hill is washed on each side by the sea; and about a quarter of a mile from the ditch in which the Coins were lodged, there runs out a little tongue of land, called Dinas, and (to distinguish it from a much larger fortification, on the other side the bay called Pendinas) this is called the little Dinas, in Cornish, Dinas vean. This little Dinas has several modern fortifications on its Eastern point (erected in the great Rebellion) but nearer to Condurrah it has an old Vallum stretching from sea to sea, which is the remainder of a very ancient fortification, and in all likelihood Roman; for it is rightly observed by Mr Horsley [*Britannia Romana*, 1732] 'the Romans were careful to have their stations' (by which he means I suppose their Camps and Forts) 'placed near a river; and there is no situation which they seem to be so fond of, as a *Lingula* (little tongue of land) near the confluence of a larger and smaller river.' Here I cannot but observe, that this station at Condurrah has every one of these properties; on the right hand, as you front the East, comes down the river Durrah, and with the sea makes a pretty pool, or cove, before St Anthony's Church, in which small vessels may lye with great safety; on the left hand comes down Hél river … From the front of the hill runs out the *Lingula* of Little Dinas about 500 yards long and 200 wide at a medium.[77]

It should be noted that vallums are also a defining feature of Cornish cliff castles, and that there was such an Iron Age fortification at Dennis Head is not in doubt. But, notwithstanding that attempting to conclusively identify the ditch Borlase documented is a challenging task, we should not dismiss his enthusiasm. Robert Dawson's 1811 map of the Lizard Peninsula does indeed show what appears to be a boundary of some sort running from north to south across the neck of the headland. This would appear to correlate with a current field boundary of considerable width and is probably that which the eminent military and archaeological surveyor Robert MacLauchlan noted in the mid-nineteenth century. He surmised that 'the ancient remains are a deep ditch run from sea to sea across the promontory, perhaps two, though the western ditch, at the Parsonage house, is now nearly effaced', but believed that there were 'no Roman right angled works upon it to lead to the supposition that it ever was fortified by that people'.[78] Parts of the vallum appear to be still there, concealed by hazel saplings and bramble.

Although the truth is more complicated than Borlase would have had his audience believe, it is possible his assertions were not entirely inaccurate. Moreover, that the Lysons brothers had come to a similar conclusion based upon fictitious documents does not mean that they were fundamentally wrong to do so. Rather than the deceptive *Magna Britannia* they could have equally placed their confidence in a genuine record of Roman Britain.

Aside from Ptolemy's *Geography*, the *Peutinger Table* atlas, and the *Antonine Itinerary* 'road map', the *Ravenna Cosmography* is the most detailed account of notable places in the Roman world. Created by an unknown author in the Italian city of the same name on the cusp of the seventh and eighth centuries, it was first published in 1688 from a manuscript held by the Vatican Library. Although it covers vast swathes of the Earth's surface, it was the part devoted to the British Isles that most attracted scholars eager to unravel its mysteries and secrets – a challenging task given the illogical scattershot approach employed by the author while working from older, now lost documents.[79]

Within the section that details the south-west of the British Isles there are a small number of entries whose modern identities are manifestly obvious. *Tamaris* clearly relates to the Tamar or a settlement somewhere upon it. *Scadum Namorum* is *Isca Dumnorum*, the former name for Exeter. Others are more enigmatic and open to interpretation: *Uxelis* has been variously identified as Launceston and Axmouth, and *Vertevia* at locations as distant as Land's End and Tavistock (the latter on account of the River Tavy which flows through it).

There are two names, however, that have a possible connection to the Helford River. The first of these is *Moriduno*. Why this should be so notable is that *Moridunum* is the Latinised root of *Meredin* and from which *Merthen* is also borrowed. In all cases the meaning is 'Fortress of the Sea'. Unfortunately, before one might even consider this all-too-plausible explanation it is important to stress that there is also a Merthen at Carlyon Bay near St Austell, and a Merthen Point at St Loy's Cove in the far west of Cornwall, near St Buryan. It is not unique to the Helford. Secondly, *Moriduno* appears in a part of the *Cosmography* where there is greater sense to the aggregation of names leaving it more likely to be in Devon. However, we should not lose sight of the fact that similar names to *Moriduno* appear on several occasions as *Milidunum*, *Morionio* and *Melamoni*.

There is one other listing that is yet more mysterious: *Duriarno*. Given its situation in the south-west, such a name is far more likely to be derived from the old Brittonic for 'water' – *dowr*, *dour* or *dŵr* – than it is from any classical source. Thus Condurrow means 'the neck of the water', being as it is between Gillan Creek and the main estuary.[80] Meanwhile, the suffix -*arno* has the same ancient derivation as the Florentine waterway, just as *arna* in Sanskrit means 'river'. We are therefore faced with the possibility, albeit fanciful, that *Duriarno* meant 'the two rivers' – the Durra and the Arno. This could relate to both Gillan and Helford, or to the split between the main channel to Gweek and Polwheveral Creek at Merthen. Such a suggestion may be absurd, but no more so than those suggesting Dorchester, or even Truro, as the site of a long-lost entry in the *Ravenna Cosmography*.[81]

Wherever *Moriduno* and *Duriarno* might have been, the Condurrow discovery needs to be placed into context. Even the same Henry MacLauchlan who poured scorn on the idea of a Roman vallum at St Anthony believed that the mouth of the Helford was a far, far better fit for Ptolemy's *Cenion* than the River Fal as others had postulated. Each and every one of these theories might be preposterous, but someone within the shadow of the Palatine Hill would have spoken its name, whatever it was. It would not have been an unknown.

That which underpinned the belief in the Helford's significance during Roman times was not so much that to be found in books, but rather the evidence from the ground. It remains that more Roman coin hoards have been found in the vicinity of the Helford than any other Cornish estuary. This is not to dismiss the extraordinary number of stray finds and small assemblages close to the Hayle (especially around Gwithian), or the impressive examples close to the Fal such as the Lamorran hoard. It is simply that those found in the parishes around the river – in relatively undisturbed land compared to other parts of Cornwall – are particularly impressive. Numerous others must still lie undiscovered within the fields, woods and meadows close to its shores.

In the same year as the Condurrow hoard had been discovered another came to the surface on the north bank of the river. Although their whereabouts today are unknown, Borlase was once again fortunate enough to catch sight of them before their disappearance:

> … up on one of the Creeks which run up into the parish of Constantine, were found forty Roman Coins. Four of the largest size, by the favour of the Rev. Mr. Collins of St Erth, I have by me. The first of copper, IMP. CAES. DOMIT. AVG. GERM. COS. XIII. CENS. P. F. A bold impression, *Head* laureate; graceful. Reverse, FORTVNAE AVGVSTI. S. C. Plenty, with her *Cornucopia*. The second of Trajan: bright brass, IMP. CAES. NERVAE TRAIANO AVG. GER DA Reverse, *figura galeata sedens*, S. C., the third defaced. The fourth FAVSTINA DIVA, the younger Faustina. Reverse *figura dextrita serpentem, sinstra bastata*.[82]

Borlase was reluctant to go into further detail about the other coins, but thankfully Dr Stephen Williams in *Philosophical Transactions of the Royal Society* in 1744 was more forthcoming. From his observations we know that it contained pieces minted under numerous emperors such as Vespasian, Antoninus Pius, Marcus Aurelius, and Valens – an unusually large date range spanning from AD 69 to 378. Dr Williams also kindly elaborated as to the location of the hoard: the finder had been a 'labouring man at plough', and that the custodian of the coins at the time had informed him they were discovered close to a 'circular camp'. Despite the vast number of Iron Age rounds in the area, there is only one possibility that would have stood out so much as to act as a geographical marker at that time: Goongilling. This is located on high ground between Polwheveral and

Polpenwith Creeks, slightly closer to the latter, and less than a mile from the present-day village of Constantine.

Dr Williams also discussed another collection of coins found approximately ⅔ mile south of Helford Village at Tregonwell. Although it is not clear how many were in the hoard, he described having 'had the sight but of three, which are Copper, and of a small size, very fair and legible' and coming from the reigns of Constantine II and Constantius II between AD 317 and 337.[83] Perhaps there is more than meets the eye to this little hamlet given the historian William Penaluna's assertion of 1838 that Roman coins were regularly found in its surrounding fields.[84]

The story of a yet another labourer discovering a hoard of coins, this time at Trevassack in the parish of Mawgan-in-Meneage, was reported in the *West Briton* of 15 March 1822:

> Last week as a man named Harry was ploughing a field about a mile from Trelowarren, the seat of Richard Vyvyan Esq., the ploughshare struck against an earthen vessel or urn and scattered about a number of coins which on examination were found to be Roman, many of them of the first Emperors. They are of various sizes and in general in good preservation. The number found is upwards of 1600, and the man who discovered them being ignorant of their value, sold them at a penny apiece to all who would purchase them. He has since become sensible of his folly but too late to retrieve it.

Although some doubt must be cast on the claim of more than 1,000 coins, it is fortunate that at least a handful of them fell into the custody of the Rev. Alfred Hayman Cummings. From his testimony we know that the hoard covered a large period of time, from Vespasian (AD 69–79) to Constantinopolis (AD 330–335). Cummings also tells us that the field in which the St Mawgan hoard was found was known as Chygarkie, which means 'fortified house', and only 2 miles from Gear Camp.[85]

By the end of the same year yet another group of coins had been found, this time *antoniniani* near Maenporth to the north of the Helford. In December of 1822 the *Royal Cornwall Gazette* announced that:

Last week some men who were working in a quarry at Penrose in the parish of Budock discovered about two feet under the surface an earthen vessel containing 250 pieces of ancient Coin; the greater part of them were copper, of the size of a farthing, but in what reigns it is difficult to make out, as they have no date. Unfortunately the jar they were in was destroyed, one of the men having thrown the pick into it.

Further finds were made during the 1830s in very similar settings at the parish churches of Constantine and Mawnan. Very little is known about the former save for the fact that a small group of three were discovered. More details are known about the latter, where ten *antoniniani* were found in the prehistoric earth bank enclosing the church. These, it is said, dated from between AD 253 and 274.

It was not until February 1865 that a group of coins as numerous as those at Condurrow were unearthed once more. As always, it would be working men who happened across them, in this case two farm labourers working above Sunny Cove at Pennance midway between the Helford and Falmouth. It is known that they came across an unspecified number of coins, but when further excavations took place in the spring of the same year the spectacular nature of the hoard became clear. This, according to the *Royal Cornwall Gazette* of 21 April 1865, had been found on Tuesday, 11 April, perhaps by one of the same men named only as Tripp and Tallack who had been responsible for the first:

… he discovered about two feet below the surface, on a foundation made of stone, a quantity of second brass roman coins, of the reigns of Constantine, Diocletian, and Maximianus. There are about 20 different types of the above reigns, but the Genio Popoli Romani type of Maximianus is greatly in excess. There are several varieties of the reign of Constantine, amongst which may be noticed the Principi Inventors – the Prince standing between two standards, and one type with P.L.N in the exerge, struck in London. There are about 8 or 10 third brass, some of which are attributed to Gallineus. The second brass are in excellent condition, and are beautifully palmated. Many of the coins are at least 1,500 years old.

Almost 1,000 coins were unearthed in total. They had been wrapped in some form of decayed organic material, perhaps leather or a wooden box, and appeared 'to have been placed in rows, side by side, four rows in breadth, sloping upwards on the hill-side'.[86]

It is regrettable that the Pennance Hoard is no longer complete. Indeed, the whereabouts of the vast majority of the coins is a mystery. A little more than 600 of them had soon after been displayed at the polytechnic in Falmouth following their purchase by local geologist and businessman Robert Were Fox. Other smaller sets fell into private ownership. Today, the Royal Cornwall Institution is in custody of only fourteen when it should arguably be in possession of every single one. But records have at least provided us with some detail, this mostly derived from the work of Thomas Hodgkin who penned a report to the *Royal Cornwall Polytechnic Society* in 1867, a mere two years after the discovery.

What becomes clear from even the most cursory investigation of the contents of these hoards is how they fall into two distinct types. Those from Polwheveral Creek, Maenporth, and Trevassack each have extremely broad date ranges. Meanwhile, those of Condurrow, Pennance, Mawnan, and perhaps Tregonwell, are considerably narrower in this regard. For example, that at Pennance spans little more than fifty years from the reign of Gallienus (AD 253–268) to that of Constantine I (AD 306–307). Hodgkin even suggested a narrower window between August and December of AD 306 on account of the lack of coins of Maxentius and Licinius, who had become emperors in October AD 306 and November AD 307 respectively.

One of the reasons most often cited for the existence of coin hoards is that they were concealed during times of unrest, of which there was certainly a great deal during the Romano–British period. Once safely in the ground they could be retrieved once the threat had passed, assuming, of course, that the owner survived the upheaval. Another theory is that some were buried as votive offerings *as per* the modern-day wishing well, although this is unlikely. However, the most logical reason must surely be that concealing wealth in a safe subterranean place was not unlike the practice of a secure deposit box in a bank vault today. They could be accessed by the owner for both deposit and withdrawal purposes and, in an age where the metal value of a coin was more important than the date of issue, it did not much matter whose Imperial head was upon it.

The most sensible conclusion to be drawn is that those finds at Polwheveral, Maenporth and Trevassack were deposited or hidden by indigenous local tribal leaders or members of their families. The coins were almost certainly the by-product of seaborne trade, be that between the Helford and other ports along the British coast or across the English Channel. They may also have had *some* value in the local economy, and their presence indicates that those living around the Helford were relatively prosperous. The likely source of this wealth was tin and gabbroic clay pottery, even though the latter seems to have been largely confined to the domestic market. But this would not have been all. Writing in the first century BC, Strabo noted that Britain was renowned for its exports of 'grain, cattle, gold, silver, and iron ... also hides, and slaves, and dogs that are by nature suited to the purposes of the chase'. As such, we cannot assume that those living around the Helford during the Romano–British period gained their wealth purely by noble means. It is entirely possible that, for some, their last view of Britain were the cliffs of the river mouth as they departed in chains for exploitation elsewhere. It was a brutal time indeed.

It should be noted that not all discoveries of a Roman nature have been numismatic. For example, glass gaming counters have been found at Tregidden and Tregiddris in the parish of St Martin in Meneage.[87] Similarly, in a field on the western bank of Polwheveral Creek was found a brooch of the time, albeit one that was almost certainly locally made and worn by the locally born.[88] However, another brooch uncovered at the north end of Merthen Downs is of more uncertain provenance but probably of the second century AD.[89] Most mysterious of all, however, was a supposed head of a Roman standard found during the ploughing of a field near Carlidnack Round. It is recorded as having been shown to children at Mawnan school in 1908, but its actual identity and when it was found are unknown.[90]

But one question remains, why are the largest hoards also those of narrowest date ranges? Further, why should the majority of these caches – both of diverse and comparable coin types – appear to have been deposited in the ground during the early to mid-fourth century AD?

In all likelihood, the early Roman Empire acquired most of its tin from Iberian sources, with domestic demand in the British Isles met by alluvial and underground deposits in Cornwall. However, by the mid- to late third century AD most of the mines in present-day Spain had ceased to be worked. Why this should have been so is open to debate, but the result would have been increased output from sources in the far south-west of Britain.[91] Moreover, the demand for pewter – an alloy comprised primarily of tin – reached its peak between the third and mid-fourth centuries AD, meaning that already prized sources of the metal would have become invaluable and fiercely guarded. Furthermore, a fragment of a pewter mould found at Boden, near Manaccan, also hints at a thriving cottage industry around the river at the time. The Helford had been *one* of the most important tin trading locations in Cornwall from the Iron Age to Roman conquest, but by AD 300 it was arguably its pre-eminent point of export.

The Condurrow and Pennance hoards bear the greatest similarities, and not only in both having been found close to the open sea rather than inland. Leaving aside the possibility that they were concealed after having been stolen, there seem to be only two likely reasons for their deposition. The first, of course, is that they were the product of an honest exchange between supplier and merchant, even if the value suggests a transaction quite out of the ordinary in both cases. However, John Rogers, MP for Helston at the time, came to a different conclusion, being struck by how at Pennance 'all the pieces seemed new, as if they had not been in circulation, and the notion has been suggested that the deposit may have been that of a military chest concealed near the shore'.[92] They had been stored carefully in rows, too, a practice that would not have been particularly important to a local chieftain or trader.

That sites such as Mount's Bay, the Carrick Roads and the Helford River were strategically important cannot be doubted. Ensuring these distribution points for tin ingots remained secure would have been one of the most pressing concerns of Roman authorities and their client leaders in the west. The hoards at Condurrow and Pennance, above all others, seem to have been linked to financing this endeavour, and Borlase came to much the same verdict in the mid-eighteenth century:

These Coins found on banks of Helford Haven, belonging to the Soldiery, and deposited near one time, will lead us to enquire whether there is any incident in history which may support the conjecture of the Roman soldiers being planted hereabouts in the age assigned to these Coins. I think there is. The Saxon depredations were come to such a height in the time of Constantine the Great, that he thought it necessary to erect an office unheard of before, the sole business of which should be to protect the shores of Britain from those pirates; it may, therefore, be a probable conjecture, that the soldiers were placed at Condorah (where no Coins but those of him and his sons appear) in the time of Constantius and his brothers for this very purpose, as the others were deposited in the following reigns of Valens and Valentinian, by soldiers on the same errand ... When we find several gallons together of this small Coin, as Mopas [Malpas] and Condorah, we cannot suppose them the property of single persons (every particular person being willing, for his own conveniency, to reduce Brass into Silver, or Gold) but may conclude them part of the stores of the Quaestor, or Paymaster of the Army, kept by him for the conveniency of the soldiers, and buried there where we find them, upon some unexpected alarm, when they could not be carried off. In short we owe the greatest part of kind of treasure, to the confusion and fatal events of War, plundering Camps, burning Temples, Streets, and Cities.[93]

In truth, it is doubtful that a large detachment of auxiliaries or legionaries defended the area alone. It is far more likely that the task was left to local recruits under the leadership of a small group of military experts, not least as it was in the former's interests to ensure the Helford remained a safe place from which to conduct their lucrative trade. Hoards from both the local area and wider Cornwall suggest that Roman concern in, and influence over, the far south-west intensified from around mid-third century onwards. Although the distinguished Iron Age historian Hugh Hencken believed that Roman officials 'were very few, and perhaps did no more than exercise some supervision over the industry and buy the tin from the native streamers', the evidence for a far greater presence in the Helford River area seems strong.[94]

As Borlase suggested, the anxiety was perhaps due to the increasing presence of Saxon pirates in the western English Channel at that time. However, nor should we overlook that it would have been around the very period during which most of the Helford River hoards were deposited that Imperial authorities were countering another threat. It is thought that by AD 275 the settlement of South Wales by the *Deisi* of Ireland had begun, and raids along the coastlines of Pembrokeshire and the Bristol Channel may have taken place for several years beforehand. In response, the Roman military constructed a fort at Cardiff, and another at Caer Gybi on Anglesey. That there were raids on both the north and south coasts of Cornwall in the late third century AD therefore seems likely.[95] They would continue, and intensify, in the centuries following the end of Roman rule in Britain.

Although it is a matter of pure conjecture for which there is no observable evidence whatsoever, the Helford *might* have become part of a wider maritime defence network. Along the south-east coast of England between the Solent and the Wash are a number of stone forts seemingly designed with the protection of the surrounding coast in mind. The earliest of these were constructed in the early third century but most, including those at Dover, Portchester, Richborough, and Lympne, were built during the latter half. They are collectively known as the forts of the Saxon Shore, the *litus Saxonicum*, although why they should have come by that name has long been a matter of debate.

It is known from a document relating to the administration of the late Roman Empire, the *Notitia Dignitatum*, that by the end of the fourth century there was a *Comes Litoris Saxonici per Britanniam*, a 'Count of the Saxon Shore', under whose command these outposts fell. But were they to defend *against* Saxon brigands, or were they actually garrisoned *by* them? Perhaps it was a combination of both given the Roman military's habit of bolstering its ranks with those from conquered territories. But perhaps of more relevance are the words of Eutropius who, writing in *Breviarium historiae Romanae*, describes the appointment of a Menapian warrior to counter a seaborne threat in the 280s:

> During this period, Carausius, who, though of very mean birth, had gained extraordinary reputation by a course of active service in war, having received a commission in his post at Bononia, to clear the sea, which the Franks and Saxons infested, along the coast of Belgica and Armorica, and having captured numbers of the barbarians on several occasions, but having never given back the entire booty to the people of the province or sent it to the emperors, and there being a suspicion, in consequence, that

the barbarians were intentionally allowed by him to congregate there, that he might seize them and their booty as they passed, and by that means enrich himself, assumed, on being sentenced by Maximian to be put to death, the imperial purple, and took on him the government of Britain.[96]

The danger posed to the islands by belligerent sailors from outside Roman dominion would have certainly been of deep concern to the authorities. Unlike the Mediterranean Sea, which was bounded on all sides by conquered territory, the English Channel had been nothing but a problem since the time of Julius Caesar. It was one of the Empire's most vulnerable points, accessed with ease by tribes whose motives were rarely above suspicion.[97] It is no surprise, therefore, that it was considered necessary to create heavily defended points from which merchants and military personnel alike could transit safely. But less well known than the Saxon Shore forts of Hampshire, Sussex and Kent were their counterparts along the northern coast of France as far west as Brest and Vannes. As such, it seems implausible to believe that the entire coastline of south west England, from Dorset to Land's End, was without some maritime defensive infrastructure. And certainly not when the west was the prime source of certain coveted commodities.

All the Saxon Shore forts in the south-east of England controlled natural havens within which Roman naval vessels could anchor in safety. The forts themselves would also have offered protection for the sailors and their provisions while not on patrol.[98] Could it be therefore, that at Helford was a more provincial version from which the western approaches to the English Channel were kept in order? The site of such a hypothetical base could have been Merthen, but might equally have been closer to the river mouth. Indeed, it is one of several plausible explanations for the enigmatic name of one small cove in particular.

In the 1830s Helston Grammar School had gained something of a reputation as a place where pupils were allowed freedom to pursue their own interests as well as receiving a sturdy education. As such, it became the ideal destination for the Rector of Clovelly in Devon to send his shy, stammering son. The schoolmaster was Derwent Coleridge, son of the great poet Samuel Taylor Coleridge, and his new student in 1833 was the young Charles Kingsley.

One of Kingsley's early passions was botany, and in the second-master of Helston, Charles Johns, he found an able tutor. Johns regularly took extended walks around the Lizard Peninsula, and upon these he was frequently joined by pupils from the school, Charles Kingsley among them. It would have been during these outings that the boy who would one day write books such as *The Water Babies* came to know the Helford. Three decades later he would use the river as a setting for part of his novel *Hereward the Wake: Last of the English*.

While Kingsley's account was a work of fiction, it is an established fact that Hereward was a real-life character. Accounts are drawn from several sources but most notably from the *Gesta Herewardi*, which dates from the twelfth century and documents the adventures of a Saxon fighter who leads a rebellion against the Norman conquerors of England. Reputed to have been a troublesome young man, he was exiled by his family and deemed an outlaw by Edward the Confessor at the age of just 18. The *Gesta Herewardi* tells us that before the guerrilla warfare exploits that would make him a legendary figure amongst the English, Hereward spent time in Ireland, Flanders and Cornwall. Some scholars have claimed that the stories associated with his banishment are embellished at best and complete fiction at worst, but we cannot entirely rule out that he did indeed travel to the West Country.

Charles Kingsley's novel is clearly based upon the *Gesta*. However, the medieval text does not specify the precise location in Cornwall where Hereward is supposed to have fought and killed an intimidating thug called 'Rough Scab', who had hoped to marry the daughter of a Cornish Prince. Kingsley, on the other hand, and for reasons unknown, places the events around the Helford. Here, at the beginning of chapter three, entitled 'How Hereward Succoured a Princess of Cornwall', he describes his arrival:

> He [Hereward the Wake] went into port on board a merchant ship carrying wine, and intending to bring back tin. The merchants had told him of one 'Alef', a valiant 'regulus', or kinglet, living at Gweek, up the Helford River … He sailed in, therefore, over a rolling bar, between jagged points of black rock, and up a tide river which wandered and branched away inland like a landlocked lake, between high green walls of oak and ash, till they saw at the head of the tide Alef's town, nestling in a glen which

sloped towards the southern sun. They discovered, besides, two ships drawn up upon the beach, whose long lines and snake-heads, beside the stoat carved on the beak-head of one, and the adder on that of the other, bore witness to the piratical habits of their owner. The merchants, it seemed, were well known to the Cornishmen on shore, and Hereward went up with them unopposed; past the ugly dykes and muddy leats, where Alef's slaves were streaming the gravel for tin ore; through rich alluvial pastures spotted with red cattle; and up to Alef's town. Earthworks and stockades surrounded a little church of ancient stone, and a cluster of granite cabins thatched with turf, in which the slaves abode.

The author's selection of Gweek as the Cornish location associated with the Saxon folk hero begs the question as to whether he was influenced to do so solely through childhood association or, perhaps, because he was also privy to long-lost oral or documentary evidence. The latter is highly unlikely but cannot be entirely discounted. Moreover, was it purely by accident that he chose to use one of only a few settlements in the area whose name is not obviously Cornish in origin?

As is so often the case with history, reasoning is influenced by the cultural zeitgeist of a given time. During the early part of the twentieth century when it was fashionable to believe that British history prior to the arrival of the Romans was dour and unimportant, the emphasis was on highlighting connections to exciting foreign civilisations. So it is unsurprising that when the Camborne Old Cornwall Society considered the etymology of Gweek in 1923, a link to Norse was considered: 'There are a cluster of camps around the Helford River. Here too are Scandinavian remains. Gweek itself may be perhaps Gwick, or Wick – Danish enough.'

Times change. With the resurgence of Cornish language the answer is now deemed to be closer to home. There is no need for invaders or traders. It is, the theory goes, clearly derived from an old Brittonic word relating to a 'forest village' or similar; variously *guic, gwyk*, or *gwik* depending upon which part of the Celtic-speaking world one considers. Indeed, given the sizeable ancient woodlands that still thrive to the south-east and east of the village, such a suggestion would appear perfectly reasonable. And yet there is some confusion.

The earliest reference to the settlement occurs in 1201, when it was then known as *Wik*. A century later when it had become the port for Helston, some 3 miles distant, it was recorded as *Wyke*. By 1506, however, it is known as *Gweke*. While the more recent appellation surely suggests a connection to the Cornish language, the earlier does not. More to the point, why would a settlement whose defining attribute is its being at the head of an important navigable waterway derive its name from a far less distinguishing feature? If this were so then there would be a great many more *Gwiks*, *Guigs* or *Gweeks* all across Cornwall and Wales. There are but a few.

Curiously, a place known as 'Celliwig' is mentioned in two separate surviving examples of ancient Welsh literature. The first, the story of *Culhwch and Olwen*, is thought to have been written circa 1100. In the second, the *Welsh Triads*, it is called 'Celliwig in Cernyw'. This is evidently 'Celliwig in Cornwall'. The name also appears in surviving Cornish manuscripts as *Kyllywyc*, which effectively translates as the multi-language hybrid 'dwelling place in the grove'. The whereabouts of the mysterious *Gelliwig* have been variously suggested as Callington or the Kelly Rounds hillfort in Egloshayle.[99] However, the case for a possible site on the banks of the Helford was once advanced only to be subsequently forgotten. Could it be that somewhere in the woods around Gweek, literally *kelly wic*, is to be found this long-lost site?[100]

Why the location of *Gelliwig* (or *Kyllywyc* depending upon personal preference) should be such a matter of debate is due to it having been a court of King Arthur. Of course, Arthurian legend is precisely that, and many doubt that he was anything more than the product of the cleric Geoffrey of Monmouth's imagination. But this notwithstanding, if there ever was a man upon whom later fable was based then the Helford River would most certainly have been the perfect place for one of his strongholds. It would have been deep within the territory of the Britons, with easy access to the seas along the south coast. Should there once have been a real *Gelliwig* then it may well have been the camp in the Gweek Woods clearing. And if not there, we know that Gear and Caer Vallack were both places of great importance during the early first millennium. Furthermore, the Helford River area can claim one other notable connection to Arthurian fable, and specifically the story of *Tristan and Iseult* – an Anglo–Saxon Charter of 967 makes mention of *hyrt eselt*, Isolt's Ford, crossing the stream above Porthallow.[101]

Arthurian myth aside, Charles Henderson seems to have agreed with the sentiments of the Old Cornwall Society. Bearing in mind his willingness to demonstrate the Cornish derivations of place names throughout the area at every opportunity, he too believed that Gweek owed its title to a more distant culture. 'It is certainly the Latin *Vicus*, a town,' he wrote, 'but whether derived through the medium of the Anglo–Saxon *Wyke* or direct from the time of Roman occupation is doubtful'. We should take Henderson's advice; searching for the linguistic root of 'Gweek' is a fool's errand. Anyone seeking Saxon connections to the Helford River will find far more stimulating possibilities than this.

There are, of course, a small number of settlements within its catchment whose names are distinctly more English in nature than the Tre-, Pol-, and Pen- majority. One of these is the small estate of Bufton, a mile to the north of Gweek. We can be certain that its title is not a post-medieval creation given that it was referred to as *Bocketon* as early as 1318 while part of the ancient Manor of Tucoys. Why it should be so named is unclear, although it seems likely that a Saxon family were settled there by the thirteenth century at the latest. A similar story might account for Tresize in St Martin-in-Meneage, where the medieval spelling of *Treseys* implies it was once the 'farmstead of the Englishman'. More notably, the nearby town of Helston, which for centuries used the Helford River for trade, owes its name to the melding of the Cornish *hen* and *lis* meaning 'old court', and the Saxon *tun*, which denoted a manorial centre. So it was in 1086 and Domesday in which '*Rex tenet Henlistone*': 'the King holds Helston'.

Overall, however, Saxon place names are more prevalent in the east of Cornwall than the west, Helford included. The Cornish language was effectively extinct to the east of the River Fowey by the end of the medieval period, but it was still the dominant tongue of the Lizard Peninsula as recently as the early eighteenth century. But there are still some interesting English names given to landmarks around the estuary: Coneysburrow Cove close to the entrance of Gillan Creek points to an obvious source, while Bream Cove and Grebe Beach may have come from the English tongue and an association with animal residents. The latter, however, may simply be derived from *grib*, Cornish for 'ridge'. How Robin's Cove between Durgan and Helford Passage came about its name is unknown, and nor can the source of 'Gincle Point' to the west of Trebah be ascertained. The latter, noted by William Borlase in 1736, has unfortunately fallen wholly out of use.

However, there is one particular place whose name is especially conspicuous: Porth Sawsen. This small cove between Durgan and Toll Point on the north bank of the river derives its title from the Cornish word for Saxon, variously *saussen, sowsen* or *sowsneger.* And while both Ordnance Survey maps and navigation charts have both tended to label it as Porth Saxon, locals have tended to call it by its traditional name. But why it should be so called in either language remains a mystery. Some suggest, with great conviction, that it was once the site of a confrontation between invading Saxons and local inhabitants. Indeed, the *Cornishman* newspaper of May 1881 even linked the event to Helston's most famous celebration:

> Monday is next Furry Day; a festival touching the origin of which opinions widely differ. Traditions say that the Saxons once effected a landing at a cove between Helford Passage and Durgan, and called Porth Saussen or the Saxon's Port, but were routed by the Britons, who bravely defended the surrounding precipices, with great slaughter.

Despite the poetic fervour of the author, the connection is profoundly unlikely. Helston's famous festival is almost certainly a melding of an ancient springtime celebration and a later Christian one concerning the town's patron saint, St Michael. Instead, those who previously advanced the case for a long-forgotten battle on the Helford's shores based their argument on a short, tantalising entry in the *Annales Cambriae.* These 'Annals of Wales' are made up of several manuscripts, many having been written in the early medieval period, of which one makes reference to three battles which took place in AD 722:

> Bellum heyl apud cornubiam. Bellum gard mailauc. Bellum pentum inter britones et saxones. sed britones uictores in hiis omnibus fuerunt Iuor existente duce eorum. (The battle of Heyl in Cornwall. The Battle of Garth Maelog. The Battle of Pencoed between the Britons and the Saxons. And the Britons were the victors in all three battles.)

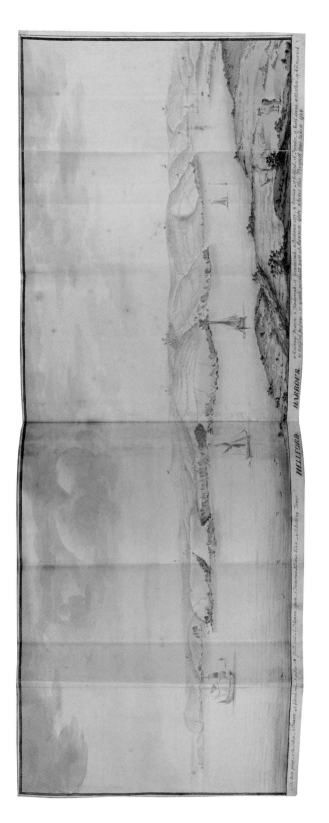

1 A sketch of the Helford drawn by the antiquary William Borlase in 1736 is one of the earliest detailed depictions of the river to survive. (Devon Archives/South West Heritage Trust)

2 The ancient oak woodlands lining the banks along the upper reaches are rich in flora and fauna. They are the precious remnants of forests that once covered the Lizard Peninsula. (Christian Boulton)

3 A Palaeolithic hand axe discovered to the north of the river at Constantine is perhaps the oldest man-made object yet found in Cornwall. It is likely to be at least 200,000 years old. (Royal Institution of Cornwall)

4 A watercolour by an unknown artist depicts the revered Tolmen stone before its destruction in 1869. Its demise led to the establishment of the Ancient Monuments Protection Act and the subsequent preservation of prehistoric sites across the country. (Constantine Museum)

5 On the southern boundary of the Helford's catchment stands the Three Brothers of Grugwith, a half-natural Neolithic ceremonial monument dating from between 3500 and 2600 BC. (Christian Boulton)

6 Located between the villages of Mawnan and Constantine, this upright stone could equally be of prehistoric or medieval origin. Another megalith was recorded as having stood nearby, but unfortunately it no longer exists. (Christian Boulton)

7 The landscape surrounding the estuary abounds with Iron Age and Romano–British settlements. One such is Carlidnack at Mawnan – well preserved in spite of a twentieth-century dwelling being built at its centre. (DroneScope)

8 Rosemullion Head marks the northern entrance of the Helford. The Iron Age cliff castles that stood upon both it and Dennis Head across the water guarded the river, both symbolically and practically, during its trading zenith. (Christian Boulton)

9 The purpose of Cornwall's mysterious Iron Age underground chambers known as fogous are uncertain, but the most celebrated of all is to the south of the river at Halliggye, near Trelowarren. (Christian Boulton)

10 A little clapper bridge of unknown date crosses the stream under the cover of ancient woodlands at Polanguy above Gweek. The sediment is one of the richest sources of alluvial tin in the world and would have been prized by Roman traders. (Christian Boulton)

11 There are several possible reasons why Porth Sawsen – the Saxon's Beach – should possess such an enigmatic name, including it having been the site of an eighth-century battle. (Christian Boulton)

12 One of many Celtic crosses to the north of the Helford, this unusual example stands guard within the ancient religious 'lann' site and medieval cemetery of Merther Uny. It is at least 1,000 years old. (Christian Boulton)

13 Trelill Holy Well, Cornwall's first Scheduled Ancient Monument, is to be found close to the source of one of the river's many small tributaries. (Christian Boulton)

14 William Borlase would still recognise the scene at Gillan Creek and St Anthony-in-Meneage recorded in his sketch of 1733. Even the small spit of land in the foreground is unchanged. (Devon Archives, South West Heritage Trust)

15 A map within the 'Lanhydrock Atlas' shows land at Trebah and Helford Passage at the close of the seventeenth century. The small circular field, now lost, was once a medieval plain-an-gwarry theatre. (National Trust Images/Chris Bowden)

16 The robust little bridge crossing the stream at Polwheveral, pictured around 1920, has barely changed since its construction in 1572. The man sat upon it is the historian, Charles Henderson. (Museum of Cornish Life, Helston)

17 Literary connections have made secluded Frenchman's Creek the most famous of all the river's branches. However, it once went by an entirely different name: Caullons. (Christian Boulton)

18 A coastal defence map drawn up circa 1539 during the reign of Henry VIII shows the Helford to have been considered susceptible to invasion. Dennis Fort is illustrated but yet to be constructed, while St Keverne was clearly the most populated village in the area at the time. (The British Library Board)

19 The Helford, its importance waning, is merely an afterthought on a colourful map of Falmouth Bay created during the latter years of Elizabeth I's reign. The Manacles, however, are disproportionately represented to emphasise their threat to ships. (The British Library Board)

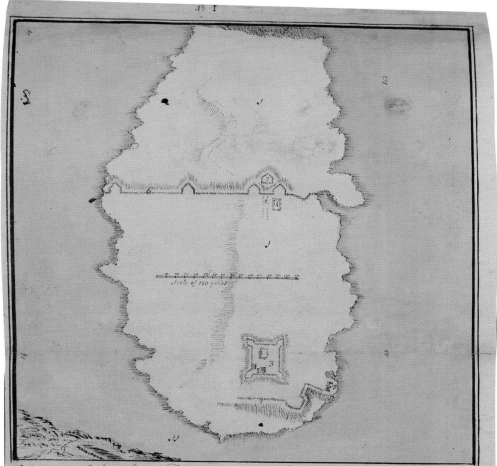

Scale of 180 yards

Nº 1 *Plan of the Little Dennis with the Fortifications* taken on the spot May 4 1736

Nº 2. a small breastwork in the declivity of the Hill and as near the level of the sea as it could well be placd. Flankd by a Bastion, and ending to the North in a little Platform, for cannon. Nº 3 A square Fort on the highest ground of the hill; the Curtains have a ditch and Glacis, with 4 Regular Bastions on the Angles; within it, near the Entrance is a square place of arms, with 3 or 4 vaults or little buildings for the Ammunition. Nº 4 A Place of arms. Nº 5 Entrance thro the line. Nº 6 A Curtaine flankd with 4 Bastions, running in a Strait line from Sea to Sea, over the Hill. Nº 7 A little Ravelin defending the Entrance into this Line. Nº 8 A large mound, reaching also from Sea to Sea, and seemingly the Remainder of some very Ancient Fortification. Nº 9 The Errah, Urreh or Orah, a small tongue of Land formerly defenced by cannon, forming the narrow strait by which the sea runs into Gillan's Creek. Nº 10 Sea running into Helford Harbour. Nº 11 The Strait. Nº 12 Course of the Tyne going up towards Mawgan. Nº 14 The Pool calld Gilland Creek.

20 A plan of Dennis Head defences by William Borlase illustrates not only the site of the long-disappeared Civil War fort, but also ammunition stores and platforms for cannon. (Devon Archives/South West Heritage Trust)

21 The unforgiving Manacles rocks guard the southern approaches to the Helford. Their collective name probably derives from the Cornish *Maen Eglos*, meaning 'church stones' – an apt title for a graveyard of mariners. (Mark Milburn)

22 The magnificent *Bay of Panama* was driven ashore close to the river mouth in 1891 during one of the worst blizzards ever to have struck West Cornwall. More than half its crew either drowned or froze to death in the rigging. Photograph by William Marsden Harrison. (Museum of Cornish Life, Helston)

23 The harrowing aftermath of the SS *Mohegan* wreck of 1898, seen in a print of a Gibson and Sons photograph, with the drowned lying in the parish church of St Keverne awaiting burial. (Museum of Cornish Life, Helston)

24 The Victorian Bosahan House, pulled down and rebuilt to more modest plans in the mid-twentieth century, was the grandest building ever to have stood above the Helford's shores. (Museum of Cornish Life, Helston)

25 Durgan might look idyllic in the twenty-first century, but many of its impoverished Georgian and Victorian inhabitants found themselves either in gaol or sentenced to hard labour for infringing fishing rights in the river. (Jo Penn)

26 Many of the river's old ornamental estates are well known to horticulturalists around the world, but that to be found at Meudon is far less so, despite being one of the finest Cornish valley gardens of its type. (Christian Boulton)

27 A schooner lies off Helford Creek at low tide in 1912, when the river's importance as a place of maritime trade was all but over. Photograph by Herbert Hughes. (The Royal Institution of Cornwall Collection)

28 Airships from RNAS Mullion would have been a familiar sight above the Helford during the First World War as they headed out over the English Channel in search of enemy U-boats. (Museum of Cornish Life, Helston)

29 Mulberry Harbour components being towed from the Helford prior to D-Day in June 1944. This is a rare image and the local photographer took a significant risk in recording the event as the operation was conducted in great secrecy. (Sylvia King)

30 Seen around 1905, the 'old' Ferryboat Inn would ultimately be replaced by a larger building in 1933. A great many famous names would visit during the turbulent years of the Second World War. (The Royal Institution of Cornwall Collection)

Notwithstanding that we must assume that the Saxons were involved in all cases rather than at Pencoed alone, the whereabouts of the Heyl encounter, or *Hehil* as it is sometimes known, remains unresolved. The Georgian clergyman John Whitaker, however, was quite sure that the Helford River was its location:

> … they landed here, were here attacked, and here defeated with a slaughter so memorable as to fix the name of *the Saxon Port* for ever upon the place, and to be recorded with two other defeats of the Saxons in the same reign, even by the pen of a Welsh chronicler. The historical notice comes with a decisive sway to mark the signification of the name; and the name with a striking propriety to indicate the sense of the notice. The port lies on the *northern* side of the Heyl but in the Great Map of Cornwall has no denomination at all … it is marked, however, in the former as a nameless creek a little east of Durgan.[102]

While making such a connection is very tempting, most historians have preferred to focus on potential sites further east such as the Camel estuary in north Cornwall and the Culm Valley in east Devon. It is generally held that both the Helford River, and the similarly named Hayle Estuary, were too far west for Saxon incursions during the early eighth century. However, such a view overlooks one crucial factor: the Saxons were accomplished sailors. As such, it is surely not too far-fetched to entertain the idea that a seaborne raiding party were ambushed on the Helford. After all, not every battle from that particular period need only have involved belligerents travelling on foot. Even the sober and pragmatic military surveyor Henry MacLauchlan was prepared to entertain such a notion:

> It seems probable, that, whenever the Saxons visited this creek, 'the Dennis' was in possession of their enemies; and on examination of the ground on the western entrance, some faint traces of an encampment will be seen on a round hill, close to the creek, with a wood on the declivity next to the stream. This hill still goes by the name of 'the round', and it is not improbable that the works were destroyed on the defeat of the Saxons.[103]

There is much to commend immersing oneself in the river's clear waters at Porth Sawsen, especially on a late afternoon in August after the tide has risen over slate stones baked by the sun. At such times it is almost impossible to conceive that it might once have been visited by violent conflict, but that it might indeed be the site of a long-lost engagement between local Britons and Saxon raiders cannot be discounted. If so, it would surely be the prettiest battlefield in the land.

There are, however, two more probable explanations for its name. The first is that here was a temporary settlement or trading outpost whose foundation and length of occupation is unknown. The shingle bank through which the stream has been diverted would not have existed a thousand years ago and, while sea levels would have been lower, a small tidal creek would have extended northwards. The ridge immediately to the west of the cove that MacLaughlan observed would have provided an easily defended settlement site, with Porth Sawsen itself a safe place of anchorage during savage easterly gales. Unfortunately, only detailed archaeological investigation would prove either settlement or battle site theories correct.

The second, of course, is the aforementioned imposition of Saxon mercenaries along the southern coast by Roman authorities. Rather than shore forts being established to defend *against* Germanic raiders from the east, such a long-forgotten example at Helford might have been garrisoned *by* them. Charged with maintaining the security of the waterway, the belligerent Saxons would have found the otherwise unassuming little cove at its mouth to be the perfect place from which to conduct their business. As such, the prelude to the final collapse of Roman rule might be responsible not only for the coins found at Pennance and Condurrow, but also the origins of Porth Sawsen's curious name. Here was a river of such extraordinary importance that the Empire considered it necessary to protect it at any cost and from any threat, perceived or actual. The hoards of disparate coin types are the product of ancient trade, and those of least variety the cost of defending it.

Whatever the truth, there can be little doubt that 'English' dominance crept westwards in the centuries immediately following Roman withdrawal. This unrelenting march of a new warrior elite is held by some to be wholly responsible for the supposed exodus of Britons to Armorica – now Brittany – from the late fifth century onwards. It is a migration described by numerous sources including Gildas and the sixth-century Byzantine historian Procopius. The Welsh religious figures of Nennius and Geoffrey of Monmouth also alluded to this decampment of the people of the southwest, but the underlying cause has never been fully understood. Some have argued that it was undertaken by a burgeoning population seeking new opportunities, as Procopius suggested in his *History of the Wars*:

> Three very populous nations inhabit the Island of Brittia, and one king is set over each of them. And the names of these nations are Angles, Frisians, and Britons who have the same name as the island. So great apparently is the multitude of these peoples that every year in large groups they migrate from there with their women and children and go to the Franks.

Another explanation for the movement is based upon evidence within the *Historia Brittonum* of the eighth century, believed by some to have been the work of Nennius. This states that the late fourth-century Western Roman emperor, Magnus Maximus, took with him an army of Britons to Gaul, where they subsequently settled. Alternatively, those in Devon and Cornwall might have fled multiple outbreaks of diseases that are today difficult to identify in a fragile archaeological record. A famine not unlike that which saw a million souls leave Ireland in the 1840s might also have been responsible, the climatic deterioration known to have taken place in AD 535 and 536 precipitating departure in pursuit of survival. This downturn was probably caused by a volcanic eruption whose aftermath was feeble sunlight and rapid global cooling. But aside from Gildas' clear hatred for the Saxon invaders there is no documentary evidence that pins clear and unequivocal blame upon them for the Cornish diaspora of the Dark Ages.

Irrespective of the actual causes of the exodus, its impact on the Helford River would have been profound. What had evidently been one of the most densely populated areas of south-west Britain during the Iron Age and Romano–British periods fell silent. It is likely that most of the round settlements around its shores and amid its surrounding countryside were deserted during the mid-first millennium, and thousands more Cornish people from further inland must have taken their final look at their homeland while sailing out of its protective embrace.

Many descendants of these *émigré* Britons would later return to the homeland of their forebears. Charles Henderson noted how the parish of Constantine Subsidy Roll of 1544 showed that no fewer than fourteen of its families were of Breton stock at the time. Why the Helford River region, as elsewhere in Cornwall, should have been so popular was not only due to the higher wages available to workers in England compared to France, but the convenience of language – Breton and Cornish were almost indistinguishable.

The arrival of Saxon families between the seventh and ninth centuries AD was the last notable migration event to have befallen Cornwall. Although human beings had already lived by the Helford for thousands of years, it was the Bronze Age that fashioned its landscape, the Iron Age that saw it populated, the Roman era that made it rich, and the early Dark Ages that returned it to obscurity. The agents of change had come across the sea in every case, and so would the small number of souls who would ultimately establish a culture that would endure for a million tides more.

4

HOLY WATERS

When the distinguished scholar of Celtic literature Caerwyn Williams passed away in 1999, his collection of manuscripts was donated by his family to the National Library of Wales for permanent safe-keeping. In amongst these forgotten works of Breton and Gaelic was discovered a lost play written in 'Middle Cornish', a dialect used during the medieval period. Although incomplete and lacking a title, the concerted efforts of emboldened scholars of the language — by then enjoying a long-overdue revival of its own — brought it back to life and bestowed upon it a formal name: *Bewnans Ke*.

Believed to have been penned during the early sixteenth century at Glasney College in Penryn, *The Life of St Ke* is one of only a handful of plays written in Cornish to have survived into the modern era. Others include the *Ordinalia* (a collection of three mystery plays based on both Old and New Testaments), and *Bewnans Meriasek* (concerning the life of the patron Saint of Camborne). They are precious texts.

Split into two parts, of which the latter focuses on the court of King Arthur, the first describes how Ke, or *Kea*, arrived in Cornwall from Brittany and entered into conflict with a notorious king, Teudar Maur. A colourful part of the story recounts how Kea gives sanctuary to a deer being hunted by Teudar, only for the ruthless potentate to seek vengeance for this insolence by having the saint's oxen taken from him. However, stags soon appear from the woods to help pull the plough in place of the stolen livestock.

Given the fairytale twists to the story it is easy to forget that both St Kea and Teudar Maur were real people, not merely characters in an old Cornish play. The latter became known in his homeland of Brittany as *Tewdwr Mawr*, 'Theodore the Great', while his grandfather, Budic II, had once been the King of *Cornouaille* in western Brittany during the late fifth century AD. When the neighbouring Veneti tribe invaded, the young Teudar had no option but to escape across the sea to safety in Cornwall.

Teudar went on to establish himself as the ruler of Penwith, but his acts of wickedness against Irish Christian missionaries became legend. The fortunate were simply denied safe-landing, the unfortunate brutally put to the sword. One such victim of Teudar's rage is said to have been St Ia, an Irish princess whose burial place reputedly lies below the present-day parish church of St Ives. Saint Gwinear was another supposedly martyred by Teudar in AD 490, probably at Roseworthy, close to his stronghold near Hayle.

The notorious despot is also said to have dispensed tyrannical justice from two other sites, one of which was reckoned to have been at Goodern, near Truro. The other, however, was at the mouth of the Helford River, where its name remains to this day: Lestowder. A corruption of 'lys' and 'Twdwr' – the 'court of Tudor' – it was variously referred to as Lestewdar in 1403 and Lestuther during the middle of the sixteenth century. Charles Henderson also noted that a stretch of road near St Keverne had once been known by the name of 'Vounder Tudor', or 'Teudar's Lane'.[1]

Of course, place names should never be assumed to provide definitive proof in such matters. The site close to Nare Point might boast *some* attributes becoming of a coastal defensive position from the first millennium AD, but cursory inspection suggests no features indicative of actually being one. There are no obvious earthworks to be seen at ground level, or anything else to propose that it might once have been something other than a simple working farm. However, surveys undertaken during the late twentieth century cast new light on Lestowder and proved, beyond reasonable doubt, that defensive ditches did indeed once exist to the south-east of the farmhouse.

Writing in the journal of the Cornwall Archaeological Society in 1995, the historian Michael Tangye described finding an outer defence work and inner enclosure some 30yd apart, the area between which sloped gently downwards towards the latter. The ravages of modern agriculture and infilling have covered or obliterated most of the structure, but the site was surely of some significance at one point in history.[2] What is more, the cove below Lestowder was denoted on the late nineteenth-century Ordnance Survey map as Caermenow, meaning the 'Fortress of the Rocks'. Sometimes toponymy really is irresistible.

Although Charles Henderson was unable to discern the physical evidence of the 'Lys Teudar' that has since been identified, he was his usual inquisitive self when it came to documentary and oral testimony. In his unpublished *Antiquities of Cornwall IV* of 1917 he noted that it was once locally held that 'a small nunnery was founded here by the Convent of Beaulieu, and it was for the sake of its occupants that the Bishop licensed the chapel in 1403'. It would be a supreme irony should it be true that a stronghold of Teudar Mawr, scourge of Christian missionaries, later became an ecclesiastical settlement. Justice would have been done. But if there really was a religious community at Lestowder, it was merely one of many to have flourished in the countryside around the Helford.

Quite when the first people to identify as being 'Christian' came to Cornwall is an unanswerable question. It is possible that they arrived by boat in pursuit of trade in the century following the death of Christ and, if so, an important Romano–British export hub such as the Helford would surely have been one of their first ports of call. However, we should not overlook the legend of Joseph of Arimathea who, it is said, came to Cornwall in search of tin ore. His ship anchored in the River Fal close to the church of St Just in Roseland, or at least so the story goes, and some even believe the young Jesus travelled with him. It is highly improbable, but not wholly impossible.

Writing in his *Adversus Judaeos* in the early third century AD, the theologian Tertullian asserted that 'all the limits of the Spains, and the diverse nations of the Gauls, and the haunts of the Britons – inaccessible to the Romans, but subjugated to Christ'. The Britons in question were most likely those in the far north of Scotland, but we cannot discount contact with the far south-west during the same period. It is also recorded that two heretical bishops known as Instantius and Tiberianus were exiled to *Insula Sylina, quae ultra Britannias est*, namely the Isles of Scilly, in AD 384.[3] Given that Emperor Constantine had decriminalised Christian worship throughout the Empire in AD 313 via the Edict of Milan, we can be reasonably confident that at least a handful of Cornish people must have become followers by the end of the fourth century.

It was another 'Constantine' who Gildas made much of in his *De Excidio et Conquestu Britanniae* of circa AD 520. In this particular work (which translates as *On the Ruin and Conquest of Britain*), the cleric excoriated the early sixth-century king, calling him 'the tyrannical whelp of the unclean lioness of Damnonia', and condemned him for the murder of two young royals in a church. It seems likely that this was the very same Constantine of Cornwall who laid down his crown for a life of piety at St David's Monastery in Pembrokeshire. He also lent his name to the settlement above the Helford.

Charles Henderson believed that the village represented the focus of his 'cult' and that the site of the present-day church was his *lann*, or religious centre. Once known as *Langostenton*, the churchtown and outlying estates such as Bosahan, Trebarva, Trewardreva and Goongilling collectively formed the endowments of the monastery. This continued until the Norman invasion of 1066, after which it 'lost all traces of its collegiate character and became a parochial benefice'.[4]

The term *lann* is derived from an old Brittonic word for 'clearing'. So too is the English word 'lawn'. *Lanns*, however, were concerned solely with the growing of Christianity, and far more likely to have been small working communities rather than generally uninhabited places of worship. It has been suggested that the development of these sites took place over an extended period of time, commencing with the enclosure of an existing graveyard, the building of a chapel, and finally the construction of a larger church.[5] Alas, ascribing even the vaguest date to the foundation of these religious sites is fraught with difficulty, not least as some appear to have been established upon the remnants of previous Iron Age or Romano–British settlements. The parish church of Mawnan is one such example, as indicated by the discovery of Roman coins within the outer bank. This curvilinear boundary, running west around the oldest part of the churchyard from the lych gate, is one of several associated with parish churches in the Helford River area. A fragment of another appears to be extant at Mawgan-in-Meneage, where it is 'fossilised' in the wall to the north and east of the church.[6] Both Constantine and Manaccan also seem to be encircled by oval enclosures, albeit ones greatly altered by the work of many hands over the past 1,000 years.

Not all *lanns* possess a rounded boundary, but it is thought that those that do represent the oldest examples at which ancient burial sites have been enclosed.[7] In fact, it is entirely possible that the presence of these 'pagan' cemeteries actually facilitated the growth of Christianity; a pioneering missionary full of zeal would have easily exploited any pre-existing reverence for departed ancestors at such places.[8] Enclosure would also have firmly distinguished holy ground from the world outside, further underlining a sense of the sacrosanct.

These early Christian sites tended to be founded either in sheltered valleys or close to the sea, and especially around the estuaries of Cornwall's south coast. Was this due to a need to maintain contact with other religious communities across the water, near and far? If so, the most prototypical must surely be that at St Anthony-in-Meneage, a place first recorded as *Lanynteneyn* during the fourteenth century and whose name is preserved in that of the adjacent farmhouse, *Lantinning*.[9] Indeed, it has been suggested that this exquisite churchyard by Gillan Creek was the site of an enclosed burial ground as early as AD 650.[10] A carved stone uncovered nearby during the late twentieth century exhibits what appears to be a Chi-Rho symbol, the implication of which is that St Anthony could have been a religious centre as long ago as the fifth or sixth centuries AD. People worshipped God at these humble places by the Helford many centuries before the first stones of Westminster Abbey were laid.

There are two other parishes along the southern bank of the Helford that share 'Meneage' as part of their name with St Anthony: St Martin and Mawgan. Additionally, Manaccan and St Keverne are both considered to be part of 'the Meneage', even if not being formally titled as such. It was once suggested that the word was derived from the old Cornish for a stony or rocky place, *meynek*, but it does not seem particularly apt for a part of Cornwall so considerably more fertile than elsewhere. The curator of the Royal Cornwall Institution during 1889, Henry Crowther, came to a similar conclusion, describing the suggested derivation as being 'much out of place' in such an area of 'vegetative productiveness':

A little further, a red patch of stonecrop, flowering sorrel, and sea-thrift; again a bed of dog-daisies, bedstraw, heather, scabious, wild carrot, bladder campions, and mouse-ear; beyond a patch of eye-bright; a little further, and then in that direction we stopped, for immediately below us was a precipitous cliff, with a cave below. Yet its slaty grimness had a floral border that words cannot paint, nor photographic art render patent. The blue scabious, held aloft like buttons, had a lower setting of ruddy stone-crop, yellow trefoil, and mouse-ear, white carrot, white and yellow dog-daisies, and pink sea-thrift, embedded in a carpet of fine green grass, blended so exquisitely that the finest blend of dyed wools would never perfect a tweed as rich in tints.[11]

Crowther's beautiful portrayal defies the centuries. It is still the same in May and June as it ever was. The Meneage could never have been described as being especially 'stony', with so many other areas in Cornwall far more suited to such an explanation. However, in some instances the name was used to describe the whole peninsula between the Helford and Lizard Point, taking in a total of twelve parishes. The seventeenth-century cartographer John Norden described it as 'a parcel of lande containing the most part of this Kirrier hundred; a frutefull and plentifull place for people, corne, fleshe, fishe, tynne, and copper', although on the last counts he was wrong, perhaps mistaking the mining area to be that in the north of Kerrier district.[12] Moreover, in the early nineteenth century it was written that 'Goonhilly Down (in Meneage) was formerly famous for a breed of excellent horses occasioned, it is said, by a Barbary horse being turned loose there'.[13] Those thin-soiled lands of the Lizard plateau are indeed strewn with rocks, even if the Helford's enveloping fields are not.

If the old Meneage did include all land south of the river rather than merely the north-eastern corner, it would add credence to the theory that the name was derived from *meneog*, meaning 'kept in by the sea'.[14] Yet this is by far the least likely explanation. In any case, early documentary evidence of the word is to be found in an episcopal register of 1269 where it is written as *manahec*.[15] In fact, there is even mention of it more than three centuries earlier in an Anglo–Saxon charter relating to a grant of land in the parish of St Keverne. This gift, from King Edgar to the fearsome-sounding Wulfnoth Rumuncant, concerns property *in loco ubi uulgariter uocitatur lesmanaoc et pennard*, meaning 'in the place where it is commonly called Lesneague and

Pennare'.[16] As with Lestowder, *Lesmanaoc*, is derived from *lys* meaning 'court' and *manach* meaning 'monk'. We can therefore say with some confidence that the true meaning of Meneage is 'the land of monks'. Lesneague must once have been an important religious administrative centre, but is today a farm whose bucolic surroundings belie its former significance.

One particular eleventh-century charter written shortly after the Norman Conquest finds Earl Robert, Count of Mortain, gifting land in the area to Mont St Michel. Once again, Lesneague is mentioned – this time as *Lismanoch* – while the locality is referred to as *Ameneth*. The latter is probably an Anglicised term for Meneage.[17] These documents suggest that the effectively autonomous nature of Cornish monasticism, and the ownership of land by small religious groups on the Lizard Peninsula, was coming to a close. We might speculate that it had held sway through this part of the county for perhaps 600 years or more, but why should it have developed such deep roots to the south of the river in the first place?

The answer as to why these 'monkish lands' should have flourished is largely one of geography. Clearly, Cornwall is below both Ireland and Wales and to the north of Brittany, with Celtic Christianity having thrived in all three. It follows, therefore, that the far south-western tip of mainland Britain would have been visited, and eventually settled, by those bringing the word of Christ from beyond its shores. Their legacies are to be found within the names of many of Cornwall's towns and villages, with St Piran surely the most famous – the patron saint of tinners is thought to have died around AD 480 having given his name to the likes of Perranporth, Perranzabuloe, Perranwell and Perranuthnoe. Indeed, the small beach at the foot of Budock Vean valley was once known as Perran Cove, although how it came by such a title is unknown and a matter only for those with particularly inventive minds.

As with elsewhere in Cornwall, the Helford boasts many connections to religious missionaries of the 'Dark Ages'. The most obvious are those whose names are preserved in the parish churches of the area, a striking example being St Mawgan. Sabine Baring-Gould believed him to have been of Irish origin – albeit via a sojourn in Wales – as were many others associated with the Meneage. The son of Dubhtach, Chief Bard to King Laoghaire, Mawgan is reputed to have lived during the fifth century and is venerated not only in Cornwall but also in Brittany at La Meaugon, a commune near Saint Brieuc.[18] It might well be that having landed at Mawgan Porth on the north coast of Cornwall, the saint departed for France from the creek on the Helford which bears his name. Little else is known about him.

St Mawnan was another holy man to have left a legacy by the river. Although some have suggested Breton origins, Baring-Gould was more convinced the name to have been 'the softened form of the Goidelic S. Magenn', a wandering Irish bishop of the late sixth century AD. Indeed, he appears to have been a particularly dramatic character given his propensity for cursing those who crossed him. According to legend, when the pet ram that accompanied him on his travels was killed, St Mawnan condemned the perpetrator to blindness and a bursting stomach. A similar fate befell another scoundrel who stole a cow belonging to a leper woman. Furthermore, it was Mawnan who supposedly made the curious prophecy that 'a time shall come when girls shall be pert and tart of tongue; when there shall be grumbling and discontent among the lower classes; when there will be lack of reverence to elders; when churches will be slackly attended; and when women shall exercise wiles'.[19]

A further theory as to the origins of Saint Mawnan is that she was *Mwynan*, the daughter of the fifth-century King Brychen of Wales.[20] But, rather like Mawgan, whether they founded the religious community where the present church stands is unknown, although tradition holds that the saint, male or female, constructed a little hovel by the boundary hedge.[21] In any case, the church was later given a second dedication to St Stephen, presumably in an attempt to draw it closer to the Catholic establishment and lessen its association with the old Celtic branch of Christianity. Alternatively, the village name might have more descriptive Cornish origins and simply mean 'the plain by the sea'.

One Irish missionary we can be more certain of having settled in Cornwall is Saint Achebran. It is thought that having arrived in Cornwall with a group of other 'saints' he made a temporary settlement upon the Lizard Peninsula before sailing across the sea to France. The site of this early Christian community is today St Keverne, formerly known as *Lannachebrann* and recorded as such in the Domesday Book of 1086. At that time it was held by the canons of St Achebran and consisted of 11 acres of land, enough for seven ploughs, and a further 20 acres of pasture. Local legend recounts how the saint – also known as Kevran – arrived from Kerry in the sixth century AD, building himself two huts where the parish church now stands. One was for shelter, the other for purposes of praying and religious observation. A small wooden cross marked the entrance.[22] From these humble beginnings it would go on to become an important collegiate church – a revered place of learning and biblical study.

However, it is important to remain sceptical of details contained within hagiographies of saints from that far off time. Clearly there are places with connections to religious figures to be found around the Helford and wider Cornwall, but in precisely what regard we will never know. After all, the 'Lives' of saints such as Winwaloe were not written for more than 300 years after their deaths, and those of St Petroc and St Cadoc a great deal longer after still.[23] But, as ever, amid the confusion there is often a grain of truth.

The apocryphal story of the founding of the church of St Anthony is one of the most colourful of any religious site in Cornwall. It is said that a group of sailors from Normandy were caught in a ferocious storm in the English Channel and, fearing for their lives, called upon the patron saint of mariners, St Anthony, for salvation. When they came ashore they found themselves in the sheltered waters of Gillan Creek, subsequently building a church upon the exact site of their deliverance. However, there is some confusion as to precisely *which* St Anthony it was that they directed their prayers. We must assume that, on account of his patronage of seafarers, the Anthony in question must be he who died in Padua, Italy, in 1231. However, the old name for the parish feast, 'piggy feast', suggests an association with St Anthony the Great – an Egyptian monk of the third century AD who is frequently depicted with the pig he is said to have healed. Moreover, it is recorded that the first known vicar of the church arrived at 'St Antoninus in Manahec' in 1266, a date little more than thirty years after the beatification of Anthony of Padua.[24]

There has also been wild speculation as to the architectural origins of this most iconic of the Helford's churches. It has been asserted that much of the stone within the existing structure is fine-grained granite quarried in Normandy and imported specifically for the task.[25] This, however, might be a completely erroneous claim with its provenance being confused with the famous limestone of Caen beloved by medieval masons. But the architecture *is* unmistakably Norman, and a great deal of its medieval fabric has survived, as the architect E.H. Sedding observed shortly after its restoration in 1890:

> The church, which stands on the side of a hill, seems to have been built not earlier than the thirteenth century, and consisted of only nave, chancel, and south transept. A north aisle was added late in the following century, when the five arches, with octagonal piers, took the place of the north wall of the nave. The fine granite west tower was built about twenty-five years later ... the nave and aisle are both covered by fifteenth century roofs.[26]

Glorious as it is, its most remarkable attribute is neither its age nor beauty. Such is its situation that only the most unsentimental secularist could fail to feel a modicum of divine intervention in its being where it is. It is sheltered, unobtrusive, and cushioned from the present. The church of St Anthony-in-Meneage is a paradox: it is both architecturally impressive and humble at once. There is a cathedral-like serenity to be found within, yet it is also intimate. It is patently a Christian site of remarkably early origin for these islands. The life-sustaining waters of a holy well to the north of the church probably account for it first being settled, and no doubt have been revered since before the birth of Christ.

If the origins of St Anthony-in-Meneage are an enigma, the ecclesiastical foundations of nearby St Martin are a conundrum. A chapelry to the adjoining parish of Mawgan, the good people of fourteenth-century St Martin even had to apply to Pope Urban VI for the right to bury their dead (partly because the bridges around the creek head were regularly left impassable by water damage).[27] Successful in their request, the churchyard was consecrated in 1385 by Thomas de Brantyngham, Bishop of Exeter. Alas, the original medieval church fell into a considerable state of disrepair and, in 1827, it was considered necessary to suspend services. This may have been a direct result of the rise of Methodism, occasioned sometimes by disreputable means as a letter to the *Cornishman* newspaper reported in May 1890:

> The blind bigotry of little minds is nowhere more clearly shown that in the parishes of Mawgan and St Martin-in-Meneage. Here nearly all the

farmers are dissenters; amongst whom are to be found those who will threaten their helpless labourers that if they absent themselves from chapel and go to Church there may be no more work for them … If the labouring man's child should refuse to go to the dissenting Sunday-school, or be absent from it and found in Church, the most hateful form of coercion is used by Brother or Sister Sly, from the chapel. The mother is visited and told that her husband gets his living from Our chapel-people.

The church was rebuilt in 1830 following a fire that spared only the fifteenth-century tower and its Norman font. Unfortunately, its existing architectural detail is in no way as detailed as its forebear would have been, but the flames could not erase its ancient origins. As with other churches around the Helford, it too stands upon a *lann* site as the arcing boundary to the south-west implies. The religious history of St Martin-in-Meneage is most assuredly as deep as that of any other parish around the Helford River, although it has not always been known by such a name.

In Brantyngham's register of 1385, the curious phrase *Ecclesie Sancti Martini, alias Dydemin* appears. This suggests that prior to its dedication to St Martin of Tours, the parish was known as 'Dydemin', or variants thereof.[28] It was clearly a name that local inhabitants were keen to maintain given that it was subsequently recorded as *Martyn alias Dedimus* in 1535, and *Martin alias Dedimus* as late as 1742.[29] But to what, or who, it refers is a mystery. Perhaps it relates to an obscure saint whose story is lost. Another theory is that it means 'the place of two monks', or similar.[30] If this latter argument were to be correct then it would be consistent with another piece of precious written evidence.

The tenth-century document in question relates to a grant of land in St Keverne and at Trethewey in St Martin-in-Meneage. Made between King Edward the Martyr and Aethelweard (a descendant of King Aethelred of Wessex), the boundary clause for Trethewey opens with *aerest aet pennhal meglar* – a melding of Anglo Saxon and Cornish – which roughly translates as 'first of all near the head of Meglar's marsh'. This concerns land at Barrimaylor, just to the south-east of the church at St Martin. It is reassuring to know that the 'pool of wild garlic' subsequently noted at the north-western corner of the old estate is still there, more than 1,000 years after being first recorded.[31]

Barrimaylor is a corruption of *Merther Meylar,* and to the north of where the church now stands was 'Mathiana', itself a distortion of *Merther Anou.* 'Merther' in Cornish means much the same as its equivalent in Welsh, 'merthyr'. Both are derived from the Latin *martyrium,* relating to a shrine, chapel or other building connected to the body or relics of a martyr. Here the saints are *Meylar* and *Anowe* although, as always, the spelling changes over the centuries. They are probably of Breton origin, but little is known of their lives and travels.[32] If true, these two monastic cells shared a boundary at the point where the first church of St Martin-in-Meneage was built, perhaps accounting for why it should have been so chosen.

Also in St Martin-in-Meneage and close to Gear hill fort is the settlement of Halnoweth. Its name is derived from the Cornish for 'new hall', but the earliest reference to the settlement was made as long ago as the mid-twelfth century, then being referred to as *Nova Aula Del Caer.*[33] This Latin description is fascinating as it not only validates the later name, but because it also subtly implies somewhere out of the ordinary. This 'new hall of the fort' clearly contains reference to Gear, but given that *aula* can also refer to a 'court' the site may have been of more importance than scholars and antiquaries have previously afforded it. Moreover, that there was a 'new' implies that it replaced an 'old'.

William Hals, who began compiling his unpublished *Complete History of Cornwall* in the 1680s, was quite convinced that a nunnery once existed at Halnoweth. Charles Henderson, rational as always, believed that it was a preposterous notion.[34] If so, it was a fiction that the Ordnance Survey willingly upheld with its late nineteenth-century map edition claiming it to have been the site of such. Perhaps Hals had based his observation on that made by Sir Richard Carew a century earlier, claiming that his 'not over-curious' enquiries had led him to believe there had been a nunnery at *S. Martine.* Some have latterly suggested that nearby Bishop's Quay at the mouth of Mawgan Creek offers supporting evidence but, alas, the apparently religious name is merely taken from that of a man who ran operations from the site during the early nineteenth century. Prior to then it had been referred to as Kilter's Quay.[35]

That Bishop's Quay should in fact possess absolutely no connection to pious travellers of the medieval era does not mean that such places of departure and arrival did not once exist. There would certainly have been a small number of landing places serving monastic cells all along the Meneage shoreline, with both ecclesiastical visitors and locals able to transit between the settlements along the river's route, secular as well as religious. The site of one, now redundant, is still known today.

The ferry that carries passengers on foot between Helford Passage and the southern shore is, as Charles Henderson noted, a 'very ancient institution'. The question as to when it first commenced operating as a business venture has never been answered, but it must surely be many centuries before it fell into to the hands of the Bishops of Exeter following the Norman Conquest. One of the earliest known records dates from 1316, when a gentleman called Ralph de Tregod made a grant to Walter, Bishop of Exeter, of a house at Helford Passage together with adjoining land at Trebah and the port of the ferry. Henderson stressed that the grant 'must be read as a recovery of the ferry by the bishop after an alienation by one of his predecessors', and it would be absurd to believe it had not been in existence for many centuries by that time. Other documentary evidence for its longevity comes from 1538 when one John Thomas 'held the lord's boat on lease' and paid 16*s* to monopolise the passage, a significant sum that implies a most profitable operation.[36]

Although the point of departure from the north bank seems to have always been somewhere in the immediate vicinity of Passage Cove and The Bar, exactly where it arrived on the south shore has changed over the years. Since the late nineteenth century it has operated from Helford Point, but it would have originally been from the hamlet of Treath to the east. That *treth* is Cornish for 'ferry' proves beyond reasonable doubt that it would have been the original landing place, with the sixteenth-century 'trehett alias passagium' settlement offering easier access to the Meneage than Helford village itself. The beautiful little quay, built during the 1700s using a technique imported from Belgium and Holland, stands upon the foundations of its medieval precursor.[37]

The present-day quietude to be found at Treath belies the fact that this would once have been a bustling place. Not only would there have been travellers awaiting passage, but all manner of goods and produce stacked for shipping. Horses would have been tethered behind the boat and made to swim, something that many would have been quite used to doing due to the regularity of their crossings. At low tide the distance would have been reduced to just a few hundred yards, making it a practical alternative to 10 miles or more of winding lanes around the head of the river. Once across to Helford Passage, the passengers and their horses would have proceeded towards Mawnan Smith; a village that derives part of its name from the smithies established to serve both transient travellers and rooted farmers of the district.

It seems probable, however, that passengers of an especially religious nature were landed at a separate point along the southern shore. This particular site, just to the east of Treath at Gold an Gear, was recorded by Charles Henderson as having once been known as 'Monk's Passage'. A rock-cut slipway possibly marks the location of this historic landing place where those heading for one of the many monastic communities of the Meneage would have alighted.[38]

One such important religious centre existed at Manaccan, a place whose relevance to the story of Celtic Christianity was succinctly summarised by the Royal Cornwall Institution in 1890:

> The ancient name of the old parish of Manaccan, of which the Rev. A. R Eagar is the new vicar, was Minster, Saxon for monastery. Since 1521 the parish has been called Manach-an (interpretation – in Cornish – being monks). Both names imply the previous existence of a monastery there. The great tithes were bestowed on Glasney College [at Penryn] by its founder, Walter Bronescombe, Bishop of Exeter, August 1275, towards the maintenance of two chaplains, to celebrate a mass daily in the Lady chapel, for the souls of the founders. But the great tithes of Trevose and Treath still belong to the vicary, so the titular Manaccan is a vicarage, but technically a rectory. The Bishops of Exeter had until lately, in the parish, a small tenement … it extended to the Helford River.[39]

Early pieces of documentary evidence for the old name for the village are to be found in thirteenth-century episcopal registers. When Robert de Stormy became rector in 1264, the church was referred to as 'Ecclesie de Menstre'. A decade later the Bishop of Exeter appropriated the rectory to Glasney College at Penryn after which the incumbents were referred to as vicars, something confirmed by the appointment of David de Sancta Beriana as 'Vicaria Ecclesie de Menstre' in 1277.[40] However, we should not allow our modern interpretation of the word *minster* to influence our vision of what may have once existed in this old manor. No grand building as at York or Southwell stood here. Instead, the title simply refers to a monastic church community within which members of a religious order lived and prayed. So it was all across the Meneage, a place apart from the rest of Cornwall, and one where geld had never been paid prior to the Norman Conquest.[41]

These little monastic communities most probably began as independent entities under the protection of tribal leaders during the first millennium. Given the seaborne movement of religious missionaries along the Atlantic coast between the sixth and ninth centuries, their settlement and the subsequent conversion of local people upon the Lizard Peninsula would have been almost unavoidable. It is also clear that at various times they lost their independent 'Celtic' status, many being absorbed into greater monastic bodies. St Anthony-in-Meneage became part of the Benedictine priory of Tywardreath, itself a branch of the great Abbey of St Sergius and St Bacchus at Angers in France, while St Keverne was presented by the Earl of Cornwall to the Abbots of Beaulieu in 1235. Writing in 1535, John Leland noted the remnants of what had once been an important place of worship:

> St. Keverine's, 2 miles from Gilling creake and not a mile from the se. S. Keverine's longgid to Bewle Abbay in Hampshir, and had a sanctuarie privileged at S. Keverine's. Also yn the west side of the point of hayleford haven, and withyn the land of Mencke or Menegland, is a paroch chirch of S. Keveryn otherwise Piranus; and ther is a sanctuary with x or xii dwelling howses, and therby was a sel of monks, but no goone home to their hed hows. The ruines of the monastery yet remenith.[42]

Although the building might have been in decay even *before* King Henry VIII's Dissolution of the Monasteries, the fiercely independent religious nature of the Meneage people most certainly was not. It has been said that 'St. Keverne was where everything started in Cornwall', and never more so than during the late fifteenth and sixteenth centuries.[43] Here was a poor, agrarian, economy whose population combined mainstream Catholicism with their peculiar brand of 'Celtic' Christianity. There is less than a mile between those living in the countryside beyond the north and south shores, but during the late 1400s they were different worlds. Meneage folk were rough-hewn and their geographic isolation a barrier against the encroaching tide of Anglicisation.

Across the water in Mawnan, the rector of the parish church from 1475 was Sir John Oby. It was a position he held whilst simultaneously acting as sacrist at Glasney College, a thriving seat of learning at the time. In 1491 he was appointed Provost of Glasney, a role that came with the unenviable task of collecting the taxes required to finance the military campaigns of Henry VII against the Scots. Needless to say, his actions proved unpopular, not least as it was believed he had taken more in revenue than had been passed to the King. In 1497 in the market place of Taunton, the former rector of Mawnan was killed 'piteously, in such ways that he was dismembered and cut in many and sundry pieces'.[44]

Ironically, the reason for Oby's demise was to be found just across the water in the Meneage. The reason's name was Michael Joseph, blacksmith of St Keverne, who the eighteenth-century Scottish historian David Hume described as a 'notable prating fellow, who, by thrusting himself forward on every occasion, and being loudest in every complaint against the government, had acquired an authority among those rude people'.[45] This man, now more commonly referred to as *an Gof*, Cornish for 'blacksmith', was undeniably right in principle, but his antagonism meant that in practice he provoked a great deal of bloodshed. His own blood, included.

Together with a second leader – the arguably more level-headed Thomas Flamank of Bodmin – Michael Joseph led those outraged by the taxes and suspension of the Stannary Parliament the previous year on a long march to London. Passing through Exeter (where a siege was narrowly averted) what had begun with a few thousand men from Cornwall had swelled into an army of 15,000 by the time it reached Guildford in Surrey during the early summer of 1497. Many had travelled on foot all the way from the lands around the river. Alas, by the time the rebels set up camp at Blackheath to the south-east of London only half remained. Engaged by the King's army on 17 June, they were defeated by superior numbers and superior military prowess with the loss of hundreds, if not thousands, of lives.

Having called for surrender, Michael Joseph fled the Battle of Deptford Bridge only to be captured at Greenwich. Both he and Thomas Flamank were hanged at Tyburn ten days later, their heads gibbeted on London Bridge for the population to see. At his execution, Joseph is said to have exclaimed that he would have 'a name perpetual, and a fame permanent and immortal'. As a Cornish icon whose statue greets travellers reaching St Keverne he has been proved right, even if his reputed statement suggests a man of narcissistic character resigned to his fate. The same cannot be said of the nameless hundreds whom he inflamed only to pay the price for their allegiance with their lives. As for Sir John Oby, there is some confusion as to whether he was murdered by Michael Joseph's rebels en route to London, or by supporters of Perkin Warbeck, pretender to the throne, during the Second Cornish Uprising just months later in September 1497.

Discontent fomented in the Meneage led to yet another Cornish insurrection in 1549. On this occasion it was an affront to Catholicism provoking the ire of the impoverished populace, specifically Thomas Cranmer's introduction of the English Book of Common Prayer. But much of the damage had already been done during the Dissolution of the Monasteries, an act that had undermined an important aspect of cultural life in the far south-west. The fire had been built and only a spark was needed to set it ablaze.

The prelude to the Prayer Book Rebellion began in April 1548. The government ministers of the boy king, Edward VI, had tasked the Archdeacon of Cornwall, William Body, with the removal of Catholic images, texts and ornaments from parish churches. On the fifth of the month he had reached Helston where, within hours, a large group led by the priest of St Keverne, Martin Geoffrey, arrived to protest. Those who accompanied Geoffrey were almost all working men of sea and soil, and records suggest that many of them had travelled with him from the Meneage.

Seeking refuge in a house close to the church, William Body had clearly hoped the disturbance would dissipate allowing opportunity for his escape. Unfortunately for him, word of his whereabouts had spread at great pace and he was soon dragged from the building and stabbed to death. The man who delivered the fatal blow to the back was supposedly William Kilter of Constantine. He and his brother John, together with over twenty others, were committed to Launceston gaol and hanged, drawn and quartered.

Martin Geoffrey was sent to London where he was unfairly met with the same fate. A year later a series of battles and skirmishes in east Cornwall and Devon culminated in the deaths of countless Cornish and Devonian rebels. Their demands that the church be restored to its former ways, including Latin mass, failed.

The church of St Keverne is largely as those who left for Helston on that spring day of 1548 would have known it. Much of the present structure dates from the thirteenth and fourteenth centuries, with the tower constructed in the early fifteenth and the spire atop it completed in 1450. Admittedly, the latter had to be rebuilt following the violent thunderstorm that struck the area on 18 February 1770, and whose aftermath was described by the Rector, Anthony Williams, as 'a scene presented as is horrible to think of, much more to see. The churchyard was 'almost full of ruins.'[46] But, aside from the growing number of headstones within the churchyard, it has been the unchanging backdrop to village life for more than six centuries.

The Helford's parish churches are far more than mere reliquaries of local Christianity. They are sturdy icons of the river's surrounding landscape whose presence is both a marker of ancient importance and a bulwark against the new. Furthermore, although they all exhibit Norman architectural signatures, each is essentially unique in structure and character.

That at St Anthony is a collection of architectural quirks, from a 'dog-door' in the tower to the most exquisite early Tudor wagon roof. Alongside the fifteenth-century font sits the base of its twelfth-century predecessor, found buried in the churchyard by the assiduous eye of Charles Henderson. One of the tower's foundation stones was that to which the stocks were once attached, while a carving of the Last Supper is thought to be of late-medieval German origin. Manaccan boasts similar eccentricities, not least the unusual Norman doorway that Nikolaus Pevsner described as having 'three little orders of columns and curious fluted voussoirs'.[47] Here, too, is to be found the famous fig tree growing from the south wall. It is an ancient place, fashioned almost entirely between the twelfth and fifteenth centuries. In comparison, partly rebuilt St Martin-in-Meneage is far less easy upon the eye, but certainly through no fault of those who conceived of it in the first place. We are left to wonder what might have been were it not for that fateful blaze of the early nineteenth century.

To the north, those of Constantine and Mawnan are vastly different in almost every respect. The tower of the former is 100ft tall and visible for miles around, its interior more voluminous than the average Cornish church. Constantine was built as a statement of religious intent; created to accommodate residents of one of the largest parishes in Cornwall. Furthermore, it is also one of the most 'recent' to have been constructed, being almost wholly of late fifteenth-century origin and with vanishingly few remnants of its Norman predecessor. Mawnan, on the other hand, is smaller and more intimate. Its fourteenth-century tower is little more than half the height of St Constantine's, while a lancet window and a piscina basin of the thirteenth century are indicators of the chancel's considerable age. Restorations of 1830 and 1880 could have been more sensitive to its medieval origins, but works were desperately required to rescue it from its parlous state. It was said that such were its structural problems that curious knocking noises were discovered to have been caused by floating coffins in the vault.[48] But its defining feature is its situation; Mawnan's origins as a *lann* are more evident than at any other church of the river. Only St Anthony is closer to the waves.

However, the Church of St Mawgan-in-Meneage is arguably the most evocative of them all. It stands proudly above the calm waters of the creek amid some of the most pastoral countryside in Cornwall. The robust tower is undeniably one of the most impressive in the county, although the finer details of its four pinnacles are lost on the earthbound observer. Inside, one is met with a sense of space that most rural Cornish churches lack. The fifteenth-century roof above bears all the hallmarks of the outstanding craftsmanship of that particular time, while the font and parts of the south wall are 200 years older still. In the north aisle are to be found a helmet and sword that once belonged to Sir Hannibal Vyvyan of Trelowarren, who died at Blackfriars, London, in 1610. The Lady Chapel contains touch-worn effigies of the crusader knight Sir Roger de Carminowe and his wife Johanna, both finding peace after being removed from the ruins of the long-disappeared Carminow Manor near Helston. It is a place of extraordinary treasures.

Although the existing churches are clearly set within the footprints of very ancient Christian communities, there are other sites around the river, seemingly secular, that also have religious origins. One such is Budock Vean, a place latterly given over to leisure but once one of worship and theology.

In a list of Free Tenants of the Bishopric of Exeter dated to the middle of the thirteenth century, mention is made of a *Richard de Sancto Buthock*, and a century later further documentary evidence provides us with the name of *Benedict de Sancto Budoco* in the parish of Constantine. Another written record from 1538 – this time relating to the Manor of Penryn Foreign – lists the property *Eglos bothyck-Vyan*, which means 'Little Budock Church' to differentiate it from that at Budock Water near Falmouth.

That there was once a small monastic cell and chapel dedicated to St Budoc upon the land between Helford Passage and Port Navas Creek is certain. It was probably located just to the north to the present Budock Vean house, being where 'skeletons were found, which, on being exposed to the air, crumbled into dust' during the nineteenth century.[49] They were presumably those of monks, but to whom they were devoted in life is unclear. It is generally held that the St Budoc in question was a Breton monk who subsequently became Bishop of Dol in the latter half of the sixth century. However, there were several pious 'Budocs' in the first millennium AD, with Leland, the Tudor antiquary, describing one as an 'Irisch man, who cam to Cornwalle and there dwelled'.[50] Perhaps it was here on the shores of the Helford.

There is far less ambiguity attached to the name of St Sidwell, supposedly a native of Devon who was murdered at the behest of her stepmother. Unsurprisingly, most places associated with her are to be found within that particular county, especially around Exeter, but a possible connection to the Helford River area must be suggested: Nansidwell. Located just to the north of Rosemullion Head, this old estate's name means 'the valley of Sidwell', and the spelling of *Nansudewell* upon the late nineteenth-century Ordnance Survey map should be disregarded. The Rev. Sabine Baring Gould even went so far as to suggest that there may once have been 'a church under her invocation' somewhere in the vicinity.[51] The reputed former name of *Lansidwell* offers tentative supporting evidence, and it would have been a beautiful location for such a building.[52]

Richard Polwhele wrote of some 'remains of a very ancient chapel on Tregonwell in the parish of Manaccan' although what little could be seen in the early nineteenth century has now disappeared entirely. When it was built and to whom it was dedicated will probably forever remain a mystery.

So too will that which was recorded as having stood at nearby Trewothack in 1330.[53]

Many medieval chapels are recorded as having once existed in the Helford River parishes, most attached to manor houses or other dwellings of importance. At Mawnan there were such buildings at Trerose and Penwarne, with a field name of Chapel Close still used to this day at the latter. Here too was a burial ground, now thought to lie beneath a walled garden. A Gothic arch window, possibly from the lost chapel, is set within the walls of a small cottage near the farmhouse. Another place of worship is reputed to have stood closer to the village centre at Boskensoe, but all vestiges of it were lost in a fire during the early nineteenth century that, lamentably, also destroyed the original medieval farm house.

A licence for a chapel at Tremayne was recorded in 1387, although there are no remains of such a structure today. The same is true at Bonallack, where one was supposedly pulled down in the mid-nineteenth century. It is thought to have stood a little to the east of the present farmhouse and was recorded in 1374 when the owner, James Gerveys, obtained a licence to celebrate mass within. Clearly another such chapel existed at Carwythenack as the following year the pious Gerveys had the licence renewed for one situated there as well as that at Bonallack. Following the reformation, when many such private religious houses were destroyed, it became a dwelling separate from the main house. Writing during the early nineteenth century, the Cornish historian Charles Sandoe Gilbert also made mention of a parcel of land known as 'the hospital' where burials had taken place at Carwythenack.[54]

In Mawgan-in-Meneage medieval chapels were said to have once existed at Treverry and Roskymer, just a few hundred yards apart above the woodland-covered stream leading to Ponsontuel Creek. That at Treverry was certainly in existence in 1372 although, as ever, nothing remains today. Roskymer was described by John Leland as having been 'a fair house' that 'fell to ruine in tyme of mynde' suggesting, by extension, that the chapel had largely crumbled with it by the early 1500s. However, during the early nineteenth century it was recorded that part was still standing and that 'a small font, or basin, for the reception of Holy water' was preserved in the farm house.[55]

The beautiful chapel at Trelowarren was built circa 1636, but its medieval forerunner – another victim of the Reformation – stood a little to the north of the house.[56] Thought to have been devoted to St Mary Magdalene, it is known to have been in existence in 1421.[57] Possible other long-lost places of worship to the south of the river are indicated by old field names at Kestle, Soarne, Chenhall and Carleen.[58] Charles Henderson, writing in his *Ecclesiastical Antiquities*, believed the latter to be associated with a possible burial ground located in the garden close to the house. Another, dedicated to St Cadoc of Wales, was said by William Borlase to have existed somewhere in St Martin-in-Meneage parish, but its whereabouts are a mystery that will probably never be solved.

At a few of these religious sites are to be found holy wells. Many have been lost to time, although the whereabouts of a few were thankfully written down before their demise. It is said that the erstwhile chapel at Tregonwell possessed its own divine water source, while another at St Martin was said to have once been used for christenings. Given that such springs are often associated with the cults of Celtic saints, their existence seems to further encourage the notion that the roots of Christianity in these places reach remarkably deep into the past. At Manaccan there is a well close to the church that, although topped by post-medieval stonework, might have been as revered for its healing properties as that at St Anthony. Meanwhile, the example at Caervallack is conjectured to have once supplied the Iron Age settlement there more than 2,000 years ago.[59]

Some particularly notable holy wells were to be found in the parish of Mawnan. One was part of the small monastic settlement at Budock Vean, and another possible example formerly stood in fields below Trerose, but both are now lost. Not so that within the grounds of 'the Sanctuary', a beautiful old house to the north of the church. Although Charles Henderson was at his pragmatic best in doubting its religious provenance on account of scant documentary evidence, the Rev. Baring-Gould was more certain. Indeed, this simple little well must surely have sustained the early *lann* community that flourished just yards away.

However, the most extraordinary of all the Helford's numerous religious wells is to be found many miles from its shores, closer to the source of one of its streams than its conclusion. At Trelill, near Helston, stands a diminutive rubble stone, turf-topped, structure dedicated to St Wendrona. Greatly restored after falling into a poor state of repairs, there are doubts as to whether it has always stood at its present location, even though it is known that by 1427 the vicar of Wendron had a licence to say mass there.[60] Legend has it that the people of the hamlet once attempted to build a church nearby, but crows removed the stones overnight to leave only the porch covering the well. We should thank those sagacious birds because what they left behind is as divine as any basilica.

Trelill became Cornwall's very first Scheduled Ancient Monument and is deserving of such an accolade, humble though it is. Despite close proximity to Helston it is uncommonly peaceful, and there is much to commend stalling a little while to watch the clear stream trickle past on a summer afternoon. The waters of the Helford are blessed indeed. However, there is one place above all, even Trelill, where a sense of ancient Christianity is at its most tangible.

Close to the watercourse that falls towards its end at Gweek 2 miles to the south is a special place where time feels compressed. One is acutely aware that the distant past is perhaps not quite as distant as it might otherwise be elsewhere, an impression that is due in no small measure to its being so well insulated from the hubbub of the modern world. The woodlands below are ancient, and the field boundaries unchanged for the best part of 1,000 years. Its name is Merthyr Uny, and here was once a shrine dedicated to the saint of the same name.

Saint Uny, or Euny, is believed to have been a fifth- or sixth-century Irish missionary whom the medieval antiquary William of Worcester described as being the brother of St Ia and St Erc. The patron saint of Redruth, it was once held that Euny's final resting place was on the site of Lelant church near St Ives, so why should this little oval enclosure bear his name? Perhaps relics associated with him were kept here, or even the mortal remains of Euny himself. Merther Uny was once a hallowed place. It still is.

It was not always a Christian site – fragments of pottery typical of the late Iron Age and Romano–British period found within is adequate proof of that. But all else that can be seen, or has been uncovered, is indicative of religious activity. Just inside the northern boundary stands an impressive granite cross whose age is a matter of conjecture. Over 5ft tall and bearing four unusual deep indentations on its head, its heavily weathered appearance is suggestive of a monolith ten centuries or more in age. Some have suggested pagan origins, but they are surely wrong. In 1886 it was reset into the ground in its original position, an act that uncovered human bones and remnants of coffins.[61] Moreover, another cross, but of the more familiar Latin variety, stands on the nearby lane between Wendron and Constantine; a marker for medieval travellers approaching this once flourishing religious settlement.

That Merther Uny was also once an important place of burial is certain, but how many were actually interred within its confines is unknown. Those whose final resting place is here could number in the tens, but are far more likely to be in the hundreds. Although the acidic soil has long-since erased traces of the earliest inhumations, the venerable archaeologist Charles Thomas observed more 'recent' examples as an 'extensive series of dug graves, some in rows, oriented a good 12 to 15 degrees off E–W in a SE–NW direction'. Those in a better state of preservation confirmed that it had once been a place for the inhumation of adults and children alike. Some were in cist graves suggestive of the twelfth or thirteenth centuries.[62]

Almost nothing remains of the chapel save a few rough stones that lie concealed by undergrowth for much of the year. The building was probably completed in the late fourteenth century, when it measured 30ft in length and 20ft across internally. Its door was to the west, as indeed was the original entrance to the enclosure itself. Alas, most of the structure was dismantled by the end of the eighteenth century to be dispersed across surrounding countryside and further afield:

> At a place called Merther in this parish [Wendron], to which a deer park was formerly annexed, an ancient church, or chapel, is still well known to have stood. This was dedicated to St Uni, or St Uny, which name was frequently applied to a portion of the parish. The situation of this edifice was near the village of Marooney, and its tower remained until of late years. A man named Francis Gill, lately residing in this parish, remembers to have often gone up and down its winding stairs. He says, that when it was taken down many of its stones were used in the building or repairing of Helston tower; and that others were carried to Truro for similar purposes. It appears also that some were used in the building of Marooney grist mills. The

earth was carried out on the farm, and it is said the font was put for a pig's trough. The family who occupied the estate were persons of respectability; but, after this were reduced even to parochial relief. Merther, or Merther Uny, on which this church formerly stood, retains no traces of its former greatness.[63]

Studies revealed that earlier incarnations had once stood on the site, with evidence of roofing slate and pottery of probable twelfth-century origin. These earlier stone chapels – presumably far smaller than the final one – were themselves likely to have been preceded by a simple wooden building of which no trace remains. In all likelihood, Merther Uny was a *lann* whose foundation had occurred by the tenth century AD at the very latest.

The Merther Uny crosses are not the only examples to be found around the Helford. These unusual stone monuments are primarily found at the side of old roads where they herald the way to parish churches. Sometimes they can be found standing alone, marking paths whose routes are now lost, while others accompany holy wells or demarcate similarly religious sites. There are more than 400 complete examples throughout Cornwall, although once there would have been a great many more.

The parish of Constantine boasts eight. Within the churchyard exists the head of a cross that probably once stood elsewhere within the enclosure. They are also to be found at Nanjarrow, Bosvathick, and Trewardreva, the latter having been re-erected in 1865 after lying on the ground for many years.[64] However, Charles Henderson believed that the example at Trevease in the northernmost part of the parish was the only one still to stand in its original position. Two others are to be found at Bonallack, although both were brought to the estate having originally been placed into the ground near Wendron.

Parts of what might once have been the first stone churchyard cross were unearthed at Mawnan in 1881. The remains of the head were subsequently incorporated into the west end of the north aisle, while the base forms part of a grave.[65] Tithe maps for the parish suggest that such stone markers were also once present at Penwarne and Trerose, although there is no evidence other than old field names. There are similarities in the case of a small wheel-headed cross built into the wall of a round tower on the approach to

Trelowarren House; the adjacent field was once known as 'Cross Close'.[66] Other possible sites of long-disappeared crosses in the Meneage district are also to be found at Treworgie and Trezebal in the south of Manaccan parish.[67] Another is thought to have stood at the crossroads close to Mudgeon.[68] On the whole, however, it is a fair to conclude that the Meneage is curiously lacking in these religious monuments compared to the rest of Cornwall, despite its reputation for monastic settlement. This may be due in part to the relatively unworkable nature of the Lizard rocks in contrast to granite, with items carved from the latter earmarked for reuse as gateposts and other projects during the late medieval period onwards.[69]

However, at Mawgan is to be found one of the most enigmatic inscribed stones in the south-west of England. It is not a cross, but rather a rudimentary marker upon which a cross head *might* have been set – a socket at the top is suggestive of such an arrangement. The inscription, now greatly eroded, once read *Cnegumi fili Genaius*, which translates as 'Cnegumus, son of Genaius'. These letters, together with its shaping and position, proved to be too tempting a target for the wild speculation of some antiquaries. One suggestion was that it referred to a local chieftain of such great importance that the whole area had been named after him – the stone *Maen* and the name *Cneg* being combined to form *Meneage*. Another was that it was a form of Old Cornish that meant 'what lieth here is not the soul'; a beautiful and enduring theory that is, alas, untrue.[70] Another believed that the syntax was 'not that of an Aryan language' and was rather more than of 'agglutinative languages such as Basque'.[71]

In actual fact, the inscription *is* Latin, albeit in a brutalised form that Richard Polwhele more charitably described as 'farther departing from the Roman exactness, and consequently more distant from the Roman times'. Commenting in 1884, the learned Rev. William Jago concluded that 'the style of writing agrees with that of the sixth century manuscripts' and little evidence has been proposed since that convincingly overturns his argument, even though it could feasibly date from any point up until the tenth century.

Although we might ponder who Cnegmus and Genaius might have been – and perhaps whether the final resting place of either really is to be found below – it might be better if we leave the secrets of this remarkable 6ft tall monolith intact. Fate permitting, it will stand for another 1,000 years and hopefully still provoke the contemplation of passers-by. If only other medieval treasures had fared so well as the mysterious Mawgan stone.

As the lane down towards Helford Passage becomes steeper and narrower stands a gateway to a track across fields declining towards the river. A small enclosure once existed just inside this boundary, but it is no more. Its surrounding hedge was obliterated during the Second World War through constructing a concrete road down which American troops walked for D-Day embarkation in 1944. Under such circumstances the minor despoliation of a landscape is entirely forgivable, but that which was extirpated was not an ordinary field.

The collection of maps known as the Lanhydrock Atlas was produced in the late seventeenth century, ostensibly as a record of the estates held by the Robartes family. These little windows into the landscape of the time are exquisite in their detail, and remarkably accurate even by modern cartographic standards. One such map includes holdings between Trebah Wartha and Helford Passage, and surviving field boundaries are clearly delineated. That close to the top of the hill, however, appears very different from subsequent maps. It is not at all angular, but rather more circular. Such an appearance suggests an Iron Age round or small medieval pound for livestock, but neither explanation would be correct. The reason for its original shape is to be found in the old names for both it and the adjoining field: *Plain-an-Wartha* and *Higher Plain-an-Gwarry*.[72] The latter means 'playing place' and, as the name suggests, it indicates that here once stood a form of amphitheatre: a *plen-an-gwari*.

'Playing places' are generally held to have flourished during the medieval period, although there is no dating evidence to support such a theory from either of the only two surviving examples at St Just-in-Penwith and Perranzabuloe. The former was heavily restored during the mid-nineteenth century, and the latter probably created from the remnants of an Iron Age round. However, the Cornish mystery plays known as the *Ordinalia* were clearly written to be performed, and these fourteenth-century relics suggest that many of these open-air theatres must have been in existence at that time. Indeed, it seems that they were still being used as recently as the early seventeenth century, as the antiquary Richard Carew noted in 1602:

The guary miracle, in English, a miracle-play, is a kind of interlude, compiled in Cornish out of some scripture history, with that grossness, which accompanied the Romans 'vetus comedia'. For representing it, they raise an earthen amphitheatre, in some open field, having the diameter of his enclosed plain of some 40 or 50 foot. The country people flock from all sides, many miles off, to hear and see it: for they have therein, devils and devices, to delight as well the eye as the ear: the players con not their parts without book, but are prompted by one called the Ordinary, who followeth at their back with the book in his hand, and telleth them softly what they must pronounce aloud.[73]

It is unlikely that religious plays would have been the only entertainment on offer at a *plen-an-gwari*. Musical performances, dance, and sports such as wrestling may also have occurred within their confines, each a place within which medieval Cornish culture was celebrated with impunity. 'It is clear that the language was then on the point of disappearing,' wrote the Victorian philologist Edwin Norris, 'and it seems extremely probable, that it was owing to their attachment to it, as the only surviving mark of their race, that the Cornish adhered to these plays with such pertinacity.'[74] Norris suggested that an outsider would be unable to comprehend the plays and, it follows, those attending would be solely of Cornish stock.

The logic that dictated a 'playing place' be created above Helford Passage must have been influenced by the existence of the ferry crossing below. Not only would it have made the theatre readily accessible to the resident laity from both sides of the estuary, but also to those travelling south to the religious settlements of the Meneage. Here they would have been afforded both cultural and physical refreshment prior to their journey across the water, and perhaps it was one of these pilgrims who lost the tiny silver half groat of Henry VI, minted in Calais during the 1420s, which was recovered from the soil just yards from where the Trebah Wartha *plen-an-gwari* once stood.[75] If not, the only trace of what would have been a site full of medieval Cornish activity may be the ghostly outline preserved within a short section of curving hedgerow. It would have been around 80ft in diameter, not at all unlike those described by Carew.

There would have been many others. At Nansidwell in Mawnan is a field denoted on the 1840 tithe map as 'Plain Close'. Likewise, the name 'Plain an Gwarry Crofts' was given to an enclosure at Lower Treglidgwith, Constantine.[76] The parish of St Keverne seems to have boasted two, one at Tregoning and the other at Laddenvean, and there were others at Wendron and Helston.[77]

Even taking into consideration that these examples were unlikely to have been in existence simultaneously, the inference is that the countryside around the river was fairly populated during the medieval period, or at least relative to the west of Cornwall as a whole. There were clearly enough people able to use pick, shovel, hammer and chisel to create them, the free time to do so, and plenty to fill them when finished. That which once existed above Helford Passage would have been able to comfortably accommodate 200 or more spectators.

How many might have lived in the parishes surrounding the river at any one time during the medieval period is difficult to estimate. In 1086 the population of the whole of Cornwall was probably in the region of 30,000, but this figure would have almost certainly doubled by the mid-fourteenth century.[78] A population of 60,000 would have been higher than that of Oxfordshire or Berkshire at the time, but still significantly lower than counties of the east such as Lincolnshire and Norfolk. Others have suggested an even greater Cornish population, perhaps as high as 100,000 by 1330, even if such a figure would surely represent the most optimistic upper estimate.[79]

Given that a prerequisite for sustaining healthy communities would have been the quality of agricultural land and access to other food sources, the area around the river would have been particularly conducive to growth and thus a buffer against the intermittent famines that swept the land. The distribution of settlements of known medieval origin suggests a thriving rural landscape, with the sheltered terrain up–river used for crops and the more exposed coastal fringes for grazing.[80] As such, we might speculate that perhaps as many as 4,000 or 5,000 souls lived close to its shores in 1340, but by the end of that decade the number would have collapsed dramatically.

It is believed that the pneumonic plague pandemic known as the Black Death reached the British Isles in the summer of 1348, probably in Dorset where a French sailor died of the disease in June of that year. Over the following winter it slowly spread across the country, entering Cornwall in the early spring of 1349. At Calstock, on the western bank of the Tamar, well over half of the inhabitants died from the 'Great Pestilence'. Curiously, there then appears to have been a sudden leap westwards where, at Helston, the first victim passed away on 11 April. As with elsewhere the plague arrived by boat, this time passing up the Helford River to the port of Gweek.[81]

Well over half of Cornwall's clergy are thought to have perished in just a few months, something that implies a catastrophic collapse in the population as a whole. Most were in parishes around the coast, especially estuaries, where contact with the wider world was at its greatest.[82] Sporadic outbreaks during the following centuries would continue to hit these areas the hardest, as evidence from a report sent from Penryn in 1536 suggests.[83] Local folklore once maintained that a small square pit close to Merthen Quay contained the bodies of local plague victims, probably sailors, although the sceptical would suggest a diminutive quarry of some sort.

An outbreak of bubonic plague across England between 1556 and 1563 almost certainly accounts for the high number of burials at Mawnan in the final year of the epidemic. On 16 November that year a girl named Jane Chinhale was interred, only to be followed by Margaret Chinhale the next day. Less than a fortnight later another lady called Jenet Chinhale – possibly the mother of the aforementioned – was laid to rest. During the same November two men, Rowland and Matthew Britten, were buried a day apart, while in December Florence and Christian Tangye died within days of each other. Nor was the plague the only epidemic to blight the area, with the register of deaths indicating that entire families were devastated by smallpox during the seventeenth century. A crippling influenza outbreak also ripped through the Helford River area on several occasions during the seventeenth and eighteenth centuries, most notably in 1732–33. A marked increase in the number of burials at St Keverne, Mawnan, and nearby Budock in 1742 also indicates the spread of a particularly virulent strain of scarlet fever.

If waves of pestilence accounted for many abrupt changes in population both during and after the medieval period, the subtler variations in climate had a far more dramatic, if gradual, effect. There can be little doubt that the generally benign conditions between AD 800 and 1300 resulted in an expanding population throughout the British Isles. This 'Medieval Climatic

Optimum' was by no means a global phenomenon, but there is some evidence to suggest that annual temperatures in north-west Europe might have been up to a degree higher than those of the late-twentieth and early-twenty-first centuries. It would be no coincidence if many of the dispersed settlements of the Helford River area were discovered to have been founded during this period.

Of course, there were still adverse weather events during this otherwise agreeable climatic period. The winter of AD 1114 to 1115 was one such negative episode, quite possibly on account of a distant volcanic eruption.[84] However, it was otherwise a time of plenty in which the health of the general population was as good as it had likely ever been. Studies of skeletons from those who lived during the Middle Ages suggest that the average height of an adult male was not at all dissimilar to that of their twenty-first-century descendants, and more than 2in taller than those of the seventeenth century.[85] Anyone who survived the diseases of infancy and dangers of childbirth could expect to live well into their 50s and beyond, especially if they were members of wealthier households.

If we were able to see the Helford's landscape during the eleventh or twelfth centuries we would be struck by one manifest difference to the present: the fields 800 years ago would be full of human activity. Agricultural labour underpinned all else, and almost every man, woman and child would have been engaged in some form of farming practice. The enclosures of the Bronze and Iron Ages would have been greatly extended, with many 'new' boundaries still standing to this day. On some of the river's farms it is still possible to travel back to that time, to behold fields just as they were almost a millennium ago. Those at Norways Farm in Mawnan are largely unchanged, most between 1 and 2 acres in area, each bounded by dense vegetation within which nature thrives. The opposite side of the valley to the west once looked the same, but the hedgerows were sacrificed to profit many years ago. Those that do remain often exhibit the tell-tale curve induced by the old ploughman's customary arc to the left at the end of each furrow.[86]

The ghosts of farming past are still visible from above, not least when the heat of a particularly warm summer parches the ground to reveal what lies beneath. At Budock Vean there are remnants of medieval ditches that once bounded small fields worked by those whose bones were unearthed nearby.[87] Such field systems reveal themselves as crop marks in every corner of the Helford River valley, from Calamansack to Trevaddra, Boswidjack to Gwarth-an-Drea.

Those who toiled upon the land during the medieval period would have invariably lived in longhouses within the estates of the owner. These buildings would have been by far the commonest type to be found dotted across the Helford's landscape, most built of coarse stone and a few of cob. Each would have contained one living space for the family and another for the livestock upon which they depended for survival, the twin domains of man and beast separated by a cross passage allowing easy access for the human inhabitants. Although thatched roofs would have dominated the village skyline, a few would have been fashioned from turf in the more remote upland districts. How these twelfth- and thirteenth-century settlements around the river might have been arranged can be seen where remains still exist at Hound Tor on Dartmoor and Trewortha on Bodmin Moor. Deep in the ground below the present village centres of Mawnan, Manaccan, Constantine and Mawgan will lie such remnants, never to be seen again.

There are no domestic buildings from that time still standing anywhere around the Helford, but many houses constructed during subsequent centuries contain their recycled fragments. Bonallack Barton in Constantine and Penwarne Barton in Mawnan are undoubtedly examples of such, although the rubble-stone walls of many modest Georgian and Victorian cottages probably also contain pieces of their thirteenth- and fourteenth-century forebears.

Despite a lack of detailed archaeological assessment of domestic settlement sites of the early medieval period, we can still conclude with certainty that the land around the estuary was full of small communities and farmsteads 1,000 years ago. Most are still inhabited today and have been, without interruption, since their foundation. Indeed, the Meneage area possesses the highest concentration of *Tre-* place names in Cornwall. This prefix, meaning 'farmstead', was possibly in use as far back as the sixth or seventh centuries AD and is, as such, a generally reliable marker of a settlement's pre-Anglo–Saxon establishment and anciently enclosed land.

Many names tell a forgotten story. For example, Tremayne is derived from *Tremaen*, which means 'stone farm' or similar. Perhaps the original dwelling was a particularly striking building for its time, or it could be that a long-lost menhir stood in the vicinity. There are settlements called Trewince to be found on either side of the river, both containing elements derived from *gyns*, meaning 'wind'. Meanwhile, Trengilly, in the parish of Constantine, was once the 'farmstead in the small wood'. However, most contain words whose meanings are unknown and may, in most cases, relate to the names of those who founded them. Trebah is probably one with such origins, it having been documented as *Treveribow* in the early 1300s.[88, 89] However, it has also been suggested that its title meant 'the boar's town', which, while appealing, is inexplicable and dubious.[90]

Those settlements whose names begin with *Bos-* are also of early medieval origin. This prefix, meaning 'house', is to be found with regularity throughout the catchment of the Helford, the most obvious example of which, Bosahan, occurring in two entirely distinct locations. One, in the granite-quarrying district of Constantine, was first documented in 1302, while the second, near Manaccan, is mentioned in 1327. Both were probably of great age even then. These titles probably meant 'dwelling in the dry place', although it is tempting to believe the latter is 'the house on the haven' given its grandeur and proximity to the southern shore.

Of course, dwellings and churches were not the only structures to have been built during the medieval period. A 'lazar house' for the treatment of lepers might once have existed close to Polwheveral Creek, while another is thought to have stood on the periphery of the Helford's catchment at Argal in Budock parish. If true, both these establishments would have existed at some time between the eleventh and fourteenth centuries (but certainly not before that of tenth-century St Mary Magdelene in Winchester, the earliest known example). Their existence also suggests that the disease was as prevalent in the Helford River area as anywhere else in the British Isles.

The river's bridges are largely the products of early nineteenth-century engineering, most being rebuilt to replace late medieval structures that, in turn, had been constructed upon the foundations of more ancient crossings. It is probable that elements of earlier structures exist in some, most notably at Gear and the southernmost of those to be found at Gweek. Indeed, the vertical shale rubble upon which the latter stands is probably the remnants of a far, far older bridge.[91] There was once a medieval clapper bridge at Gweek, too, and a single-span example still exists under the cover of woodland near

Merthyr Uny. It is unsophisticated and of unknown origin, but none the poorer for it. As it is, only that at the head of Polwheveral Creek can be said to be an almost complete example of pre-seventeenth-century craftsmanship. We know this because the contract for its construction still exists:

> May 24th, 1572. Memo: that one Roger Hallard of Tregony Borough, Mason, hath bargained to make of new-hewed stone of moore stone one Bridge, now decayed in Polwheverall before the day of St James the Apostle next ensueing under the manner and form following:-

> First, the same Bridge is to be made with an arch of hewn stone, the water course between the two side walls to be 7 foot broad with two squinches on the upper side and the walls of every end of the side walls to be of length 12 foot, and to make two crests of every side of the passage and ye Bridge, to be hewn stone above the bridge rising 2 foot; and between the same 2 crests to be clear 7 foot way for wain-carriage and the Bridge and the Arch to rise in altitude 7 foot and the parish to pay him for his labour £3 6s. 8d. And to find cleavers and all lime and sand … he must enclose the way on the back of the Bridge with hewed stone to be well pinned and he to cleave and occupy in the same work such rocks and stones as now lye in the way in Polwheverall Lane annoying the passage.[92]

Roger Hallard was clearly an exceptional artisan. Notwithstanding that some minor works were undertaken in the intervening centuries, it is exactly as he left it during that summer of 1572. Neither the endless flow of the churning stream nor the pressures of traffic passing over its stones have exhausted it. They are unlikely to for hundreds of years to come, such is its stoutness.

Although most sites of medieval mining activity were obliterated by subsequent extraction and processing, there are fragmentary traces still to be found. The most notable of these is a mile to the north of Constantine at Retallack, where the remains of a 'blowing house' for the smelting of tin ore lies on the side of a wooded valley. Their existence was documented as far back as 1506, although they would surely have flourished for centuries beforehand. It is an invaluable piece of Britain's industrial heritage.[93] Alas, nothing remains of a similar enterprise believed to have once operated on the other side of the river at 'Manaccan Moor'.[94]

Aside from the church towers, some of the most obvious man-made landmarks would have been windmills. There would have been one or more in every parish, with three believed to have operated in St Anthony-in-Meneage alone. One probably stood on the higher ground behind the church, and was recorded as *Melynen-Mara* – 'the sea mill' – in 1390.[95]

Wherever those who lived during the turbulent medieval period might have laboured by day or slept by night, the constant for both rich and poor was God. But it had been ever thus, and the existence of the Meneage monastic communities ensured that it was especially pronounced throughout the lands to the south of the river. And yet the collective determination of the Cornish people to 'do things differently' far outlasted the demise of feudalism. The suspicion of anyone, or anything, that posed a threat to the religious *status quo* was irresistible. Despite early reservations – and occasional outright hostility – both Quakerism and Methodism came to prosper in the county. John Wesley, founder of the latter, made more than thirty visits to Cornwall but rarely ventured south of the Helford. A journey to Mullion in 1762 was a notable exception to the rule. Local tradition holds that he stayed in Mawnan Smith at some point during the mid-eighteenth century, the present chapel built on the site of his 'preaching meadow'. Although this particular visit is not mentioned in his otherwise comprehensive journal, it is held by oral tradition that he sustained himself by collecting berries from the surrounding hedgerows and sheltered at the grace of a humble labourer and his wife.

However, while the Helford's enclosing lands have long been a place of religious fertility, we should not neglect the water itself. Although there are no written words to substantiate the sacred importance of streams, rivers and estuaries to prehistoric people, the archaeological evidence is unarguable – the deposition of votive offerings in such contexts throughout the world proves their significance in this regard beyond any doubt. We might also contemplate the relevance of its tributaries to those who were born, lived and died beside them. Similarly, those with an interest in the sun, moon and stars would surely draw attention to their rising at the mouth and setting at the head.

No doubt the Helford's earliest inhabitants venerated, indeed feared, otherworldly beings who dwelt below the surface. Deities surely once inhabited the river's depths, and we are still drawn to it for the same primitive reasons. It is the threshold between the known and the unknown, a place of rejuvenation and contemplation. A sense of calm can be as easily instilled by the sound of winter waves upon one of its coves as the murmuration of one of its many streams during the dog days of summer. The Helford's waters – salt and fresh – have washed away much sadness, and they always will. It is a divine place in every sense.

The Helford's most conspicuous religious monuments might well be its churches and Methodist chapels, but there is one humble little place whose charm is rarely lost on those who come across it. It is also the most recent to have been built, and done so at the request of a former owner of Pengwedhen house above Penarvon Cove. Begun and completed in 1930, the tiny chapel dedicated to St Francis of Assisi is a place of uncommon serenity. The statue of the patron saint of animals within shows him cradling a hare in one hand and embracing a wolf with the other. There is a crow upon his shoulder, a frog upon his foot, and even an earthworm upon the ground. It is exceptional as only the modest can be. Otherwise, nothing but the Gothic-arched door and window suggest a connection to faith.

Only the wooden steps from the shore hint at its existence when the trees are in full leaf, and in the depths of winter very few pass by and chance upon it. No roads lead there, just a lightly trodden woodland path. It is best this way. Sturdily built of local killas stone, it will likely stand for as long as any of the river's Norman churches. Looking out from its doorway through the branches to the shimmering water below, the past is the present. The kindly man in whose memory it was built, Leo Norton Knight O'Neill, is sailing while his sister, Sybil Jerram, watches from the shore. She adored him so much as to remember him in stone. In such places it is easy to feel the presence of those who once loved the river. They are still here.

5

DARK CURRENTS

The life of the medieval tenant farmer was a gruelling one indeed. However, most who endured those difficult times could at least comfort themselves with the prospect of a premature death by disease or famine rather than violence. Unfortunately, the latter fate befell a man recorded only as John, son of Matthew, in the parish of St Keverne in 1283, a written record of the event being preserved in a Crown Plea Roll penned during the reign of Edward I.

It is said that together with several bailiffs, a certain William le Waleys journeyed to the Meneage from Restronguet ostensibly to seize cattle belonging to John. Although no detail is given as to why this should have been so, the confrontation ended in tragedy with the farmer slain by the sword of Waleys. Panicked, the wrongdoer fled to the church at St Keverne where he claimed sanctuary, only to escape with the assistance of associates early the following morning. It is recorded that local tithing men chased the villain and his friends 'as far as an arm of the sea called Monhonyer, which they crossed in a boat belonging to Richard le Pastur'.[1]

The *Monhonyer* mentioned in that ancient legal document was almost certainly the Helford River. It is a coarse name for so beautiful a place. For how long it should have been known as such we cannot be certain, although it would not have been the first title ever given to the waterway. There seems to be no clear viable translation from the Cornish language, although the word *mor* means 'sea', so perhaps there was a misspelling by a scribe, thus making *Morhonyer* possible. Indeed, this may also be the case with what was described in 1316 as the 'Water of Mawonieck', for which Charles Henderson proffered an alternative explanation in his book *Old Cornish Bridges and Streams*:

> Mawonieck may have some connexion with Manahec, now Meneage, the name of the beautiful country on the South side of the river. Meneage has clearly some connexion with Monks, for the district in Celtic days was covered with little monasteries.[2]

Alternatively, the prefix *maw-* may have had the same meaning as that of the River Mawddach in North Wales, namely 'broad', or 'wide'.[3] But whatever the truth, it was being recorded as *Hailforde* by the mid-sixteenth century and has been known by variations of that title ever since. Why it should be so named has been pondered by numerous historians and linguists over the years, and even a deputy speaker of the House of Commons once attempted to throw light upon its origins. When Sir Leonard Courtney MP addressed the Penzance Natural History Society in 1888 he was quite certain of its derivation. It was, he thought, 'not a ford in the ordinary sense, but a road-stead for ships, like Wexford, Waterford and others'.[4] While this might have found credence with some listeners, the truth is more likely to have been exactly that which Sir Leonard dismissed. As it is, the Ordnance Survey 25in series of the late nineteenth century shows a ford at the head of the creek – the same feature that endures to this day.

The very name perfectly encapsulates the rich history of the river from a linguistic standpoint. It is a melding of the Cornish word for estuary, *heyl*, and the obvious English term for a shallow water crossing. As the village within which the pedestrian ford exists grew in size and importance, so the water as a whole took its name. Alternatively, some have logically argued that it simply refers to the ferry crossing, this coming into use during the medieval period despite the Cornish language being the dominant tongue of the area at the time. There would have been a mixed ethnological population in the waterside communities following the Norman Conquest and, unlike terms such as 'passage' and 'ferry', the word 'ford' was already recorded as being in use in Cornwall by the time of the Domesday Book.[5]

However, while it is quite correct to observe that *heyl*, and other variations such as *hayle* and *hele*, are indeed words in the Cornish language, it is arguably a little simplistic to ascribe them as having their roots solely within it. Perhaps it is better to recognise and thank Cornish for being a custodian, something best evidenced by the relative profusion of variations of the word still in use today. The most obvious of these is the Hayle estuary in West Cornwall, but it is also captured in places such as Egloshayle ('church on the estuary') on the River Camel in North Cornwall, and the little River Menalhyl ('mill on the estuary') which flows out across the sandy beach at Mawgan Porth near Newquay.

Indeed, hydronymy – the naming of rivers – is of great benefit to the study of ancient language and culture. After all, the capacity to understand and communicate information about the geographic environment would have been of the utmost importance to Britain's early inhabitants. Perhaps this is why we find similarities in river names such as the Thames, Tamar, Teme and Taff, which are believed by some to be derived from the word *tamesa*, meaning either 'smooth' or 'the dark one'.[6] However, just as these variants of Thames are to be found distributed across the islands, there is reason to propose that so too are those of *Hele*.

Clear connections are to be drawn with several locations in Wales, specifically those whose names include the element *-hal*. So it is that Rhyl means 'place upon the salt marsh', and Pwllheli 'the salt water pool'. And although a link to English rivers such as the Hull of East Yorkshire or Hele (now the River Dene) in Warwickshire are tenuous, it is to be suggested that the Mersey once shared a common name with the Helford. Notwithstanding that, its present title derives from the Anglo–Saxon term for 'boundary river', it seems reasonable to conjecture that an earlier term for the estuary has been preserved in the ancient settlements of Halewood, Halebank, and Hale village. Some, however, insist that they are borrowed from the Old English word *halh*, meaning 'nook'. But while this might be the case, the presence of certain Celtic place names such as Penketh and Sankey further upstream lend credence to the theory that this most iconic northern river was once the *Heyl*, too.

Put simply, the descriptive word *hele* and its variants was probably inherited by Cornish from Common Brittonic, an ancient language assumed to have been spoken throughout most of the British Isles and which subsequently also evolved into Welsh and Cumbric. And yet Brittonic probably borrowed it from an earlier pre-Celtic source. In fact, its origins might not be Indo–European at all. Perhaps it even pre-dates the Bronze Age and, if so, Hayle – and thus the root of Helford – will be one of the oldest words still in use.

The Hailforde of the Tudor period was depicted in some detail by the antiquary John Leland. Staying as a guest of the Reskymer family of Merthen during the reign of Henry VIII, the 'father of English local history' clearly spent several days exploring the river and recorded many of his observations within his *Itinerary* – a series of notes thought to have been taken during his travels between 1538 and 1543. Although they remained unpublished until the eighteenth century, they have been of inestimable value to historians ever since. And while many of the places he described have changed beyond recognition, the Helford has fared better than most, as his description of the old medieval Gear bridge proves:

> … I cam to a Causey of stone, in the midle wherof was a Bridge having but one Arche. It flowith above this Bridge: and at the Ebbe there resortith a Broke thorough this Bridge that cummith doun from South Weste. A litle beneth these Bridges both thes Brokes in one ren into Wik [Gweek] Water.

Aside from descriptions of features encountered during his wanderings, the most fascinating aspect of Leland's account are place names. Some are familiar, such as the aforementioned Gaire (Gear), while Mogun (Mawgan), Gilling (Gillan), Poul Wheveral (Polwheveral) were also transcribed from the spoken word to the written with little care for accuracy. However, others are more perplexing, and without Leland's fairly accurate depiction of geographical distance it would be difficult to identify them. Of the creeks on the south bank – which he describes as being on the west – two possess rather mysterious names. The first of these is Pencastel ' … whither shipes do resorte' and where there is 'a trajectus [ferry] from one side of the haven to the other … This is a Mile from the Haven Mouth and here Shippes communely do ly'.

Pencastel can only be Helford Creek. There is no alternative. But why it should broadly translate as 'Castle at the Head' is intriguing. No remains of any ancient defensive structure exist at the immediate end to its course and, as such, there are only two logical reasons as to why it should be so named. The first is that it refers to a once sizeable Iron Age round covering some 3 acres slightly to the south-east near Treath. All that remains today is part of its boundary fossilised in 'modern' hedges, and the field name of 'Gears' – Cornish for 'Fort' – on a tithe map. Perhaps antiquarians, archaeologists and historians have thus overlooked one of the most important sites in the area. But if this ghost of a fortress is not the reason for the long-lost name of Helford Creek, what is?

The second, and most likely answer, is the settlement of Kestle a little over ¼ mile to the south-west of the furthest tidal point. First recorded as Kestel around 1300, it too suggests the presence of a defensive structure, but there are no obvious signs. However, by 1577 Helford Creek is recorded in *Holinshed's Chronicle* as 'Penkestell', so the influence of the medieval manor rather than the enigmatic Iron Age round must be considered the strongest.

Yet more questions are raised by the title Leland provides for another of the river's little branches: Caullons. This he describes as being ½ mile upward of Pencastel, i.e. Helford, which signifies that it can only be the old name – or at least that during the sixteenth century – for the sliver of water now known as Frenchman's Creek. Perhaps it was the surname of a local family that once inhabited the immediate area, although both it and anything similar are rare anywhere in the world and almost non-existent in the south-west of Britain. Neither does there appear to be a firm connection the Cornish language in which words starting with the letter 'c' are strangely uncommon, and anything beginning with 'Ca-' all but absent.

While the author Daphne du Maurier is responsible for making the name familiar to millions, she cannot be held liable for the transformation in title from Caullons. Even a late nineteenth-century map created more than sixty years before the publication of the famous novel in 1941 clearly shows it being delineated as 'Frenchman's Creek', with the slightly more Cornish 'Frenchman's Pill' (*Pyll* meaning creek or inlet) describing the area at the head where a small cottage still stands. Instead it may simply be that poor orthography, coupled with gradual Anglicisation, is to blame for the change.

After all, in the aforementioned Elizabethan *Holinshed's Chronicle* the creek is named as Callous rather than Caullons, so it seems perfectly reasonable to hypothesize that at some point the initial letter 'G' was mistaken for a 'C'. Its name might therefore have been Gaullons or suchlike, with the implication that it referred to a person from Gaul, or present-day France. In effect, Frenchman's Creek might have the same meaning today as it did more than 500 years ago. Alternatively, a parallel could be drawn with Cowland's Creek on the nearby River Fal, whose name could be an Anglicised 'Caullons'. The origin of the name could therefore feasibly be *kewnans*, meaning 'hollow valley' or similar.

Further supposition, speculation and guesswork is required for Port Navas creek's old title. In Leland's *Itinerary* it is called Cheilow, which once again is a slight misspelling of its correct title, 'Chielow'. This, it is suggested, translates as 'the house of the elm trees', and one might initially be tempted to ascribe the title to one of the obvious creekside settlements known to have been in existence in the early medieval period. These include Inow (first documented as Iwenau in 1269); Ponsaverran (extant in the early fourteenth century); and Calamansack (founded by the thirteenth century at the very latest). Furthermore, given that William Borlase describes it as 'Chielow, alias Calamansake Creek' in his *Natural History of Cornwall* of 1758, it would be tempting to discount the others in favour of the latter. However, the Rev. John Bannister, a notable nineteenth-century enthusiast of Cornish place names, was more certain that it meant 'house by the lake'; an ill-fitting description for Inow, Ponsaverran *or* Calamansack.

In reality, Port Navas Creek almost certainly owes its original name to a property, or properties, which once stood near to the shore at Budock Vean, close to where it enters the main channel of the estuary. It is the only place in the immediate vicinity at which freshwater can pool. However, we must once again defer to the studies of Charles Henderson and his *History of the Parish of Constantine in Cornwall*, for it is there that we find more evidence:

> In a Rental of the Manor of Penryn Foreign, dated 1538, among the free tenants in socage we read that *Sanctus Budocus* or *Eglosbuthok* or *Eglos bothyk-Vyan* had formerly consisted of three Cornish acres held by Richard Chaylou ...

Whether the creek took its name from the family or vice versa is not known, although the former is the most likely – the French *caillou* means 'stone', and it is very possible that Richard Chaylou was simply the descendant of Norman invaders.

Whatever the truth behind the names of the Helford and its subsidiary branches, we can be certain that its toponymy was of comparatively little interest to anyone during the reign of Elizabeth I. As the Age of Sail reached adolescence, the river became a paradox. It was still the haven offering safety from the wild south-westerly winds it always had been, but it had equally become a perilous place for unacquainted civilians and figures of authority alike. The stories of nefarious seafarers and illicit dealings in contraband around the Cornish coast have been romanticised and embellished, but those of the Helford are authentic. Perhaps only with the exception of the River Fowey – whose state-sponsored piracy and privateering is well documented – the Helford was the most lawless length of coastline in the south-west of England for a significant period of time.

Richard Carew was a gentleman of some standing in the West Country during the late sixteenth century. A Member of Parliament for Saltash in 1584, and High Sheriff of Cornwall between 1583 and 1586, he is still most celebrated for his *The Survey of Cornwall* published in 1602. It is a work of great value as, much like Leland's *Itinerary*, it provides us with a vivid picture of Cornwall in the Tudor period. Unfortunately, his description of the Helford was far more terse and far less flattering than those for most other locations:

> Hailford, so called of the fordable river Hail, if elsewhere placed, would carry the reputation of a good harbour; but as it now standeth Falmouth's overnear neighbourhood lesseneth his use, and darkeneth his reputation, as quitting it only to the worst sort of seafarers, I mean pirates, whose guilty breasts, with an eye in their backs, look warily how they may go out, ere they will adventure to enter; and this at unfortified Hailford cannot be controlled; in which regard, it not unproperly brooketh his more common term of Helford, and the nickname of Stealford.

Why the river should have come by such a nickname is, as Carew suggests, an indirect result of it having been an inferior harbour in terms of size to

Falmouth. Here grew a vibrant port, able to hold many ships and accommodate their crews, while the Helford became a mere point of import and export for tin and other raw materials. Notwithstanding that it provided superior shelter from the worst Atlantic storms, it had little else to offer the transitory merchant or naval vessel. There were no sizeable settlements on its banks, and the local population largely sustained itself on the proceeds of fishing and agriculture. In contrast, the early seventeenth-century Carrick Roads and River Fal possessed an ever-expanding Falmouth at its mouth, the county town of Truro – which had received a new charter under the reign of Elizabeth I – at its head, and the ancient Borough of Penryn on its western bank. The Fal was mercantile, the Helford a subsistence economy in comparison. With fewer eyes to watch comings and goings, those of a less salubrious nature were effectively free to take advantage of its relative isolation.

Even before the founding of Falmouth, the Helford's decline towards association with maritime ne'er-do-wells had begun. In the British Library exists a remarkable map drawn by an unknown cartographer at some point during the latter half of the 1500s. Although the town is conspicuous by its absence, Arwenack Manor and Pendennis Castle are both depicted. In contrast, ancient villages such as Budock, Mawnan, Manaccan, Mylor and St Anthony-in-Meneage are all included, as indeed are Penryn and Truro. But it is the superfluous elements that make this particular map both a work of art and remarkably informative.

Oddly orientated such that the south is at the top and the north to the bottom, the open sea is a hive of activity. There are whimsical sea monsters, and ships of various sizes and rigs – details modern Ordnance Survey editions sadly lack. The 'Careck Roode' and its offshoots are also full of animation. Even rowing boats are to be seen under oar off St Mawes, Mylor, Tolverne and St Clement. Not so in the Helford, where only two sailing vessels are depicted in contrast to more than twenty in the Fal. Moreover, the relative size of the two estuaries is awry; the Helford is perhaps less than a quarter of its true scale against the Carrick Roads. It is almost an afterthought to the map. It looks darker and more secretive, somewhere best not spoken about.

Clearly the Helford had a reputation for lawlessness as far back as the late medieval period. Gweek had served as Helston's port from the early fourteenth century after Loe Pool had become inaccessible, and documentation from the middle of that particular century suggests that the authorities were keen to assert control by brutal means. Of particular interest is one section of the Exemplification for King Edward III of May 1356 (based upon proceedings at the Royal Eyre Court in Launceston in 1302) in which the fate of those committing criminal acts was made clear:

> As to the liberties, they say that the Burgesses of Helston claim to hold in the same borough pleas of Forbidden Distraint and to take fines for breaches of the assize of bread and ale, Infanganthef and Outfanganthef [felons seized within and outside the borough], and to hang their thieves, when adjudged, on the gallows at Gweek outside their Borough; they claim also sullage of ships anchored in the water of Gweek aforesaid, and to hear and determine all quarrels and attachments which arise on the aforesaid water between the merchants and the sailors and their servants whoever they may be.[7]

Where the scaffold and noose were erected we can only surmise, although it was probably at the head of the creek close to the junction between the main road and Chapel Hill. Places of execution were most often situated away from the centre of the settlement, but still in a prominent position whereby they would act as a warning. Moreover, the medieval mind, awash with superstition and religious fervour, believed that a crossroads would confuse the spirits of the executed. Many disorientated wraiths must have wandered Gweek during those years when thieves and murderers met their end there, but no records exist to say how often the gallows bore the weight of men.

The medieval period was a brutal time, and the early post-medieval era little better. Within Star Chamber records from the reign of Henry VIII there is a mention of how a number of named men, together with 'other evyll disposed persons with swerds, bucklers, byllys, bowys and arroys, shepells, pyke-axes and other abyliments of war', drove out a tenant from land at Inow, Port Navas, in 1530.[8] Such events would not have been unusual. Those living during the thirteenth and fourteenth centuries were more than ten times more likely to be murdered or the victim of violent crime than those born during the Georgian period. Savagery was endemic, and there is absolutely no reason to suppose that those living in Cornwall were especially more peaceable than elsewhere in Britain.

Perhaps the small communities around the Helford were, relatively speaking, quieter than the towns in terms of civil disobedience and criminal behaviour. But whatever the truth, the sea and those who came across it were the most malevolent factors in the day-to-day lives of those who lived before the modern era. The trials and tribulations of the land were nothing compared to those of the water.

Those travelling along the road towards the parish church of Mawnan will no doubt observe that for some 350yds of it course it is peculiarly straight – a rare phenomenon given the famously circuitous lanes of Cornwall. Situated upon a ridge that is amongst the highest points in the immediate vicinity of the river, drainage ditches to either side cease to exist where the route curves at either end.

Were you able to look along its course in the late medieval period then the reason for its linear nature would become clear. Where today stands a farmhouse and barns would have been a building as imposing as any other private residence in Cornwall at the time. The approach was once its drive, intended to leave visitors in no doubt as to the power and influence of its inhabitants. Its name then and now, Trerose Manor, roughly translates as 'estate of the promontory'. Its domain was once all the land between Maenporth and the eastern bank of Port Navas creek, and it was bounded to the north by the Manor of Penwarne where the dead of the yet-to-exist Mawnan parish were buried prior to the founding of the old church upon the cliffs.

By the early seventeenth century little of the original medieval building remained. Its stone had been plundered for other buildings, and much of the extant manor – a pretty and endearing country house of modest size – contains elements of the old within its fabric. Although the foundations of the medieval house lie mostly beneath the farmyard, its ancient well still exists in the entrance hall of the 'new'. It is a substantial yet beautiful structure whose clear water rises and falls according to the seasons and weather. Powerful figures from Cornwall's past drank from it and were probably no worse for the experience.

Quite when Trerose Manor was first constructed, or the settlement established, is uncertain. A coin of King John, minted in Shrewsbury between 1200 and 1204, found just a few yards outside of its perimeter walls suggests a date identical to the first documentary record of 1201 at the very latest.[9, 10] The first known owner was Sir Roger de Carminowe who, legend has it, took part in the Crusades to the Holy Land. In 1313 the manor passed through marriage to another illustrious Cornish family, the Whalesboroughs, and by 1468 it had fallen into the hands of yet another family as a result of the marriage of Elizabeth de Whalesborough to John Trevelyan of Nettlecombe.[11] One of their sons, George Trevelyan (or Trevilian), was rector of Mawnan church from 1510 before becoming chaplain to King Henry VIII.

The once famous names of Carminowe, Whalesborough and Trevelyan have long slipped from the public consciousness, but not so that of the family who came to own Trerose Manor in 1578: the Killigrews. Although not a particularly frequent visitor to the area, its owner, Sir William, was the son of the notorious John Killigrew of Arwenack Manor in Falmouth. Both John and his wife, Mary Wolverston of Suffolk, were both widely held to be involved in iniquitous maritime deeds, something made all the more remarkable given that John Killigrew was simultaneously serving on the Commission for Piracy in Cornwall. Mary even stood trial for seizing a Spanish ship that had taken shelter in Falmouth and murdering its crew while the captain and first mate were being entertained by her husband. Two of her servants were found guilty and executed, but she received a pardon at the eleventh hour from Queen Elizabeth; families such as the Killigrews, corrupt as they might have been, were best kept on side given England's susceptibility to seaborne invasion.

With guardians such as these the coast was quite literally clear. Even if the authorities *were* present, bribery could be employed to have them look the other way. In 1595 John Killigrew 'the Third' was brought in front of the Privy Council to answer a charge of assisting a pirate known as Captain Elliot who was hiding in the Helford. It was alleged that he not only warned of the approach of the twenty-four-gun HMS *Crane*, but bribed its senior officer, who he recommended 'enjoy a little excursion inland' at his expense. Elliot escaped with his prize of a captured Dieppe ship; John Killigrew escaped without as much as a reprimand, quite probably because his uncle was a respected diplomat who had the Queen's ear at court. However, the Killigrews were not the only high-ranking officials who had come under suspicion. In 1587 the Vice-Admiral for Cornwall, Sir Edward Seymour, was ordered to appear before the Privy Council if he refused to offer up the sub-ordinate who had been purchasing stolen goods from pirates operating out of its creeks.

It should be stressed that the river was a very different place to Fowey further along the coast. Here had been based the 'Fowey Gallants', a group of privateers indulging in state-sponsored piracy during the Hundred Years' War of the fourteenth and fifteenth centuries. By contrast, the Helford was largely a bolt-hole for rougher nautical brigands, probably tolerated by local fishermen who turned a blind eye to their comings and goings. In 1578, for example, Plymouth pirates called Grainger and Morris were supposedly landing goods in the estuary, but little else is understood about them.[12] It is also recorded that a notorious Scottish raider known as Captain Herriot was apprehended by a Dutch ship in the Helford river in 1624.[13] Meanwhile, State Papers of May 1631 suggest there was another unnamed pirate, prob-ably a 'Dunkirker' from north-east France, who had 'the whole coast in fear' and had gone to ground in the upper reaches of the river.

Of all the piratical events associated with the river to have been docu-mented – and most would not have been – one particular example of May 1636, observed and recorded by the Lieutenant of Pendennis Castle, John Tresahar, is by far the most colourful:

On the 11th inst. there arrived in Falmouth harbour two frigates of Dunkirk, with four French ships taken at sea by them as prizes. On the 14th they set sail, and were encountered by the *Black Bull of Amsterdam*, John van Galen captain, which chased one of the frigates to the entrance of that harbour under Pendennis Fort, continuing shooting at the frigate until there was a shot made from that castle at the Hollander, which then tacked about and chased the other frigate into Helford, and followed her above a mile into the river until they both touched ground. The frigate was then near a musket shot of the Hollander who continued shooting at her with his ordnance, and landed thirty musketeers on the south side of the river, who shot with their muskets into the frigate from the land, and killed one of their men. The Dunkirker yielded his ship, which is now in the harbour of Helford in the custody of the Hollander. The captain of the Hollander has been required to deliver the Dunkirker into the hands of his Majesty's officers but refuses to do it. At the time of this conflict there was in Helford Mr Timothy Harte who carries the merchants tin from those parts, who at his arrival in London can make a full relation of the conflict.[14]

It is difficult to say with any certainty where this particular fracas took place, although the description suggests somewhere just to the east of Treath. But lawless acts were not the sole preserve of visiting maritime brigands. The river seemingly had a few of its own, as is proved by the case of a Helford man known as Diggory Priske. Said to have been 'a desperate person and one who formerly had had some command of the seas', Priske stood trial with others in 1624 for plotting to seize a ship laden with tin valued at £60,000 and sail it to foreign shores. The ship in question, the *Larke*, was to be taken by men purporting to search it for runaway sailors from the navy, but some of the conspirators failed to hold their nerve and informed the authorities.[15] It would have been a spectacular heist indeed.

Of course, even more famous names in the lexicon of piracy would have known of the Helford and perhaps even partaken of its hospitality. After all, Captain Henry Avery, who 'was master of a stout squadron of ships, manned with able and desperate fellows of all nations', is supposed to have buried plundered treasure somewhere on the Lizard to the south.[16] According to a mysterious document held by the Cornwall Records Office – and probably written more than a century after Avery's death as a pauper around 1700 – three boxes of precious stones, gold and bullion were hidden 'on his return from India'.[17] There Avery had attacked two ships, the *Fateh Muhammad* and the *Ganj-i-Sawai* belonging to the Mughal emperor Aurangzeb, as they returned from pilgrimage to Mecca. His wicked treatment of those on board made him the most wanted man in the world, but the spoils made him the richest pirate by far.

For the most part, however, armed vessels making use of the river during the seventeenth, eighteenth, and early nineteenth centuries were invariably those belonging to privateers. Carrying government 'Letters of Marque' enabling them to plunder enemy vessels with impunity, they were regular visitors to a safe haven that served well the approaches to the English Channel. In 1665 the privateer *Success*, captained by Edward Manning, brought in a captured ship that had been taken during a journey between Nantes and Hamburg. The vessel, *Golden Crown*, was laden with brandy, wine and tobacco.[18] Captain Manning appears to have been remarkably successful in that particular year as he is also recorded as having claimed another prize, the *Mary of Bordeaux*, also carrying brandy. Another privateer was Captain Wilkes who, in November 1780, brought in an American brig called the *St Luke*, which had been en route from L'Orient in Brittany to Philadelphia – it was found to be full of linen and other fine articles, some of which were bound for the French ambassador.[19] Others merely used it as a place of rest before and after engagements with foreign vessels, such as the *Young Raven* of Dover and the *Jolly Tar* of Guernsey, the latter having returned from a cruise off the Canary Islands in June 1803.[20,21] When the London brig *Active* arrived at Helford in May 1808 after action off Cape Finisterre, she did so having beaten off a French warship in a battle that lasted for nine hours.[22]

Friendly gunships were not the only ones frequenting the Helford. On one occasion in October 1756 during the Seven Years' War it was reported that a French privateer had been particularly bold by coming so close to the coast:

> Yesterday afternoon a sloop from Plymouth with stores was taken a few miles from this harbour by a French sloop privateer, who after taking out the people and the sailors, cutting her rigging, etc. let her drive. She was soon after taken up by some fishermen, and put into Helford, a small harbour in our bay, without any defence, and a few miles from this place. The privateer appeared off this harbour again, and has continued all this day in sight of numbers of our people, and chased a small privateer (which had put into Helford and was now sailing from thence) ashore at Coverack, another small defenceless harbour in our bay. There is another vessel, a ketch, which keeps at some distance from the sloop, and by their motions they appear to be consorts.[23]

Ten years earlier the brigantine *Mary* had made a narrow escape from two French privateers, only just reaching the security of the Helford in time.[24] It was a similar story in 1794 during the French Revolution when the *Violet* of Sunderland put into the Helford after an encounter with a French lugger sporting ten or twelve guns. Her captain reported that he and another brig had encountered the hostile vessel, which they 'engaged for three hours, during which time both ships received considerable damage in their materials, and some shots in their hulls'. Fortunately a British naval ship came to their aid and gave chase to the belligerent.[25] Earlier, in 1740, seventeen men from five different ships had come ashore in the river after being set adrift by a Spanish privateer off the Lizard.[26]

Those who made it home after such encounters were the fortunate ones. Men who plied their trade from small boats around the south coast of England in the mid-seventeenth century were in a perpetual state of fear, with those causing the alarm the 'Barbary' pirates – corsairs operating from North African ports such as Algiers, Tripoli and Rabat, and who plundered European maritime communities while encountering little resistance in the process. Their target was not specifically the ships or the valuable cargo they conveyed, but the very people who sailed them. Some were ransomed and returned home, usually only those from wealthy families whose finances could cope with such exaction. By contrast, men and women from humbler backgrounds were destined for servitude in the Ottoman Empire. Although by no means as badly affected as European countries along the Mediterranean coast, the number of captured Britons would have been in the tens of thousands. It is known that some of them came from villages around the Helford River.

State Papers of 1636 contain the harrowing testimony of a barge captain from Plymouth who had arrived at St Keverne in June of that year. Upon his arrival he had been met with 'sorrowful complaint, and lamentable tears of women and children' as the very day before many men of the parish, fishing from boats 'less than three leagues from the shore', had been taken by Turkish pirates. Three fishing boats from the Helford and another from Mullion had also disappeared, leaving perhaps fifty men unaccounted for. What happened to them we do not know, but reports of the hardships endured by those from elsewhere who ended up in Tunisia, Morocco, Algeria and Libya suggest a dreadful fate. The account by a local man, Thomas Pellew of Penryn, who was captured in 1716 in the Bay of Biscay is harrowing, and he was 'fortunate' enough to become an elite slave of the Sultan Mulai Ismail. Those from local communities probably fared much worse 'undergoing most unsufferable labours, as rowing in galleys, drawing in carp, grinding in mills; with divers such unchristian like works, most lamentable to express and most burdensome to undergo, withal suffering much hunger and many blows on their bare bodies'.[27]

In the months following the raids of June 1636, Barbary pirates were frequently seen around the Cornish coast and left fishermen 'fearful not only to go to the seas, but likewise lest these Turks should come on shore and take them out of their houses'.[28] Fowey, further up the coast, was particularly affected in 1645 when a raiding party landed and carried away more than 200 men, women and children. Although the number of 'Sallee Rovers' patrolling the channel decreased as British naval power grew stronger once again, the threat was not fully extinguished until a combined English and Dutch fleet laid waste to the maritime defences of Algiers with a devastating bombardment in August 1816. Around 3,000 slaves were emancipated.

The depravity of slavery aside, much of Cornwall's disreputable maritime history has been misleadingly romanticised. For example, that ships were specifically lured on to the rocks in pursuit of plunder is a mendacious myth, and one that unfairly portrays coastal communities as being full of rapacious thugs who would deliberately endanger the lives of mariners. They would not, and did not. That said, there is little doubt that the misfortune of some was often a boon to others, as records from all around the British coast testify. Aside from the gathering of washed-up cargo of wrecked ships that inevitably took place after many tragic events, there is scant evidence for the looting of stricken vessels in this particular corner of Cornwall. However, as far back as the thirteenth century it was recorded that a ship called *All Saints* was driven ashore in the river during a storm. Its captain reported that the vessel was subsequently ransacked by locals who took all thirty-six tuns of wine on board.[29] Alas, we do not know whether it was the parishioners of Mawnan, St Keverne, St Anthony or Manaccan who made merry on the proceeds.

More prevalent by far was the practice of using the Helford to circumvent paying duty on a whole manner of goods. Indeed, the value of the contraband landed in its coves and creeks during the eighteenth and nineteenth centuries must have been colossal. What is more, it is likely that almost everyone in the little communities around its shores were involved in the enterprise, whether they realised it or not. This was not a choice, but a necessity. The people of the Isles of Scilly, for example, were almost brought to the brink of starvation when customs and excise measures were tightened in the archipelago. The lower cost of certain goods meant survival, not luxury, for those around the Cornish coast.

It is also important to stress that unlike many smuggling enterprises elsewhere in England, those operating around Falmouth and the Helford were probably small in scale. There were certainly no brutal cartels equivalent to the Hawkhurst Gang of the South-East – an organised crime mob not averse to punishment beatings, torture, and even murder. But this does not mean that violence was entirely absent in this part of Cornwall. Writing to his superior in 1597, one Randall Ingerson, a deputy customs officer based in Penryn, demanded that unless some 'reformation' was made he would not continue in his post even if he 'might gett a hundredth poundes a yere, for men be lawless'. His plea was unsurprising given the threats that had been made against him:

> Thomas Sprye, dwelling at Saint Jermyns, did bringe on land six skore pounds of tobacco, almost two miles from Penryn, yet it was my chaunce to meet him, and offrenge to make stay of that, he with his Company did forceablye draw theire rapiers, and did sweare that if I did not departe presentlie, they would kill me, and he did thrust his naked rapier to my brest, above a dozen tymes … From there he did carry it to his father in lawes house, his name is Mr Thomas Ilforde, dwelling in the parish of Mawnan, being betwixt Penryn and Helforde and he is a man of good accompte.[30]

On the whole, however, violence was generally avoided. It was far better to keep a healthy distance from authority, and doing so often proved rather easy. A noted smuggler of the late seventeenth century, Richard Upton, boasted that he could anchor in the Helford for days without ever seeing a customs officer. His task of loading with tin destined for the Netherlands was thus a straightforward process.[31] Even the establishment of a customs house at Gweek did little to stifle smuggling enterprises, despite making life a great deal easier for both the merchants of Helston and inbound shipping. In February 1689 it was agreed by the Commissioners of Customs 'that there should be a limited collection established at Gweek, in the harbour of Helford, for the entry and exportation of their native comodityes of tynn and fish'.[32] Prior to this decision it had been necessary for masters of vessels to pay dues at Falmouth before proceeding onwards to Helford – places 'so obliquely situated that no one wind will serve for sailing from one port to the other'. Similarly, Helston traders no longer needed to travel to the customs house at Falmouth before shipping out of Gweek.

The officers stationed on the Helford were met with some success, although the contraband seized by them during the eighteenth and nineteenth centuries must have represented a tiny fraction of that which passed into the area undetected. In March 1754, for example, officials from Gweek seized 'a quantity of wrought wool, designed, as supposed, for France; a traffick that must be highly prejudicial to these Kingdoms', but little else appears to have been confiscated around that time.[33] By the end of the century, however, they were stretched to the limit as the smuggling gangs became more fearless in their approach, as an extract of a letter sent from Falmouth in December 1785 confirms:

On Saturday the 18th instant, a large smuggling lugger, mounting upwards of twenty guns, commanded by a noted outlaw, appeared off Helford. Two revenue vessels were then at anchor in the harbour. The smugglers assembled on shore, and the captain began to land his cargo, which was very valuable. On seeing this, the revenue vessels (not daring to face this desperate outlaw) manned their boats, well armed, and made towards the people employed in landing the goods, in hopes of seizing the boats coming on shore. This manoeuvre being seen from the lugger, her boats were instantly filled with desperadoes, who attacked the boats belonging to the revenue vessels, drove them off, mortally wounded some of the men, forcing others to jump into the sea, and swim to shore, etc. The smuggler's loaded boats were then ordered back with the goods, which were taken on board, and the lugger stood out to sea again, the captain fearing an alarm might be given. He is hourly expected again on the coast. As nothing but a frigate dare come near him, he visits where he pleases with impunity.[34]

We do not know the identity of the captain, although it is tempting to believe it was the infamous Harry Carter of Prussia Cove. After all, he courted a Helford girl, Elizabeth Flindel, and married her on 19 April 1786.[35] Perhaps Carter was also behind the brazen act of stealing the customs boat from its moorings in the river in 1791, for which a reward of ten pounds was offered to anyone 'discovering and apprehending any one or more' of those guilty of the crime.[36] Whoever was responsible, their efforts must surely have raised a few smiles amongst those gathered in the little waterside hostelries once news of the act became public.

The early years of the nineteenth century seem to have been more successful for the King's men. Notwithstanding that there was an attempted break-in to the warehouse on 1 December 1804, the frequency and size of the sales of confiscated goods by customs officers attests to their impact.[37] For example, on 9 September 1805, 350 gallons of brandy, 28 gallons of rum, and 20 gallons of Geneva were sold to the public at Gweek.[38] In August 1809 another 32 gallons of brandy went up for auction, and an inventory of September 1814 included twelve pairs of silk gloves, eight grey pantaloons, eight dozen gilt watch chains, fifteen telescopes, and a pound of snuff.[39, 40] Sometimes it was not even necessary to threaten force to acquire contraband; one officer is reported to have accidentally stumbled across a cache of 63 ankers of brandy in undergrowth while shooting game in January 1807.[41]

The proceeds of smuggling were clearly in general circulation during the eighteenth and nineteenth centuries, whether they had been acquired by honest sale at the customs house or through unlawful transaction. The vicar of Manaccan, Richard Polwhele, observed that some of the victuals inherited from his predecessor bore the hallmarks of seaborne provenance:

> On coming to the vicarage, I found the cellar (almost as large as the breakfast parlour) stored with wines and spirituous liquors – some very bad and some of the best quality – all which were appraised at no more than £20. The Coniac-brandy, Claret, and Frontiniac, were excellent. But the binns were full of wine and salt-water, picked up at wrecks by my predecessor. The salt, indeed, so much predominated in some bottles, that it was almost *merum sal*.[42]

By 1822 the customs house had been moved from Gweek to Treath, near Helford, seemingly as a direct result of requests by the masters of ships who regularly plied their trade in and out of the river. In any case, the decade following the relocation seems to have been a particularly active one for attempted smuggling. In 1825 a man was arrested for lighting a warning fire in one of the coves – a tactic regularly employed by shore parties to warn incoming boats of the presence of the authorities.[43] The following year a preventive boat apprehended three men crossing the main channel who threw their cargo of Geneva overboard in the hope of avoiding arrest. Unable to pay the prohibitive fine of £100, the three farm labourers were sent to Bodmin Gaol.[44] Already impoverished families slid further into penury.

Officials were met with further resistance in November 1828 when a large party of men 'armed with pistols, bludgeons, and knives' were intercepted by customs officers in the village of Constantine. A reward of £300 was offered to bring those to justice for 'feloniously assaulting and ill-treating the said Officers so that the life of one of them is despaired of'.[45] However, perhaps the most infamous act in local legend occurred in September 1840 following the confiscation of brandy from a ship called the *Teignmouth* at Coverack, as the *West of England Conservative* reported:

> On the 18th instant, H. M. Customs-house at Helford within the Port of Gweek, was attacked by a body of men, consisting, it is supposed, of upwards of thirty persons, who broke open the heavy doors and strong locks, and robbed the cellars of 126 kegs of contraband brandy, each keg containing four gallons and a half of spirits. The smugglers commenced their work about 1 o'clock, and in the course of half an hour succeeded in removing all the kegs except three, which they left for the benefit of the officers at Helford. From the tracks of wheels, it is supposed there were at least three wagons employed in removing the spirits.

The event had been witnessed by a man and his wife who lived above the cellar but, fearing for their safety, wisely decided against raising the alarm. In any case, to have done so would have involved a journey of more than ½ mile on foot to Helford village itself. The incident resulted in the customs house being relocated once again, this time to the head of the creek and closer to the centre of the community.[46] This little building by the ford is today a pretty cottage, but within its walls were once stored great quantities of contraband. In March 1843 the Controller of the Port of Gweek seized a ship containing more than 100 kegs of brandy and placed the cargo under lock and key here. The smuggling gang, comprised of three Frenchmen and one Englishman, were also apprehended.[47]

It is hard not to feel some sympathy for those who were unsuccessful in their disreputable exploits, but neither should we condemn those tasked with preventing them. They were onerous times for all except those of inherited wealth or good fortune. Indeed, the only leveller was the very water itself.

On 14 May 1845 an experienced mariner called George Barnes set off from Durgan bound for Falmouth with three of his sons. As was the case with all men of the waterside hamlet, the former chief boatman of Her Majesty's Coastguard Service knew well the perils of the sea, and few would have doubted his ability to sail through anything except the most fearsome storm. On their round trip the party called in to Swanpool where Barnes and his youngest son took tea with a coastguard colleague while the others walked into the town. Later, the two eldest boys returned with a girl of 13 called Ellen Retallick, also of Durgan, who seemingly preferred the pleasures of a sea voyage home to a long walk with her mother. Grace Retallick clearly had no qualms about entrusting the safety of her young daughter to such an experienced sailor. After all, her own husband had been a fisherman, and the families had known each other for years. The weather was fair, the boat more than 20ft long.

When Mrs Retallick arrived home in the hamlet, neither her daughter nor the Barnes' were to be seen. The alarm raised, her son and another local man, John James, took to the sea in search of the missing travellers. They eventually found the boat 'in which was old Barnes, alone, a corpse … His watch stopped at six o'clock'.[48] The official inquest concluded that it had been a most unfortunate accident: 'something dropped overboard – they then lowered the mast and pulled back for it, and in picking it up, they all rushed on one side and she filled', they suggested.[49] Rumour had it that an infirm George Barnes must have tried desperately to save Ellen as her collar was found still in his hand. All were washed ashore in the days following the accident. At the funeral it was said that 'scarcely an eye was to be seen in which tears did not start', and all five were buried in a single grave in the parish church of Mawnan.

It was a similar story thirteen years later when yet another respected member of the coastguard service, Samuel Lark, drowned along with two of his children. They had merely headed across the river from the now disappeared station at Porthallack only to overturn in a squall. Samuel and his daughters, Ellen and Mary, were buried at Constantine. Such tragedies testify to the fact that the sea can confound even vastly experienced sailors on the most benign of summer days.

A further headstone at Mawnan churchyard records how 35-year-old Richard Rashleigh, also of Durgan, drowned with his son 'Little Willie' off Rosemullion Head in 1882. Six years later the bell tolled for another resident of the hamlet lost to the water, this time James Downing. Other victims of the sea's fickleness no doubt lie in unmarked plots. However, in another quiet corner of the churchyard are three headstones beneath the shade of a tree whose growth has distorted the ground below and entirely toppled one memorial. Although it lies in three pieces its inscription is still entirely legible. The second remains upright, but the poorer quality of carving and the years of subsequent weathering make it difficult to read the epitaph today. The third, a cross, has also been dislodged by the expanding roots, but it bears the most detailed description:

> In Loving Memory of
> Charles Wassell
> Who was drowned in the wreck of the S.S. Mohegan
> On the Manacles rocks
> Oct 14th 1898
> His body was found in the Helford River Oct 16th
> And interred in this churchyard on Oct 23rd

Wassell was one of ninety-seven crew members aboard the 6,900-ton SS *Mohegan* when she left Gravesend for New York on 13 October 1898. It was the Atlantic Transport Line ship's second voyage. By the time she reached the coast of Cornwall the following day she was at her full speed of

13 knots, passing close to Falmouth and the mouth of the Helford without slowing. Too late to save her, the crew realised the terrible danger the ship was in and shut off the engines. At approximately 7pm *Mohegan* slammed into the Vase rock, her rudder torn away, before drifting on to the Maen Varses reef. Despite heroic attempts by the Porthoustock lifeboatmen, fewer than a third of those aboard the ship survived. It was dark, strong winds were blowing, and her hull so terribly scarred by the collision that her sinking commenced almost at once.

Why *Mohegan* should have been so close to the coast and not 10 miles or more further to the south was never fully ascertained, but a navigational error was undoubtedly the cause of the disaster. With no officers left alive it was impossible for investigators to acquire the verbal testimony required. The official Board of Trade inquiry the following month also concluded that the 'deplorable loss of so many lives, amounting to 106, 51 only being saved, was in consequence of the vessel taking a very sudden and serious list to port, her going down in not more than a quarter of an hour from the time of striking, and of there being no light to indicate her position through the electric light having gone out'.

Many of those who perished were interred in the parish church of St Keverne, the majority in a mass grave close to the church walls. So tightly packed with coffins was the huge pit that a careful plan of their positions was made should relatives subsequently wish for an exhumation. The bodies of some American passengers were embalmed at St Keverne before continuing their journey across the Atlantic, but twenty-eight other souls were never accounted for.[50]

Charles Wassell, on the other hand, has his final resting place at Mawnan where he is in the company of three other crew members: Henry Pinfold, a carpenter; Leslie Aston Blake, an able seaman quartermaster; and E. Fieldhouse, an assistant steward. All four were young men in their 20s. The funeral of Blake was attended by his grieving sweetheart, a Miss Powell of Woodbridge in Suffolk, as well as his brother and a great many villagers.[51]

There were reports of other victims being found in the river, including a married woman 'with dark hair and eyes, dressed in black silk dress and wearing a rose diamond ring with the initials "E.W" on it' whose corpse was discovered close to Helford Passage the day after the wreck. The following day another two were pulled from the water at Durgan.[52] The bodies of two young women came ashore at Maenporth, presumably those of Helena Mary Cowan of London and Ellen Elliot of Hertfordshire. Both were subsequently buried at Budock Church, as was the former's brother, Herbert Francis Cowan.

But there were even younger victims. As one survivor told *The Times* newspaper 'a little girl begged me most piteously to save her, as she "did not want to die yet," but I was powerless'. So dreadful and shocking was the disaster that the poet William McGonagall was moved to write a verse on the event. And yet it was not the first time a great loss of life had occurred on the Manacles.

It is perverse that such a safe haven as the Helford should have such wicked sentinels to its approaches from the south. Some are never to be seen above water at any state of the tide, often just a few feet below the surface with their sheer sides falling down to the seabed hundreds of feet below. Others are more obvious, such as the Carn-Du rocks to the south-west of the main cluster and the Varses to the north-east. To the north are the outliers of Maen Garrick and the Gwinges. They are all made from hard, unforgiving igneous Gabbro rock. A bell buoy marks their outer limit a mile from the safety of the shore, its toll is equally a warning to the living and a lament to the dead. Their collective name of 'The Manacles' is portentous, although it is actually derived from *Maen Eglos*, meaning 'Church Stones'; apt enough given both the visibility of St Keverne's spire and the countless lost souls in the depths below.

One poetic correspondent to the *Royal Cornwall Gazette* in 1838 described them as:

Neptunian Altars ... polluted with many a hecatomb of human victims. Many a homeward-bound bark with her goodly company, exulting in the prospect of a few hours sail, has here struck, and with one fell crash delivered up fathers, husbands, and brothers to the offended element over which they had so fondly and so proudly stalked.[53]

Others have reckoned that there must be at least a hundred shipwrecks on the rocks, but such a number is a gross underestimate. There were few areas of water around the British coast with a more formidable reputation, and the names of countless vessels lost in the distant past will never be known. Only those from more recent centuries are remembered, and the greater the horror endured by those on board the greater the recognition. Despite its infamy, the wrecking of the SS *Mohegan* was by no means the worst to have taken place on those ungodly Church Stones.

During the early hours of 22 January 1809 in fierce, bitter winds, two ships were lost within just a few miles of one another. The first was *Dispatch*, a transport ship out of Corunna, Spain, heading for the safety of Falmouth with more than 100 exhausted men of the 7th Dragoons on board. The ship floundered on Black Head near Coverack with all but seven drowned or dashed upon the rocks. Hours later the 380-ton Brig Sloop of War HMS *Primrose*, heading in the opposite direction towards Iberia, struck the Minstrel Rock on the Manacles reef. One hundred and twenty six men perished. There was only one survivor, a boy called John Meaghen, who had lashed himself to the stump of one of the masts above water and was rescued by fishermen from Porthoustock.[54] Most of the dead from both *Dispatch* and HMS *Primrose* – or at least those given up by the sea – are buried at St Keverne. An 18-pounder carronade recovered from the latter symbolically guards the churchyard and the drowned. Tragically, the exact site of the mass burial for those from *Dispatch* was lost until excavations for another grave almost half a century later uncovered the remains of the soldiers, their distinctive coats and buttons still intact.[55] Thankfully, they are commemorated now.

However, of all the ships known to have met their end on the Manacles, the name of the *John* is surely the most infamous. Built in Chester in 1810, the barque of 464 tons was of fair age by 1855 and had been employed in transporting emigrants between Plymouth and North America for many years. But it was neither her structural maturity nor the weather that would be the cause of her demise on 3 May that year. Instead, the fate of those on board was determined by the actions of the very people charged with their safe passage, and it remains one of the most contentious maritime disasters in British history. Not only was there a serious navigational error that led to her striking one of the eastern rocks of the reef, but the captain, Edward Rawle, refused to deploy the lifeboats until it was far too late. He survived when others did not, and although a charge of manslaughter against him failed, he was still found guilty of gross negligence. Many survived by clinging to the rigging and awaiting rescue, but almost 200 souls were lost. More than sixty were children. Instead of beginning a new life in Canada most were buried, like others from broken ships before, in the ground of St Keverne church. The body of a little boy, name unknown, was also interred at Mawnan having come ashore in the Helford in the aftermath after the disaster. Two others were laid to rest at Budock Church.

Perhaps the only consolation is that those within the churchyards have a known resting place. Many shipwreck victims from earlier centuries were not afforded such a dignity, and it was only with the passing of the Burial of Drowned Persons Act 1808 that the practice of unconsecrated cliff-top interment was abolished. It is likely that anyone walking the coast path between Falmouth and Manacle Point passes several maritime graves lost to history along the way. Perhaps those of the forgotten naval ships HMS *Rinovia*, *Spencer* and *Olive Branch* lie in such unmarked plots assuming, of course, there were indeed fatalities. All that is known is that these three vessels went ashore in the vicinity of the Helford during 1754.[56] Why this should have been so is a mystery. There are no known engagements with foreign ships in the area in that particular year, and the possibility that three should fall to a navigational error is unlikely if not impossible. More likely is that the weather for the early months was bitterly cold, suggesting strong icy winds from the east.[57] That they were in convoy and struck the Manacles is also feasible.[58] Another which definitely fell victim to fierce easterly winds was the sloop, *Endeavour*. Bound for Falmouth, she was wrecked along the coast between Rosemullion Head and Meudon on 21 December 1804, with reports stating all on board had perished.[59]

In addition to ships which have foundered below the cliffs at the mouth, a few were reckoned to have come to grief further up the river's course where they ought to have been relatively safe. One such was the *Ida* of Newquay, which appears to have put into the Helford during her voyage between Plymouth and Padstow on 6 October 1820. Three men drowned in the early hours of the morning and only the captain survived having been found in the lifeboat in an exhausted state.[60]

Those who died on the *Bay of Panama* may have been relatively modest in number, but their demise during the winter storm of 1891 is a matter of legend. This huge steel-hulled sailing ship of more than 2,000 tons was one of the finest square-riggers ever to have been constructed by the famous Harland & Wolff yard in Belfast. She was renowned for her speed and, as such, regularly plied her trade as a long-distance cargo vessel between India and Britain. Indeed, it was from Calcutta that she had set sail in the preceding November, laden with thousands of bales of jute and the port of Dundee her destination. It is a tragedy that she should have been so close to home when struck by the full force of the worst blizzard to have befallen south-west England in centuries.

By the time the *Bay of Panama* reached the Cornish coast on 9 March 1891 the weather was already deteriorating rapidly. Knowing that they were probably sailing up the east coast of the Lizard Peninsula but not certain of their exact position, the captain chose to heave to and take depth soundings. It was too late for such measures and, shortly after, the ship was hit by the full force of the relentless snow storm. Although the crew desperately furled the sails in the hope of riding out the violent seas, the ship crashed into rocks below Nare Point at the mouth of the Helford. Waves washed over the decks and swept the captain, his wife, and several other crew members overboard to their deaths. Others took to the rigging, high above the churning water. One was seen to throw himself into the waves, an act of certain suicide to escape the pain of the biting cold.

It was not until the next morning that the wreck and those who had survived the night were discovered by a farmer. It is said that the survivors were so weak they were unable to move until rescuers could board the vessel. Their deceased shipmates were frozen solid. Fewer than half of the forty crew survived the ordeal and all were taken to St Keverne where they were given lodgings, food and warmth for the night. The next day they set out for Falmouth but, with snowdrifts impassable to the horse-drawn bus, the men were soon forced to continue by foot from Gweek. By the time they reached the Royal Cornwall Sailor's Home – some of them without shoes or boots – they were in a most wretched condition. It is a most extraordinary tale of the human spirit that these poor souls should have survived two ordeals, either of which would have defeated lesser men. The same could be said of brave Joseph Hendy James, who attempted to get to Helston to telegraph news of the wreck, but was forced to effectively crawl his way to Falmouth as all other means of communication were impossible.

The *Bay of Panama* was not the only ship to have been lost to the great storm of 1891. The immediate coastline to both the north and south of the Helford was littered with broken hulls and drowned mariners. Some survived, but only through a combination of remarkable good fortune and the courageous efforts of those ashore, as in the case of the sloop *Dove*:

> Just after daybreak, in company with several other vessels, she left for Falmouth. There was a strong wind blowing, which, as time went on, increased with much violence, and was followed by a blinding snowstorm. The captain and the mate of the *Dove*, who were both at the helm, could, they said afterwards, scarcely see their hands before them. At about three o'clock in the afternoon the vessel was near the Manacle rocks, and off Porthoustock Cove, and here, while in a most critical situation, the tremendous sea lifted the little craft clean over the rocks, and she was washed up on the beach. The skipper threw his little boy overboard, he and his mate following the same way, and all were rescued by those persons on shore.[61]

Those aboard the ketch *Catherine* and the Jersey schooner *Acquilon* were not so fortunate. Both ships were wrecked near to where the *Dove* had come ashore but neither of their crews survived the ordeal. Another schooner, *Agnes and Helen* of Beaumaris, was pounded by violent waves at Bream Cove, Mawnan, with the wind being described as storm force and from the northeast.[62] All hands were saved.

Like the *Agnes and Helen*, many shipwrecks in the vicinity of the Helford mercifully resulted in no loss of life. In November 1860 a barque of 467 tons from Porsgrunn in Norway came ashore in an easterly gale. Owing to poor visibility the captain had mistaken Maenporth for the river where they were to unload their cargo of timber at Gweek. Realising the error, the crew cut away the foremast and let go both of the ship's anchors but without success. It was the bravery of local residents, putting themselves in extreme danger while climbing down a sheer cliff, which would once again save many lives:

The crew, seeing their perilous position, shouted, being close to the shore, for help, when their cries were heard by Mr. Freethy, who immediately procured ropes and endeavoured to get a communication from the barque to the shore. The Rev. W. Rogers, rector of Mawnan, and a number of farmers and their labourers in the vicinity of the wreck were also present and rendered every assistance. At one time the crew had almost given up all hopes of ever reaching land, having thrown overboard three lifebuoys, to no avail; they also tied a string around a dog's neck, and attempted to send it on shore but the dog, after touching the wreck of the spars, &c., ultimately returned to the vessel. Communication was at length made with the shore by the exertions of the crew, by throwing a light marling spike from the vessel, to which was lashed a line, and on its reaching the rocks it was caught hold of by Mr. T. Veail, of the Helford Ferry, and passed to the shore and secured, so that the crew by this medium were safely landed.[63]

All seventeen aboard the ship, including the dog we must assume, were taken to the Sailor's Home in Falmouth. To this day a small cove to the north of Rosemullion Head bears the name of the ship on nautical charts and maps: *Gatamala*. No other trace of it remains.

Seven years later the Rev. Rogers was caught up in yet another maritime incident. When the *John & Rebecca*, en route from London to Dublin, sank on the Manacles on 18 March 1867, the crew took to a lifeboat and rowed to the mouth of the Helford. Here they came ashore and were welcomed to a comfortable night at the vicarage. So thankful were they for their host's hearty hospitality that the captain wrote to the *Falmouth Packet* newspaper expressing his gratitude for the kindness shown to him and his crew.

On some occasions it was both the sailors and the vessel that survived. In March 1810 the *Mercury* of Portsmouth was driven onshore at the mouth of the river but later 'got off with loss of anchors and cables, and damage to her bottom'.[64] It was a similar story for the *Tiger*, sailing between Stockton and Bordeaux in March 1841, which 'got on shore this morning, at high water, during a fog, on a bed of rocks off the entrance of Helford Harbour, but is expected off should the weather continue moderate'.[65] And it was fog that also saw the *Holmrook* of Newcastle run aground at Rosemullion Head in

July 1881 during her journey back from Caen in Normandy. She was later freed by tugs from Falmouth.

However, of all vessels to have stranded and survived, the most notable must surely be the *Clara*. An emigrant ship of more than 900 tons, she had left Plymouth for Calcutta carrying 'nine married men, 188 married women, 91 boys, and 107 girls, in all 412 persons, the families of soldiers in the East'.[66] In another example of woeful navigation by captain and crew, she struck rocks close to Nare Point during the early hours of 3 October 1859 but later floated free and returned to port. Much was made of what great fortune it had been that the event had not resulted in a loss of life comparable to, or even greater than, that of the *John* four years earlier. Had the *Clara* crashed into the Manacles just to the south it might well have occasioned one of the worst disasters in British maritime history.

Of course, the Manacles were not the only hazards to present themselves to mariners of centuries past. Indeed, those particular rocks would once have been far more conspicuous to early prehistoric seafarers by virtue of lower sea levels. However, those travelling by sea during the Iron Age and Roman periods would have experienced precisely the same dangers as modern sailors.

Such hazards to boats and ships sailing in the area include *Car Croc*, a submerged rock guarding the centre of the entrance to Gillan Creek that dries out during low water spring tides. Today it is denoted by a cardinal marker buoy warning those who approach to pass to the east, but no such advice would have been available to those 1,000 years ago. Why it should have come by such a sinister name is unclear, but it seems most likely that it is a clumsy appellation for 'castle rock', where *caer* denotes a fortification in old Cornish – its proximity to Dennis Head where the Iron Age cliff castle once stood seems to support this theory. Ominously, its title might instead derive from *caer krog*, which would roughly translate as 'castle gallows', or *carn krog*, the 'hanging rocks'.

Another cardinal mark, this time demanding safe passage to the north, is to be found mid-river along the southern shore. Here a rocky outcrop known as *The Voose* extends out into the main channel and is covered by water at high tide. Under normal weather conditions it is more nuisance than menace, and its position impeding access along the shore is probably why it is so named: *fos* in Cornish means 'wall'.

The only other significant hard obstacle to navigation is to be found in the northern approaches some 400yd off the cliffs at Mawnan. Sometimes referred to as *August Rock*, but more often as *The Gedges*, this reef dries out an hour either side of low tide. Its position means it is only a threat to vessels lost in fog or without adequate night-time navigation, and there is simply no good reason for any captain or helmsman to be close to it. Arguably the most remarkable aspect is that it gave its name to another group of rocks in the Antarctic, these being discovered by the British Graham Land Expedition between 1934 and 1937.

Aside from these minor menaces, only *The Bar* along the north bank between Helford Passage and Port Navas Creek posed a challenge to navigation, then as today. Its southernmost limit is denoted by a single buoy, and those foolish enough to disregard its advice and cut across what appears to be deep water have often been caught out. But, despite the outer threat of the Manacles, various hazards to an approach, and the risk of grounding in shallows, the Helford River was a place of sanctuary. Countless ships have ridden out storms within its sheltered bays or sought its safety in times of adversity, from local coastal traders to Norwegian timber ships and naval vessels. Alas, on rare occasions not even the seclusion it offered was enough, as proved to be the case during the Great Storm of 1703. So fierce were the hurricane-force winds that the first Eddystone Lighthouse was destroyed, lives were lost as the Somerset Levels flooded, and thousands of chimney stacks were blown down across London. But one of the most unusual stories must be that recounted in Daniel Defoe's *The Storm*:

> In Helford … there was a tin ship blown from her anchors with only one man, and two boys on board, without anchor, cable or boat, and was forc'd out of the said haven about 12 a-clock at night; the next morning by 8 a-clock, the ship miraculously run in between two rocks in the Isle of Wight, where the men and goods were saved, but the ship lost: such a run in so short a time, is almost incredible, it being near 80 leagues in 8 hours time.

That they survived is miraculous, but it was in part due to the actions of one of the youths already acquainted with the Isle of Wight coastline. He requested that he be allowed to steer the ship into a particular creek 'which he according did, where there was only just room between rock and rock for the ship to come in, where she gave one blow or two against the rocks, and sunk immediately, but the man and two boys jumpt ashore, and all the lading being tin, was saved'.[67] However, those using the river as a refuge sometimes did so for more unusual reasons, such as that which the *Morning Chronicle* reported in September 1803:

> The Earl Spencer, cutter privateer, of Dover, 16 guns, Captain Chitty, arrived on Friday at Helford from a cruize, having captured a French ship from St Domingo, a brig schooner from Louisiana, and recaptured the ship Royal Charlotte of London, Captain Hamilton, from North Carolina, bound to London, which had been captured by La Venus brig privateer of Nantz, of 14 guns and 77 men. Soon after the Earl Spencer fell in with La Venus, which she engaged some time, until she made off. Captain Chitty and four men were severely wounded, and two men killed. On the 7th instant about 100 miles west of Scilly, the Earl Spencer fell in with a Swedish dogger, having on board part of the crew of the King George (late Packet); three gentlemen passengers left the dogger, and came in the Earl Spencer.

Although undoubtedly vibrant on account of the many ships arriving and departing its confines, the early years of the nineteenth century were an uncertain time for the Helford River and its communities. Despite many virtues it was also a liability. Nearby Falmouth was a bustling port whose approaches were defended by two formidable fortresses: Pendennis and St Mawes castles. The Helford, on the other hand, was a comparative back-water whose vulnerability had already been noted by Elizabeth I's Council of War in 1587. It was this body, Sir Walter Raleigh and Sir Richard Grenville amongst its number, which concluded that the river was 'one of the places most to be suspected that the Spaniards intend to land in'.[68]

The neurosis engendered by the possibility of invasion outlasted the immediate threat of the Armada. In 1595 William Cecil, Lord Burghley, observed 'of the dangerous places for the landing of the enemy upon the south coast of England' that the Helford River was one of the most notable. He demanded that 'for the defence of these places, or any other in Cornwall, where the enemy may attempt to land, it is requisite that the lieutenant of the shire, or his deputy in his absence, should make choice of so many of his most principal gentlemen of credit and knowledge in the county, as might take charge of so many bands as should amount to 4,000 men, furnished'.[69] An attack did indeed materialise that year, but further to the west in Mounts Bay. Penzance, Newlyn, and Mousehole were plundered and set alight by a Spanish raiding party that had sailed from southern Brittany during July. Such was the fear of a repeat attack that when an unidentified fleet were sighted in the western English Channel in July 1599, John Reskymer was ordered to have his company fall-to at Helford. Life along the coast of Elizabethan Cornwall was an anxious one indeed.

By the beginning of the nineteenth century the possibility of invasion resurfaced, but by a different foe. This time it was the forces of Napoleon Bonaparte that posed a clear and present threat to the nation, but the Helford still remained the same weak point in the Cornish coastline as it had during the reign of Elizabeth I. To counter this deficiency it was considered necessary to bolster the military presence, as the *Evening Mail* reported on 2 December 1803:

> Two batteries are immediately to be formed for the protection of Helford harbour. The one on a spot scared to loyalty; the *Little Dennis*, which divides Helford and Gillan rivers, and commands them both. The mount and ditches of a battery, the last that held out for the unfortunate [King] Charles, are still pretty entire on this little promontory. The other battery will be on the Eastern entrance of Helford; and both are to be strengthened by a ship of war, or gun-boats.

Later the same month a list of fire beacons for south-west England were published in the *Royal Cornwall Gazette*. The closest to the Helford was sited at Roskruge between St Keverne and Manaccan, 370ft above sea level and upon the site of a Bronze Age barrow. Constructed of furze and barrels of tar covered with a thatch to keep it dry, it was positioned exactly where another had been lit to warn of the approaching Spanish Armada on 19 July 1588. Some have claimed that it was from the top of nearby St Keverne church that Philip II's fleet had first been sighted.

The Vicar of Manaccan, Richard Polwhele, was acutely aware of the Helford's strategic failings at the time. 'I cannot but express my wonder, that the French should have left us so long unmolested,' he wrote, 'that not even a privateer should have approached us in our present defenceless state; for not one gun have we on the Little Dinas – not one vessel in the harbour of Helford to guard us from the invader.'[70] Indeed, it was precisely this strategic deficiency that had led to Polwhele's remarkable encounter with one of the most well-known characters in the history of British seafaring.

During a break between campaigns at the turn of the nineteenth century, William Bligh was sent by the Admiralty to conduct a survey of the Helford. It was a little over a decade since he had endured the infamous 'mutiny' on HMS *Bounty*, and his skills in hydrographic matters had become highly valued. Unfortunately, vigilant locals wrongly suspected his actions to be those of a spy on a reconnaissance mission, and he was forcibly brought by local constables to Manaccan vicarage and locked in a coal cellar. Tasked with getting to the bottom of the matter, Polwhele recalled his first meeting with the irascible naval icon:

> Not knowing who he was, we suffered him to remain in an outhouse, a close prisoner, whilst in our little parlour we sipped our tea at leisure. When brought before the Magistrate, Captain Bligh refused to give any account of himself, till his guard was sent out of the room, and the door shut – to which I at length assented, not without a feeling of apprehension. But a moment's conversation with Captain Bligh discovered all the gentleman. In an act of duty he had been roughly treated; and he resented it. But his anger evaporating, he even joined me in commending the loyal zeal of my parishioners, whom I dismissed; taking Captain B. under my own care. The woodcocks were produced for supper, and a variety of wines such as they were; and it was two o'clock in the morning before we parted.[71]

The friendship between Richard Polwhele and William Bligh flourished thereafter. They were regularly in correspondence, and exchanged books by post between their homes in Cornwall and London. More importantly, Bligh's survey was never needed. The threat of invasion passed by, as indeed did Napoleon Bonaparte himself on 11 August 1815 as he left Falmouth for

St Helena on board HMS *Northumberland*. Perhaps he caught sight of the Helford, unknowingly casting his eyes upon the very harbour he could have used for invasion.

For hundreds of years, those who had lived by the river would have been acutely aware of their vulnerability. The sails of a ship upon the horizon could equally have belonged to friend or foe, and the fear of being captured by enemy raiding parties – or even pirates – would have been all too real. And yet on a day-to-day basis it was the very sea itself that posed the greatest threat, not those who travelled across it. However, on occasions it was not from the water but the land that danger appeared.

When William Killigrew resigned from his role of Governor of Pendennis Castle in May 1635 his successor was Sir Nicholas Slanning. A native of Devon, Slanning had previously served on the Commission for Piracy for both Devon and Cornwall and, in 1640, was elected as a Member of Parliament for Plympton Erle, near Plymouth. He was also a staunch supporter of King Charles I, and described by Edward Hyde, Earl of Clarendon, as 'a young man of admirable parts, a sharp and discerning wit, a staid and solid judgment, a gentle and most obliging behaviour, and a courage so clear and keen, as, even without the other ornaments, would have rendered him very considerable'.[72]

While in Cornwall, Slanning lived at Trerose Manor just as his Pendennis predecessor had done. It is likely that whenever his duties required him to be present at the castle that he travelled by boat from one of the nearby coves, probably Porthallack at the river mouth. Otherwise his journey would have been on horseback along the coast road that passes Maenporth, Swanpool and Gyllyngvase beaches. However, his governorship became of little importance upon the commencement of the English Civil War on 22 August 1642, and within weeks he had been visited by Ralph Hopton, the Royalist commander. By November, Sir Nicholas Slanning had taken charge of a regiment of Cornish soldiers loyal to the Crown alongside others led by the likes of Sir William Godolphin of Helston, and Colonel John Trevanion of Caerhays. In the early months of the war they proved themselves accomplished leaders, inspiring their troops to victories at Polson Bridge near Launceston in April 1643, and at Stratton near Bude in May. By June the Cornish Royalists had joined forces with others in Somerset, where they would go on to victory at the Battle of Landsdowne on 5 July. Slanning was described that particular day as 'advancing from hedge to hedge at the head of his men, in the mouths of muskets and cannons, insomuch they thought him immortal, as indeed he was that day'.[73]

Sir Nicholas Slanning was not immortal. He was never to return to Trerose and the Helford River as, on 26 July, he was struck in the leg by a musket ball at the Siege of Bristol. He passed away shortly after. His death was greatly lamented by those fighting for Charles I, and it is not beyond possibility that had he, Trevanion, Godolphin and Sir Bevil Grenville survived that the Civil War might have tipped in favour of the Royalists. These men were the 'Wheels on Charles's Wain' during the early days of the conflict, and their loss was a crushing blow. Although those loyal to the king would continue to make gains, they would ultimately cede ground and power to the Parliamentarians. However, Cornwall did not merely send its sons away to fight in the English Civil War as the conflict eventually engulfed the county itself. On two occasions the Helford would prove to be the backdrop to the drama.

Those walking along the coast path that encircles Dennis Head are afforded some of the finest views in south Cornwall – a maritime vista that sweeps from the mouth of the Carrick Roads, Dodman Point upon the horizon, across to Nare Point in the foreground, and down to timeless Gillan Creek below. Any visitor who takes this detour to the main route is not only afforded this exquisite visual prospect, but also unknowingly passes by the remains of a long-disappeared defensive emplacement. Most do not realise that the apparently inexplicable arcs in the path trace the bastions whose towers rose perhaps 50ft above. Here once stood Dennis Fort, built between 1643 and 1644 by Royalist forces under the supervision of Sir Richard Vyvyan of Trelowarren. The war cost him greatly in both personal and financial terms.

Although documents suggest that it was originally to have been a five-sided structure with embellishments such as a gate tower to the north-west, it was patently not constructed to such plans.[74] From the sky its ghostly outline is manifestly one of a small four-sided castle, no larger than 200ft across from corner to corner, and barely enough to contain the garrison chapel reputed to have stood within.[75] However, there do appear to be the remnants of a battery to the north-east and a walkway that would have joined it to the main fort. It would certainly have been capable of defending the entrance to the Helford, with its cannons eminently capable of covering the ¾ mile across to the northern shore in addition to protecting Gillan Creek to the south. It was placed in a most strategic position, just as its Iron Age forerunner had been.

Dennis Fort did not exist for long. In the early spring of 1646, the formidable Parliamentarian army commander Sir Thomas Fairfax moved into Cornwall and, on 14 March that year, the Royalist forces surrendered to him at Truro. Only Pendennis Castle, St Michael's Mount, and Dennis Fort held out for the King. Four days later the little castle at the mouth of the Helford, with its 200 men and twenty-two guns, succumbed.[76] Over the following decades it fell into disrepair and was plundered for its stone, leaving only the foundations intact below the wild flowers.

The 'first' English Civil War effectively concluded with the arrest of Charles I, just eight weeks after the laying down of arms at Dennis Head. Within two years the nation was plunged into chaos once again, directly as a result of friction between various power-hungry factions including Scottish Presbyterians, the Parliamentarian New Model Army, and the remaining staunch Royalists. Revolts and uprisings took place all across the British Isles, beginning in South Wales and spreading as far afield as Essex and Yorkshire. In Cornwall, too, the discontent spilled over into conflict once again.

During May of 1648 there were stirrings in the far west of the county, with Parliamentarian army leaders believing that the quickest way to deal with the situation would be to confront the rebels and demand their surrender. At Penzance their requests were refused, and the soldiers under Col Robert Bennett attacked, killing around fifty insurgents and needlessly looting the town. The following day, 23 May, another Parliamentarian commander, Edward Herle, engaged another band of discontented Royalists outside Helston. This event, known as the 'Gear Rout', took place on the southern banks of the Helford River.

The Rev. Richard Polwhele produced the most well-known account of the 'battle', although the time elapsed since the actual event suggests it was derived from anecdote passed down through the generations. Still, it is enlightening enough, and cannot be dismissed as entirely inaccurate:

A number of men under the command of Mr. Bogans of Treleague in St Keverne who had accepted a commission from Charles, posted themselves in a most advantageous situation at Gear in Mawgan, with an apparent determination of defending that important pass: But the Parliament troops advancing and showing themselves in much greater force than was expected, Major Bogans' men deserted him without coming to action. Some betook themselves to the Dinas [Dennis Head], the greater part dispersed, and Major Bogans himself fled to Hilters Clift, in St Keverne, and concealed himself in a cave in the rocks.[77]

Another unnamed contemporary chronicler who seems to have actually been present at the Gear Rout provides more specific detail. He says that having been pursued eastwards towards the mouth of the Helford, many of the men 'were so desperate, that scorning mercy, they joined hand in hand and violently ran themselves into the ocean, where they perished in the waters'. Others were said to still be hiding along the cliffs a full week after the skirmish.[78]

The two occasions when the English Civil War came to the Helford River are sometimes thought to have been the same event. It is an easy mistake for the casual reader to make, despite two years separating the fall of the garrison at Dennis Head and the Cornish uprising of the Second Civil War. Moreover, both have been used to explain the existence of a curious geographic anomaly between Manaccan and St Keverne. This long mound is to be found alongside the lane near the hamlet of Tregowris, although it is now barely noticeable on account of the undergrowth that envelops it. It is known locally as 'The Deadman', and has long been held by locals as the place at which the victims of the Civil War were buried *en masse*. Indeed, a small cannonball found in a nearby field lay along an almost direct line between it and the head of Gillan Creek.[79]

This 'sepultre to the slain' may have no connection whatsoever to the conflict.[80] It has even been suggested that it simply derives its name from that of local landowners – a theory given credence by the fact that several of the surrounding fields are denoted as such on the 1840s Tithe Map for St Keverne.[81] And yet upon the Ordnance Survey map for the area produced during the 1880s there is the bleak annotation of 'Human Remains Found'. By whom and when is unknown.

The Deadman and the Helford will both keep their dark secrets for a while longer.

6

EBB

The colours of the river change constantly. The transition can be subtle or lucid, by the minute or by the hour. But those brought about by the unremitting tick of the seasonal clock offer the greatest contrast. The verdant lime hues of fresh spring leaves become richer as summer takes hold, only to ultimately fade to bronze and rust. The oaks of the upper reaches will often come into leaf later than the beech woods downstream, and maintain them long after other trees have become barren. A dry summer might provide the additional gift of a golden autumn, a cold winter steal away all hope of early buds and the optimism they instil.

On an overcast day the water can appear leaden, but profound change occurs with the appearance of the burning sun. The shallows around the coves at the river mouth become an iridescent viridian green while the upper reaches below the ancient woods a more muted olive. As the water deepens so a transition towards blue occurs, azure at first then dark and cold. The shadows of drifting cumulus clouds often appear inky blue-black against the sunlit emerald depths close to shore, but the variation is lost as they disappear on their evanescent journey out to sea.

It is to be imagined that at noon on a bright summer day that the colours would be at their most vivid, but this is not so. Wait until evening. The differences between greens, blues, browns, yellows and reds become more acute as the day wears on and shadows lengthen. Sometimes a vermilion sunset renders the river between Helford and Port Navas ablaze, the yachts moored betwixt bathing in the fading warmth. Even the monochrome moonlight that often follows these fair days changes the character of water and shore.

Of course, the skies are not always clear. But even a violent, thunderous downpour can create a scene that Monet or Eugene Boudin would have wished to honour in oils. Before the rain the water glistens and shines, but as the deluge begins it loses its lustre; the little boats seem to be resting above the matte and muffled water rather than in it, their shapes more defined than before.

However, while the sun is a blessing and the rain either an inconvenience or agricultural necessity, the element that has always affected the lives of those around the river most acutely is the wind. For most of the year it prevails from a direction between the west and the south, while in spring the gusts are frequently born of the opposite north-east. A vigorous southwesterly is most keenly felt on the north shore where, at the river mouth, maddened little waves break upon the beaches of Porth Sawsen and Porthallack. Here the slate pebbles are rounded and flattened, the largest to the west, the more eroded to the east. In contrast, Bosahan and Ponsence coves are sheltered from the choppy waters and sometimes appear unruffled even on the most blustery of days.

Winds from the south, west or north do little to affect activity on the Helford except when at their worst or accompanied by a torrential downpour. Strong breezes arriving from these points on the compass are usually more of an annoyance than a peril although, as always, those venturing out to sea must always be mindful of the unexpected threats they carry. Besides, the river is often calm, especially in summer and early autumn when any light airs that might ripple the surface are variable in direction or generated by offshore breezes after sunset.

Only a strong wind from the east leaves the river entirely devoid of human activity, and it takes an especially wrathful one at that. Such storms do their worst should their tempestuous zeniths coincide with high tides, and it is a threat that will only increase as the rise in global sea levels continues. Of all inhabited places around the river, by far the most exposed to those wicked easterlies is Durgan. Surges within living memory have accounted for repairable damage, but that which struck in January 1916 was so severe that it caused part of the cliff to collapse, taking the steps that ran up from the cove away with it. Lord Rendlesham of Bosloe House was so afraid of high winds from the east that he would demand his steam yacht *Lady Bee* be moved from its mooring to safety upriver at the slightest hint of one.[1] Thankfully, however, this little hamlet avoids the fury of the Atlantic storms that pound the western-facing coast of Cornwall during the winter months.

Durgan feels like a place that has heard all about the modern world and wisely decided against joining it. But it is no longer the little fishing community it used to be. Here are still to be found the fish cellars where pilchards were pressed into hogshead barrels, along with a yard and stables for the donkeys that would carry catches to market. But they are working fish cellars and stables no more. At the turn of the twentieth century there were numerous boats at anchor in the cove, *Milly*, *Ganges*, *Two Sisters*, *Dora*, *Stella*, *Shamrock*, *Fleetwings*, *Mabel* and *Secret* among them. The men of the village would catch the fish and their wives would take them to market, supplementing their income by digging for cockles and other shellfish which they would often take all the way to Falmouth on foot. A lamp would be left burning in the window of the reading room for those hauling nets or pots at night, each fisherman waiting until the last of his neighbours were safe before retiring to bed.[2]

To live in Durgan during those times was truly to belong. Even the donkeys were a cherished and important part of village life, with given names such as Billy, Fanny, Joey, Charlotte, Jessie and Jack. One particular Durgan resident, 'Blind' George Retallack, had lost his sight at birth but was easily able to find his own and lead him from the field and along the lane to Mawnan. Up until the latter half of the nineteenth century the community even possessed its own inn, *The Two Cutters*, which stood upon the western-most of its two quays. No doubt it was a place of great importance to social cohesion, and probably full of intrigue on many occasions.

As if the lives of Durgan fishermen were not difficult enough, the very sea from which they drew their livelihoods could not wholly be called their own. Indeed, restrictions upon fishing anywhere they chose within the river had long been a source of discontent, being as it was divided between the 'lower right' and the 'higher right'. The legal freedom to cultivate oysters in the former was leased from the Duke of Leeds, the latter from the Manor of Merthen. This valuable 'higher right' extended upriver to Gweek from a point just west of the entrance of Port Navas Creek, as a document from the mid seventeenth century affirms:

> ... the royalty and privilidge of anchorage, killadge, and bulladge, dredging and taking of oisters, fowling, fishing and setting of nets of all sorts whatsoever, in and throughout all places and creeks whatsoever in the river of Helford, from a place called Mene Brooth under Kestle Down up the river to Gweek Bridge, Gare [Gear] Bridge, and Mawgan Bridge, to be a member and part of the manor and barton of Merthen, and now wholely and solely to belong and appertain unto Sir Richard Vyvyan, Knt., as lord of the said manor and barton. And, that no person whatsoever, ought to make use of any of the said previledges without leave first obtained of the said Sir Richard Vyvyan. And we do also confess and acknowledge, that the lord of the manor and barton of Merthen aforesaid is to have and receive as his due, the head chiefe or best fish of all porpesses, thornepoles [Pilot Whales or Risso's Dolphin], dolphins and all other sorts of great fish whatsoever killed in any of the places aforesaid, and that all the said fish are to be brought to a place called the Greyne, alias Merthen Grune [Groyne Point], and there to be divided and nowhere else.[3]

This boundary was clearly a source of deep resentment as in the spring of 1654, 'Jno. Mayne, the son of Thomas Mayne, of the parish of Constenton [Constantine], in the county of Cornwall, tucker, did see Baldman, the son-in-law of Sampson Cockram, of Helford, to pull down the [marker] stone commonly called and known by the name of Mayne Brough'.[4] Nor did matters improve after the Tyacke family of Constantine leased the higher right from Merthen in 1829, given that within a decade men were being imprisoned or sentenced to hard labour for supposedly stealing oysters. But, of all years, 1866 appears to have been one of major discord, with the people of Durgan at the heart of a disagreement between lord and commoner. In fact, it was reported that there was a 'most lawless spirit' in the tiny fishing village, with legal proceedings being brought against members of the community on two separate counts.

The first of these courtroom dramas concerned a number of men who had asserted their right to fish upriver on account that the Helford was a public navigable waterway. The charge levelled by the prosecution, however, was that William Retallack, Thomas Downing, Henry Pascoe, Richard Pascoe, Richard Veal, Henry Downing, and Josiah Downing had unlawfully taken and destroyed fish 'otherwise than by angling, between the beginning of the last hour before sunrise and the last hour after sunset … from a certain fishery or water, situate in the Helford River, in the parish of St Martin, the property of John Tyacke, gentleman'. Much as they offered circumstantial evidence of themselves and others having done so previously, five were found guilty and ordered to pay a fine or be committed to prison for fourteen days each.

The second case, held at Helston Petty Sessions, was that of four female Durgan residents: Mary Richards, Martha Rodda, Susanna James and her daughter Mary. All were charged with stealing 200 oysters, again supposedly belonging to James Tyacke. Mary James was spared punishment on account of her youth, but the others were committed to six weeks' imprisonment with hard labour. One defendant already had three offences to her name and the prosecutor hoped that they would 'find that the law was too strong, even for the people of Durgan'.[5]

The threats did not work. Four years later in 1870 a young Durgan man named Abraham Downing was found guilty of stealing oysters worth 9*s* from Port Navas Creek. Again, the defence of public right in a navigable river was given, but to no avail. The case was considered to be of considerable interest because of 'the inhabitants being exceedingly jealous of the private rights claimed by the prosecutor to the valuable oyster fisheries on that river'.[6] The truth, of course, was not so much that their actions were driven by jealousy as by poverty. When eleven Durgan men had been sent to prison in 1839 for stealing oysters, it was a sentence all of them could ill afford.[7] Families would have gone hungry were it not for the solidarity of neighbours. They were not isolated cases, and many a resident spent nights at Bodmin Gaol during the nineteenth century. The injustice of the situation was not lost on many observers, with one correspondent to the *Falmouth Packet* suggesting that it was 'a disgrace to civilisation that it should be so … the claim set up that all shell fish found in the Helford River belong to a private person is bad enough, but that floating fish which come in with the tide and pass out again are private property seems monstrous'.[8] It was merely the prohibitive cost of challenging 'ownership' in the High Court which prolonged the impasse and incarcerations.

Arguably worse than being hauled in front of a judge and jailed was being caused actual bodily harm. In 1846 three of Tyacke's employees were accused of assaulting a woman searching for shellfish close to the mouth of Frenchman's Creek. One man reputedly 'knocked her down with his fist, shook her violently, and knelt on her while she lay on the ground'.[9] No doubt many more altercations which took place on the river stayed on the river, never to reach court or the ears of local journalists.

It is little surprise that the humble oyster was the source of much conflict on the river during the Georgian and Victorian periods. It was noted during the mid-nineteenth century that 'the oyster of Helford River is very superior to that of Falmouth Harbour' and that it was 'held in such esteem that in the Plymouth and other local markets the produce of the fishery finds a most ready sale among the upper of society'.[10] Perhaps their wider renown was one reason why numerous fishing boats from the east of England descended upon the river in the spring of 1849, as a Constantine correspondent to the *Royal Cornwall Gazette* recorded:

> The whole neighbourhood is in a state of excitement at the arrival of upwards of 60 smacks with their crews from Colchester, for the purpose of dredging oysters in Helford River. The parties have not yet begun, but have desired the present occupier (Mr. Tyacke) to produce his title for holding the property. Should this be refused, they intend immediately to commence operations in the lower right, belonging to the Duke of Leeds. They also intend dredging in the higher ground, which is claimed by Sir. R. Vyvyan ... Mr. Tyacke is empowered by the Home Secretary, to engage if requisite, the services of the men belonging to the Revenue Cutter at Falmouth, and the Coast Guard, to resist their attempts. The laying at anchor of such a forest of masts in our quiet little creek has attracted the attention of crowds of spectators.[11]

The following week the same newspaper reported that evidence of his right produced by Tyacke had been deemed inconclusive and that dredging had begun both above and below Calamansack. In addition to the vessels from Colchester, boats from as far afield as Jersey and Rochester were also said to have commenced fishing. Three cutters with a contingent of marines on board were 'calm spectators of the proceedings'.[12] Order was soon restored; a mixed blessing for the Helford fishermen who must have been relieved to have their territory returned to them, but also disappointed that the claim they had tried to overturn had been upheld once again.

Precisely why and when the river should have developed such an important oyster fishery is unclear. The author Herbert Byng Hall reckoned that the Phoenicians had discovered them 'to be infinitely preferable to the watery things they got at home'.[13] The Romans, too, were famously keen upon *Ostrea edulis* and all the supposed health and virility benefits they possessed. Unsurprisingly, the legend that the Helford's shellfish bounty was coveted by them has come to stick. Indeed, it is a fable not entirely without circumstantial supporting evidence. After all, as Mediterranean supplies dwindled, so a booming import industry developed, with oysters from Bordeaux, Brittany and Normandy packed in snow during the winter and tubs of brine during the summer.[14]

Some have suggested that although oyster beds occurred naturally around the coast of the Britain at that time, it was the Romans who introduced the concept of farming them for mass consumption. Shells have been found at numerous inland military sites of Roman age, suggestive of a highly organised logistics operation.[15] A tablet uncovered at the Hadrian's Wall outpost of Vindolanda contains text stating that fifty oysters had been sent to the writer from 'Cordonovi' by a friend.[16] Could it be that this mysterious source, as yet unidentified by scholars, is actually west Cornwall? Furthermore, is it entirely ridiculous to hypothesize that the preponderance of Roman coin hoards around the Helford might have as much to do with the humble bivalve mollusc as either tin or gabbroic clay?

Ancient unknowns and the suppositional aside, some of the earliest documented evidence for the Helford oysterage dates from the late sixteenth century when it was said to have been worth £2 10s a year.[17] However, it must surely have been a profitable venture for hundreds of years before that point, not least as oysters were popular with both rich and poor on account of the number of 'fish days' imposed by the all-powerful medieval church.

Those digging gardens in the oldest parts of the Helford's surrounding villages regularly turn up large numbers of shells discarded centuries earlier. Most were probably 'stolen'.

Despite the renown of the oyster fishery, the local economies of Durgan and Helford village during the eighteenth and nineteenth centuries were underpinned by the annual harvest of pilchards. The summer months were dominated by the practice of drift netting for these most legendary of Cornish fish, and the cliffs around the river mouth would have echoed to the commands of those directing the boats to the shoals visible below the surface. Almost every community on the river was involved in the industry as the proliferation of surviving fish cellars suggests. A particularly fine example still stands proudly by the water's edge at St Anthony-in-Meneage, although its counterpart across the creek at Flushing has long since disappeared. Those who have sailed around the river's middle reaches will be most familiar with the remains of the fish cellar at the mouth of Frenchman's Creek, while those at Treath are less obvious: one is now a dwelling, and only the lower walls of another remain.

Some unusual species occasionally made appearances in the nets, such as a bramble shark in 1838. Just to the south of the river mouth at Porthallow, twenty-six pilot whales came ashore in 1812 producing 'a great quantity of fine oil'; an unexpected bonus for the impoverished local fishermen, even if vexatious to twenty-first-century social convention.[18] Some fortunate boatmen even found pearls while harvesting mussels.[19] However, it is entirely unjust to assume that these were simple people without any talent beyond the catching of fish. They knew the sea and how to sail in almost every condition. So esteemed was their seamanship that one young man of Durgan, Edward Downing, was requested to crew on the *Shamrock III* during the America's Cup yachting contest of 1903 in New York harbour. What is more, this diminutive collection of waterside cottages could even claim to have been the home port of Captain George Vancouver – founder of the Canadian island of the same name. Regrettably, no one knows if he ever set foot upon its shingle beach, but only the gloomiest of cynics would pour scorn on the idea.

In contrast to Durgan, the waterside community of Port Navas grew and sustained itself not on fish but on granite. This small village had originally been known as 'Cove', a cluster of cottages and farmsteads that had grown around the medieval estate of Ponsaverran. Whether the actual name of Port Navas is a corruption of the early 'Penreveran' is open to interpretation, but some have variously suggested that its meaning is 'cove of the sheep' or 'harbour of the summer abode'.[20] Whatever the case might be, the Mayn family of Ponsaverran were instrumental in the rapid development of the village and its creek head during the nineteenth century.

Completed in 1830, the Mayn's 'higher quay' proved to be a remarkable example of nineteenth-century business acumen. No longer would the granite of nearby quarries have to be transported along the tortuous overland route to Penryn. Instead, a slow decline to sea level at Port Navas ensured minimal effort on the part of both man and beast, with the easy berthing available for sizeable ships proving attractive for their owners. From here was despatched a valuable type of granite famous for its fine grain to building projects throughout the British Isles and beyond. Stone for the Wellington Memorial of 1863 at Stratfield Saye House in Hampshire left from the village, while local moorstone from Constantine and Mabe parishes – largely shipped from Penryn – also went into the building of the first Waterloo Bridge. It was an enterprise vividly described by Cecil Lane in the late nineteenth century:

> This busy little port, having granite wharves and quays of considerable size, with cranes and derricks for the loading of large blocks of granite from the Constantine quarries. Immense numbers of these blocks are piled up forty or fifty feet high, waiting to be loaded into two or three ketches, schooners and smacks moored under the cranes or anchored in the stream.[21]

Alas, it was not to last. By the early twentieth century it had ceased to be of strategic importance due to demand for more economically produced stone from overseas. It was a story of decline replicated in that other industrial mainstay of Constantine: mining. Although by no means as productive as the ground beneath Camborne or St Agnes, six mines operated in the parish during the nineteenth century, each manned by local residents seeking sustenance for their families while the owners sought their fortune.

The most important by far was Wheal Vyvyan, close to the centre of Constantine itself. Named after the land-owning family, between 1827 and

1864 it produced more than 8,000 tonnes of copper and almost 100 of tin, all of which contributed to the rapid growth of the village.[22] In contrast, Mount Brogden Mine near Port Navas concerned itself with recovery of iron from a significant haematite seam 60 fathoms below ground. During its zenith in the early 1870s, thousands of tonnes of ore were being sold annually. Less successful was Wheal Caroline to the south of the village, where a modest lode of tin was worked without economic success during the middle of the nineteenth century. Less still is known of Wheal Nanjarrow close to the stream at Ponjeravah, although it must surely have been unprofitable given the meagre remains and lack of publicity at the time. Another mine at Naphene, north of Gweek, is similarly lacking in documentary evidence but surely once existed.

Two other mines operated close to the present-day parish boundary with Mawnan. The small Wheal Bosanath above the head of Trenarth Creek was opened briefly in search of copper, but it was the nearby Anna Maria mine that proved more fruitful. Its shafts and workings were said to have reached the 45 fathom level in pursuit of a copper lode at the head of the creek that now bears its name. Although viable during the 1830s, an attempt to reopen the site in the early twentieth century proved too costly on account of the flooded shafts being troublesome to pump dry. More than a century later the water in the creek can sometimes appear discoloured after a stormy deluge, a reminder of the drowned workings below.

The only known mining operation to the south of the river in modern times was Wheal Mudgan (a variant of 'Mudgeon') in the parish of St Martin-in-Meneage. Shares in this particular enterprise came up for sale in 1815, with a notice in the *Royal Cornwall Gazette* describing it as having 'a Lode about five feet big, in which there is Copper Ore and Mundic; and it is the opinion of experienced miners that with a fair trial it would be very productive'.[23] Where it now lies is uncertain, but two adits with which it might be linked are to be found close to Vallum Tremayne Creek.[24]

Tin, copper and gold are not the only metallic elements associated with the river's bedrocks. In 1791 a science-minded man of the cloth, the Rev. William Gregor, observed curious black sands in the leat of Tregonwell Mill at the head of Gillan Creek. Having retrieved a sample of the alluvial sediment, he returned home to perform experiments and eventually isolated a substance he named *Menechanite*, or *Manaccanite*. Later the same year the celebrated German chemist Martin Heinrich Klaproth came across the same element in a different ore and, believing it a new discovery, called it titanium. Klaproth's monumental title has endured, but one of the Helford's humble tributaries is the place we should call its home.

In truth, the Helford of the nineteenth century was far more associated with the export of metals than their actual production, just as it had been 2,000 years earlier. A small number of 'blowing houses' at which tin was smelted stood around the river, most notably at Polwheveral and Gweek. Most importantly, it was observed in the mid-eighteenth century that Helston was a 'large, populous trading town', and that it was at Helford that the ships often loaded with the tin assayed at its Coinage Hall.[25] Much was destined for the wharves of the Thames between Limehouse and London Bridge. Eighteenth-century Bills of Lading bear testimony to the value of such cargo transported from the river at the time, with around 9 tonnes leaving on one local ship, *Peter and Mary*, in July of 1703 alone.[26]

The river's industrial legacy is best evidenced by its overabundance of quays. The oldest have been reduced to residual piles of stone by the erosive action of tides and waves, but most of those constructed in the eighteenth and nineteenth centuries still stand, refusing to submit to time. That to be found at Merthen represents the highest point on the river's course to which large vessels could safely navigate. From here some would winch themselves upstream, the crew pulling the ship by its anchor upon a rising tide, while others would unload their cargo on to rafts.[27] Merthen is hushed today, but it was once one of the busiest places on the river. The existence of a large lime kiln and controller's dwelling house – now entirely derelict – would once have been prominent above the shoreline. Not anymore, hidden away in the protective embrace of watchful oaks as they are, never to be fully exposed to the elements again.

Within a curlew's call of Merthen is the grandest of them all: Tremayne. There was a utilitarian quay here once, but that which exists today was not designed for mercantile purposes. Instead, it supposedly owes its current form of neatly stacked killas foundations and robust granite topstones to a vain attempt to impress Queen Victoria. It was here that the monarch and her husband, Prince Albert, were due to disembark during a coastal tour of Cornwall in September 1846, but foul weather prevented them from reaching their intended destination of Trelowarren. Her great grandson, Edward, Duke of Windsor, at least made royal use of it almost seventy-five years later in 1921 – he would return to the Helford once again, with Wallis and Ernest Simpson, on a visit to Trebah in 1935.

Scott's Quay on the middle reaches of Polwheveral Creek is silent today, but was formerly a thriving place of export for the granite produced by Constantine's quarries. The remnants of the surviving structure's predecessor can still be seen close by, its weed-covered foundations slowly losing their form with every ebbing tide. To whom it owes its name was a 'hard and unjust' man of the law, Charles Scott of Trewardreva, whose apparition was believed by old some residents of Constantine to ride through the countryside with a pack of incorporeal hunting hounds.[28] At least the quay has outlasted his unflattering legend.

Like that at Polwheveral, many of the Helford's surviving man-made landing places are sited upon their antecedents. All the medieval communities that flourished within sight of the water would have built and maintained such structures, so we can be certain that those at Mawgan, Gweek, Helford and St Anthony have foundations that penetrate deep into the silt and past alike. Even modest farmsteads such as that at Treveador above Frenchman's Creek possessed their own landing places. Admittedly, the days of Withan quay's practical value are long-since gone, but not so those useful to the soul, especially on a languorous July evening.

Some examples, however, are still in economic use. Nineteenth-century Bishop's Quay has been employed regularly for storing fishing gear in recent years, as has the small fish cellar and quay at the mouth of Frenchman's Creek. And, of course, those at Gweek continue to be as serviceable as they have been for centuries. Indeed, unsuccessful proposals to create a canal between the Hayle estuary and Gweek at the end of the eighteenth century would have seen the port grow significantly.[29] Further suggestions for a similar waterway between Loe Pool and Gweek to include a lock above Port Navas creek in the late 1800s also failed to gain support.[30] Either would have made investors wealthy. Either would have destroyed the natural beauty of the river forever.

Notwithstanding the Helford's historic association with tin and granite exports, we must not overlook that it was a place of import, too. Accounts of Dues received 'for that part of the Harbour, belonging to Sir Richard Vyvyan [of Merthen]' during the nineteenth century show that, amongst other materials, vast quantities of coal were being unloaded in the river's upper reaches. Most ships and their masters were regular visitors, none more so than *Royal Adelaide*, which made no fewer than twelve appearances between the Lady Days of 1831 and 1832 alone.[31] Other vessels brought wheat, salt, brick, slates, potatoes, iron, and even guano. The Customs Duty collected at Gweek for the year ending 5 January 1839 totalled £7,363 13*s* – more than £750,000 today. Although a tiny figure compared to that taken in ports such as London and Liverpool, it was still a greater amount than that collected by their colleagues in places such as Swansea and Whitby.[32]

The Norwegian timber ships and their crews were especially frequent visitors: Captain Ellingsen and *Gladiator*, Nielsen and *Apollo*, Christiansen and *Janus*, Berg and *Odin*, Ludvigsen and *Apollo*, Abrahamsen and *Maria* and others. Each had made the 1,000-mile, ten-day journey from ports such as Porsgrunn, Drammen, and Longsound. However, Captain Erikssen of *Valhalla* was by far the most regular Scandinavian arrival, and especially during the 1840s. But, despite familiarity with the estuary, even he managed to inadvertently ground his formidable ship on The Bar at Helford Passage in November 1846.

Limestone was yet another notable import, the legacy of which is the handful of lime kilns that stand around its shores. Some have been lost, such as that at Helford Passage, but most remain either as ruins or having been incorporated into modern dwellings. Two served the estate of Trelowarren, with that near the mouth of Mawgan Creek still surviving unlike its counterpart at Gear Bridge. Two others existed at Gweek, although the finest of all stands proudly at Gold an Gear to the east of Helford village – its crenellations bestow it with an appearance more fitting of a Civil War fort than a place of industry.[33]

The eyewitness accounts of Alfred Fox of Glendurgan confirm that the open sea beyond the river mouth was full of maritime life during the mid-nineteenth century. On 18 June 1831 he recorded in his diary 'thirteen ships of war in sight all the afternoon', with '190 vessels in the bay' on 21 November 1847. However, not all traffic arrived for military or commercial reasons. The estuary was much more than simply a place of trade and dispatch. Ships from all around the British Isles and the world beyond continued to use it to shelter from foul weather, just as they had always done. The sloop *Phoenix* was one such refugee, seeking sanctuary in December 1807 after sustaining severe damage in a heavy gale.[34] So too did the *St Antonio* while en route for Gibraltar in February 1810.[35]

On occasions the river even represented salvation from misery. In November 1826, a Dutch ship called the *Four Sisters* arrived at Helford four months after leaving Jakarta. It was reported that one man was dead and the rest of the crew suffering greatly from scurvy.[36] Nine years later in January 1835, the brig *Caroline* put into Helford following what her captain described as the longest and most tempestuous passage in his twenty-four years at sea. Sailing from America, the ship was about a week into its voyage when it came across a small boat adrift in the middle of the Atlantic. Within it were found six men, barely alive, and another who had passed away. It transpired that they were the only survivors from a crew of fourteen belonging to another brig, the *Elizabeth*, which had run into fierce storms nine days previously. With the ship's main mast gone and hull severely damaged, the captain and seven of his men had taken to the longboat with just a few potatoes between them. Two 'could bear the pangs of thirst no longer, and in the bitterness of agony drank salt water (which their comrades tried to prevent); the consequence was, they became deranged, and died'. One cadaver was thrown overboard, but it was rumoured that the other remained in the boat and 'whose mangled body manifested the irresistible cravings of the hunger that his barely surviving shipmates were suffering under'. The survivors of this horrific ordeal were delivered to Helford village, where they were tended by a doctor from Helston.[37] How beautiful the river must have appeared, even in the depths of winter, to those frostbitten and debilitated mariners.

Despite the trade in tin and oysters, the early nineteenth-century Helford had long been in the shadow of Falmouth. With the packet ships arriving and departing daily to and from around the world, the town grew rapidly in importance. Renowned for being where news of victory at Trafalgar and Nelson's death first reached England in 1805, Falmouth was also a place of embarkation to ports around the globe, with figures such as Lord Byron sailing for Portugal in 1816 on board one of its numerous mail ships. Here too came luminaries such as Charles Darwin and Benjamin Franklin. The

Helford could not boast such illustrious company. Rather, by 1805 it was even being considered as a place suitable for the relocation of Falmouth's quarantine station.[38] It would have been a dramatic fall from grace for a river that had been so important for thousands of years.

Instead, the Helford – or more specifically the lands surrounding it – entered a period of gentrification. Notwithstanding that several fine houses such as Merthen, Trelowarren and Tremayne had been standing above its waters for hundreds of years, the early nineteenth century saw significant tracts of its landscape transformed into ornamental gardens. The chief architects of this metamorphosis were the Fox family of Falmouth; Quakers with a keen eye for both business and the sciences.

Glendurgan and Trebah are the most celebrated of their horticultural creations. Work upon the former was begun by Alfred Fox and his wife Sarah, together setting about clearing the valley from their modest thatched cottage at its head during the late 1820s. By 1833 the maze for which it is so famous had been laid out – a lasting testament to their prodigious energy and enthusiasm – and a new house, still standing today, was built upon the charred ruins of their first home, destroyed in a blaze in 1837.

Trebah, on the other hand, had been an estate of some consequence for hundreds of years before being sold to Alfred Fox's younger brother, Charles, in 1838. Although the foundations of the existing gardens were the product of Charles Fox's endeavours, much of the development for which it is celebrated today can be attributed to Edmund Backhouse, an MP from Darlington who had married the Fox's only daughter, Julia. However, the Backhouses did not limit their interest to the 26 acres at Trebah. At Meudon Vean, on the other side of Mawnan parish, exists the forgotten beauty of the Helford's many gardens. This, like all others, lies within a sheltered valley whose fertile soils are conducive to the growth of rare and exotic plants.

The grounds of Carwinion became yet another cultivated valley garden during the nineteenth century, while those of handsome Bosloe House near Durgan – a building ostensibly of seventeenth-century origin but largely a product of early twentieth labour – are understated yet pretty, especially during spring when wild flowers abound in its hedgerows. The stream around which the more exotic plants thrive is responsible for its name: 'the house on the marsh'.

Of all country houses to have looked out upon the river, the Bosahan of the Victorian period was, by a considerable margin, the grandest of them all. Alas, it was demolished shortly after the Second World War to be replaced by a more modest dwelling, but whether the landscape of the Helford is richer or poorer for it is a matter of personal opinion. The ornamental gardens established in the eighteenth century by the Grylls family have fortunately survived, indeed thrived, even if the building that some believe inspired du Maurier's 'Manderley' of *Rebecca* is no more.

The era during which most ornamental private estates were established lasted a little over a century, its end precipitated by the societal changes caused by the Great War of 1914–18. Many are now administered by charities or trusts, the old bonds between gentry and the indentured tenant workers who reverentially maintained them for their overlords long gone. It is regrettable that it took such bloodshed to sever them. Sons of the Helford River lost to the violence and tragedy of the First World War are buried far from its shores all across Europe and beyond. Their bodies lie in the cemeteries of Lijssenthoek, Adinkerk, and Bailleul amongst others, while a few are interred even further afield in Turkey and Baghdad. Others lie out in the fields of Flanders and beyond, yet to be found or identified, their names inscribed on the Tyne Cot, Arras and Thiepval Memorials in lieu of certain final resting places. Even the tiny community of Durgan lost young men, with Rifleman Norman Downing and Lance Corporal Peter Eddy buried at the Somme grounds of Warlencourt and Bagneux respectively.

The Helford went to war between 1914 and 1918, but very little came to it. Other than the prolonged absences of hundreds of men, there was scant evidence of the conflict in this far corner of the British Isles. Unlike the eastern Channel coast, no distant sound of booming guns on the Ypres Salient could be heard on the wind, and nor were many ships sunk by U-boats in this particular part of the Western Approaches. Only a training rifle range at Calamansack and the establishment of an anti-U-boat airship station near Mullion were obvious indicators of the hostilities. Those and grieving families mourning lost sons, fathers and husbands.

However, the Helford suffered equally as much as any other part of rural Britain as the war drew to a close. In November 1918 the influenza pandemic that claimed the lives of 100 million people worldwide gripped the west of England. Some were less fortunate than others, as the *Cornishman* newspaper reported in the days leading up to the Armistice:

> … few families have suffered so acutely as that of Mrs. A. Cuttance, of Trenower, St Martin-in-Meneage. Mrs. Cuttance has lost her daughter (Miss Olivia Cuttance, 19), and her daughter-in-law (Mrs. Ernest Cuttance, 26). Mrs. Cuttance is in bed with the 'flue', as is her son Roy and daughter Doreen, whilst in the same house, suffering from the same complaint, is Mrs. Stronguvist (*nee* Swaine, of Penzance). Mr. Ernest Cuttance is also laid up with influenza. The funeral of Mrs. Ernest Cuttance took place at Manaccan on Wednesday, Oct. 23, and that of Miss Olivia Cuttance at St Martin on the following Friday. Both were largely attended, and the sympathy of the whole neighbourhood has been extended to the bereaved.[39]

However, if the conflict of 1914 to 1918 was one that took place elsewhere, the Second World War was visited upon the Helford to a greater extent than almost any other rural area of Britain. Although local hotels still advertised themselves as places where the visitor could escape the vicious reality of the Blitz on the nation's major cities, even the Helford was not immune from military action. From the moment the first air raids struck west Cornwall in July 1940, the river and its people became embroiled in the conflict. As one resident of Helford observed during those early days of action, fragments of anti-aircraft shells from Falmouth were seen and heard to fall in the fields above its shores.[40]

It is almost certain that many of the bombs that dropped in and around the river did so due to poor navigation. Falmouth and its docks were the objective, and a confused pilot observing the shimmering surface of water penetrating deep inland on a moonlit night could easily mistake the Helford for the Carrick Roads. So it was that innocuous villages of no strategic value suffered. Several high explosives struck Gweek in the late summer of 1940 with one fatality and numerous casualties, while incendiary bombs fell in the fields around Manaccan.[41]

Perhaps more feared than conventional devices were the immense parachute mines that plunged not only into the sea, but also dropped on to land. They are still found in the depths of Falmouth Bay from time to time, and many more no doubt await discovery. The devastating effects of such explosives befell the village of Mawnan Smith on the night of 9 May 1941. Numerous houses were rendered uninhabitable by one, while another obliterated the property of an elderly couple whose recovered remains were interred at the parish church soon after. The same year other high-explosive devices fell across the river at Gillan, while livestock were killed at nearby Tendera and Condurrow.[42] At Helford Passage an unexploded mine washed up perilously close to the waterside cottages and inn, the bomb disposal experts of the army called in to defuse the huge device.[43]

The proximity to Falmouth and its superficial similarities to the Carrick Roads were responsible for the mouth of the river becoming a decoy site for the docks – better for enemy ordnance to fall in unpopulated countryside than upon shipping and civilians just a few miles to the north. This sacrificial 'Q site' at Nare Point was largely constructed by the special effects department of Ealing Film Studios, and its control centre, once manned by naval personnel, still lies beneath undergrowth in Lestowder cliffs. Here were placed 50-gallon tar barrels and troughs fed from tanks of paraffin, diesel and water, the combination of which, when ablaze, would appear as a successful strike upon industrial or maritime targets. Even a fake railway line, complete with signals, was constructed to lure the Luftwaffe's Heinkel, Dornier and Junkers bombers away from their intended target. It often worked.

The Second World War also threw into sharp relief once again the strategic paradox of the Helford: it was simultaneously a safe haven and vulnerable target. In the early years of the conflict, when the lands across the Channel had fallen into enemy hands, its susceptibility was foremost in the minds of locals and military officials alike. Those protective measures to have survived most intact are the pillboxes – small defended concrete blockhouses – along its northern shore at Porth Sawsen, Durgan, Polgwidden Cove, and Helford Passage. At Toll Point are also to be found faint traces of a coastal battery and searchlight emplacement, while Rosemullion Head was deemed an auspicious place upon which to site anti-aircraft guns. A boom stretching south across the main channel from Porth Sawsen was also employed as a defensive measure, as were mines anchored to the seabed whose detonation could be triggered electroni-

cally by operators at Toll Point. Most fearsome of all, however, was a flame
barrage fed from fuel tanks in the woods above Grebe Beach – test firings
would often leave scorch marks upon nearby trees.

To the south, slowly degrading anti-tank defences still exist at Gillan
Creek, while an observation post once stood on that famously strategic
site of Dennis Head.[44] Just as it had in the reign of Elizabeth I and during
the Napoleonic Wars, the river was seen to be a geographical flaw in the
nation's coastal defences. But the Helford would emerge from this period
of uncertainty and, in time, would become an asset rather than a liability. In
fact, the estuary played a leading role in two of the conflict's most remarkable
stories. Alas, as always, its isolation and the secrecy surrounding what took
place upon it meant that its importance would go largely unnoticed in the
ultimate story of national victory.

A hostelry offering shelter to cold, weary travellers has existed at Helford
Passage for 300 years at the very least. It stands at a point where boats could
be beached safely or pulled entirely clear of the shore, and where a shilling
could be made from those awaiting transfer across the water to the Meneage.
And if the weather were to suspend service for the night, the wayfarer was
at least assured of warm lodgings. As such, we might reasonably assume that
the Ferryboat Inn is an institution almost as old as the ferry itself.

The Georgian inn that stood facing south-west across to Helford Point
was replaced by a larger, more profitable complex in 1933. It was to this
expanded and refurbished establishment that a great many famous names of
the time sought escape from London and, ultimately, the stress of the Blitz.
As one journalist described the Helford in 1940, it was 'five miles from
Falmouth, and five million away from the war'.[45] It is ironic, therefore, that
one of the earliest known visitors to the existing Ferryboat Inn was the
Nazi Foreign Minister Joachim von Ribbentrop, then German Ambassador
to Britain, who dined in its restaurant in 1937 while staying briefly at
Glendurgan during a tour of Cornwall – the Fox family's best efforts to
improve declining relations between Britain and Germany came to nought.
Other notable, less controversial, names passed through its doors during the
war years, including Baron Rothschild, actor Godfrey Tearle, film director
Michael Powell, and RAF pilot John Cunningham. David Niven was so

enamoured of the location that he would return many times following the end of hostilities.

Of all, General Montgomery was arguably the most revered guest, although at the time of his sojourn he had yet to establish himself as a household name through El Alamein. One lady who worked at the inn described him as a 'very quiet man', albeit one of great charisma.[46] However, most of those with military backgrounds enjoying its hospitality in the early 1940s did not do so openly, but rather as part of a clandestine project.

In contrast to the action clearly observed by the British people between 1939 and 1945 there was, according to Winston Churchill, 'a secret war, whose battles were lost or won unknown to the public'.[47] Part of that secret war was waged from the Helford River, and with great success. During the darkest days of 1940, it was from its quiet waters that covert attempts to fight back against Nazi domination of the Continent were launched. Local residents might well have been intrigued by the new arrivals in their midst, but only those involved understood the nature and critical importance of their work.

Nicknamed 'the Ministry for Ungentlemanly Warfare', the Special Operations Executive was formed specifically to conduct espionage and sabotage in occupied Europe. One of its principal bases was established at Helford Passage, specifically within three of its grandest houses: Ridifarne, Bar House, and Pedn Billy. Lord Runciman's requisitioned yacht *Sunbeam II* became a floating headquarters, moored as she was off Helford Passage. The Inshore Patrol Flotilla was largely comprised of escaped Breton fishing boats able to cross the English Channel under darkness to arrive off the French coast before dawn. There they were able to mingle with genuine fishermen and operate above the suspicion of the German lookouts.

Those who undertook these daring missions were British and refugee French alike, with local men such as Howard Rendle of Port Navas involved in some of the assignments. These extraordinarily brave ventures often involved the rescue of stranded military personnel, including shot-down airmen from Ile-Tariec at the mouth of Brittany's Aber-Benoit river during Christmas of 1943.[48] One of those saved carried maps identifying sites intended for the launching of V1 and V2 rockets across the English Channel towards London.[49] Through such heroic deeds as these the war was ultimately won.

At the same time as the Special Operations Executive conducted their final covert assignments from the river, preparations for an assault upon occupied Europe were being made. In late December 1943 a practice mission took place, with landing craft leaving the Helford to join up with ships from other south coast estuaries for an 'attack' upon Slapton Sands in Devon.[50] Few villagers were aware of the rationale for Operation Duck, although most recognised the gravitas of the situation. Those in Mawnan were particularly affected, often being banned from communicating with servicemen and having surrounding lanes made inaccessible. So great were efforts to conceal developments that even small children who failed to carry an identity card would be escorted home by the Military Police.[51]

The build-up to the invasion of France by Allied forces had begun two years earlier. The coastline around Falmouth had been intricately surveyed, with three points of embarkation for military vehicles on to landing craft identified: Tolverne and Turnaware on the River Fal, and Polgwidden Cove on the Helford. By spring of 1944 preparations at the latter had been completed, with components for Mulberry Quays stored in the river's upper reaches away from prying eyes, and a water supply pipe installed across miles of open countryside. More noticeable to civilians were a new access road across the fields above Helford Passage, an embarkation hard across the beach, and the widened lane towards Mawnan Smith intended to allow passage of giant machines of war.

Those who left on 3 June from what has become better known as Trebah Beach were members of the US 29th Infantry Division. These officers and men of the 116th Infantry Regiment who had camped for the preceding nights in the shelter of woodlands around Trebah and Durgan would be amongst those worst affected by the carnage of Omaha Beach. The US 1st and 29th Divisions collectively suffered around 2,000 casualties, many of whom had last stood upon friendly territory at Polgwidden Cove. Just as the war claimed so many of their lives, so the river has claimed what they left behind – little remains of the concrete slipways and access road once pounded by tanks and boots, the former eroded by relentless winter waves, the latter covered by encroaching trees and shrubs.

The second half of the twentieth century was not especially kind to the natural inhabitants of the river. Such a delicate environment was always going to be vulnerable to human pressure, no matter how inadvertent. Precious eel-grass beds were dramatically reduced through the anchoring of recreational boats; fragile intertidal silt and sand habitats were ravaged by the over-exuberant extraction of cockles; and certain antifouling paints for boats had all-but rendered the once flourishing dog whelk extinct. Similarly, while the waters of the Helford were, relatively speaking, still clean, many of its tributaries had seen a fall in their quality through slurry, silage and other agricultural effluents that, however slight, had implications for the fragile biota.

In the period between the end of the Second World War and the final decade of the twentieth century many species were lost. The cup and saucer limpet (*Calyptraea chinensis*), sea cucumber, (*Labidoplax digitata*) and peacock worm (*Sabella penipilli*), had all vanished from where they had once been abundant. At Gillan Creek, formerly plentiful sea potato urchins (*Echinocardium cordatum*), and various species of razorfish were clinging to survival, while the sedimentation of parts of the river's upper reaches, often precipitated by the establishment of alien plant species, was threatening to even change the ancient topography.[52]

Were it not for the determination of those who cared deeply for the river and its humble natural inhabitants the decline might never have been fully arrested. By the dawning of the twenty-first century their efforts had proved pivotal, with some species recovering entirely and the collapse of others prevented and given hope. Eelgrass beds were expanding once again, and with them a habitat for juvenile fish of numerous species.[53]

However, without its surrounding landscape the river would not be the place of wonder it is. We overlook the welfare of the Helford's woodlands, fields, meadows, upland fringes and freshwater tributaries at our peril. The three distinct geological realms – granite to the north, slate beneath, and ophiolite complex to the south – underpin a range of diverse ecosystems in remarkably close proximity to one another. Upon the shortest of walks it is usual to encounter a miscellany of wild flowers, shrubs and trees that themselves sustain innumerable invertebrate species. Their names and peculiarities would fill these pages many times over, but their existence is invariably overlooked by most passing through their territories.

The question, therefore, is what of their future? This, of course, depends to some extent upon how gently generations yet to be born tread upon the shores, traverse the waters, and manage the land. There is much to be optimistic about in this regard. And yet change beyond the control of the Helford's caring custodians is assured. It is merely the challenge of ensuring a transition during which plants and animals might adapt that is important. It is in protecting those very ecosystems that we give hope for the time to come as the Helford grows. And grow it will.

Irrespective of the certain increase to sea levels resulting from man-made climate change, the river has yet to reach its limit. It is still in its youth. Although we know not how future layers of sediment or human interference will change the course of its channels, the warm interglacial period within which we live will ensure an inexorable rise overall. Another 1,000 years will see existing branches penetrating yet further inland, while new ones will be created. The descendants of the hallowed wild oaks of Merthen, Tremayne and Calamansack will hopefully still thrive by the water's edge, but some of their existing territory will undoubtedly have been lost. Let us hope that our own descendants have the same life-affirming opportunity to rest within them – to escape *their* present – as some of us have been afforded.

Yet in due course the Helford will ebb away. That the climate will once again cool is inevitable, and so too is a return to a river valley through which chill waters flow out into an ever-receding ocean. Such a time might be 10,000 years away, or perhaps 100,000. And then it too will end, a new estuary born within the footprint of our own. Pioneers, human or otherwise, will return and lay claim to this riverine reincarnation. It will have a new name, and new stories will unfold. Perhaps they will be as extraordinary as those of the last five million tides.

ACKNOWLEDGEMENTS

Many have contributed to the creation of *Five Million Tides*, some without even realising it. On occasions it can be the simplest kindness that makes the author's travails so much easier, and it is so often the case that those with the least have given the most.

A great many of those I would like to thank personally are, alas, no longer with us. The late Anthony Rogers of Carwinion was an exceptionally generous man whose snippets of knowledge inspired further investigation. Similarly the journalist Alan Symons – known to many older local residents as *Trelawney* – provided so much detail about the river during the Second World War. The latter would no doubt be pleased to know that the little boat in which he used to explore the Helford continues to be used by the author.

Others no longer with us but to whom I owe a debt of gratitude include Arthur Eva of Helford Passage for his sage advice, while Larry McCabe of Helford and Percy Randlesome of Mawnan provided inspiring anecdotes long before this book was ever conceived. Another posthumous thank you must also go to Stella Jackson and Pat Crisp, who helped to make me so very welcome in my first weeks living by the river as a child.

Of course, many books depend upon evidence within the works of those who have lived before, and *Five Million Tides* is no exception as the reference section confirms. I would very much like to shake the hands of old Cornish antiquaries such as William Borlase and the Rev. Richard Polwhele, but it is Charles Henderson who deserves the greatest credit. His body now lies far from the river in the pretty Cimitero Acattolico in Rome, close to the mortal remains of John Keats and Percy Bysshe Shelley.

Advice and assistance has been provided by a great many people, including Anna Tyacke and Sophie Meyer of the Royal Cornwall Museum, Dr Rowan Whimster MBE, and James Gossip and Andy Jones of the Cornwall Archaeological Unit. The enlightening opinions of members of the Meneage Archaeological Group are also greatly appreciated by the author.

Many local landowners kindly allowed me on to their property as part of my research, not least Chris Kessell who very sadly passed away as this book neared its completion. Others include Rex Sadler MBE, James Lyall, Edward and Ann Benney, James and Andrew Benney, Brian and Sarah Kessell, and Tessa Phipps. Those whose specialist knowledge has proved invaluable include Nigel Cook (trees and the Helford River woodlands); Mark Milburn (shipwrecks); and the wonderful Sylvia King (everything). Outstanding practical help with the text of the book was provided by Rachel Walker and Elma Martin, while several photographs were very kindly supplied by Annette McTavish of Helston Museum. Thanks for images and other acts of generosity are also due to Don Garman of Constantine Museum, Gaye Woods, David Barnicoat, Tamsin Hennah, Jo Penn, Roger and Annie Trevaskis, the National Maritime Museum Cornwall, and James Ward, Rachel Ponting and Mandy Caine of the Devon Archives and Local Studies Service. Mention should also be made of two old friends, Matt Pengelly and Julian Good, with whom I spent so many happy hours exploring the river (and delights of the Shipwrights Arms) all those years ago.

My sincere gratitude goes to Sir Tim Rice for providing a foreword, and to Nicola Guy who believed that this was a story worth investing ink in. Most of all, however, I am indebted to my family. My mother and father, Susan and Peter Boulton, have supported me in every endeavour I have ever undertaken, this included, and I could not have wished for more loving and supportive parents. And as for my wife and kindred spirit, Sally, there are few words that would do justice to my appreciation. Thank you.

NOTES

Preface

1   Henderson, Charles, and Gilbert Hunter Doble, *A History of the Parish of Constantine in Cornwall:* Compiled from Original Sources by Charles Henderson; Edited by the Rev. G.H. Doble. Royal Institution of Cornwall, 1937. p. 2.

Introduction

1   Vyvyan, C.C., *The Helford River* (Dyllansow Truran, Truro, 1986) p. 38.
2   Du Maurier, Daphne, *Frenchman's Creek* (Victor Gollancz, 1941).
3   Bannister, John, *A Glossary of Cornish Names, Ancient and Modern* (Williams and Norgate, 1871) p. 183.
4   Padel, Oliver. *Cornish Place-name Elements* (1985).
5   *Western Morning News*, 23 August 1905.
6   Rackham, Oliver. *The Helford River Woods: a report on their history, ecology, and conservation* (Botany School, Cambridge, 1987) p. 1.
7   Folliott-Stokes, A.G., *The Cornish Coast and Moors.* (Greening and Co., 1913) p. 292.

1 Rise

1   *Transactions of the Royal Geological Society of Cornwall: Volume the Fourth* (T. Vigurs, 1832) pp. 481–483.
2   *The Cornishman*, 3 December, 1896.
3   French, C.N. *The Submerged Forest Palaeosols of Cornwall* (Geoscience in South West England, 9, pp. 365–369.

4   Flett, J.S. & Hill, J.B., *Geology of the Lizard and Meneage*, 1912.

5   Ashton, Nick, Simon G. Lewis, Isabelle De Groote, Sarah M. Duffy, Martin Bates, Richard Bates, Peter Hoare et al., 'Hominin footprints from early Pleistocene deposits at Happisburgh, UK'. *PLoS* One 9, No. 2 (2014): e88329.

6   Simon A. Parfitt, Rene W. Barendregt, Marzia Breda, Ian Candy, Matthew J. Collins et al., 'The earliest record of human activity in northern Europe'. (*Nature* 438, 1008–1012) 15 December 2005.

7   Jacobi R.M, Higham T.F.G., 'The 'Red Lady' ages gracefully: New ultrafiltration AMS determinations from Paviland'. (*Journal of Human Evolution*, Elsevier). 2008; 55. pp. 898–907.

8   Aldhouse-Green, Stephen, Rick Peterson, and Elizabeth Walker, *Neanderthals in Wales: Pontnewydd and the Elwy Valley Caves*. Oxbow Books, 2012.

9   Wymer, John, *The Lower Palaeolithic Occupation of Britain*. (Wessex Archaeology, 1999) p. 188.

10 Polwhele, Richard, *Traditions and Recollections: Domestic, Clerical and Literary*, Vol. 1. (John Nichols & Son, 1826) p. 381.

11 De Luc J.A., *Geological Travels* Vol. III. 1811. p. 319.

12 British Geological Survey.

13 *The Cornishman*, 7 April 1898.

14 Baring-Gould, Sabine, *Richard Cable: The Lightshipman* (1888).

15 Wunsch, E.A., 'The Problem of the Lizard Rocks'. *Journal of the Royal Institution of Cornwall*, Vol. IX, 1889. pp. 353–357.

16 *Sandeman, H.A., Clark, A.H., Styles, M.T., Scott, D.J., Malpas, J.G. & Farrar, E., 'Geochemistry and U-Pb and 40Ar-39Ar geochronology of the Man of War Gneiss, Lizard Complex, SW England: pre-Hercynian arc-type crust with a Sudeten Iberian connection'. Journal of the Geological Society, London, 1997.*

17 Bates, Robin and Scolding, Bill, *Beneath the Skin of The Lizard. Seven Coastal Walks Exploring the Geology of the Lizard Peninsula*. (Cornwall County Council, 2000) p. 17.

18 De la Beche, H.T., *Report on the Geology of Cornwall, Devon and West Somerset*. (Longman, Orme, Brown, Green and Longmans, 1839) p. 432.

19 Shepperd, Peggy, *The Story of Port Navas* (second edition).'The Geological Setting of Port Navas' by Peter Scott. (Hemingfold Press, 2016) p. 17.

20 Lericolais, G., Auffret, J.-P. and Bourillet, J.-F., 'The Quaternary Channel River: seismic stratigraphy of its palaeo-valleys and deeps'. *J. Quaternary Sci.*, 2003, 18: [pp. ?] 245–260. doi:10.1002/jqs.759.

21 Massey, Anthony Carl, *Holocene Sea-level Changes Along the Channel Coast of South-west England. University of Plymouth, 2004*.

22 Bernhard Weninger et al., 'The catastrophic final flooding of Doggerland by the Storegga Slide tsunami', *Documenta Praehistorica* XXXV, 2008.

23 Gover, J.E.B., 1948, *Place-Names of Cornwall*, p. 557.

24 Harris, Daphne, *Poldowrian, St Keverne: A Beaker Mound of the Gabbro of the Lizard Peninsula* (Cornish Archaeology No. 18, Cornwall Archaeological Society, 1979) pp. 13–14.

25 Bayliss, A., Hedges R., Otlet, R., Switsur, R., and Walker, J., *Radiocarbon Dates from Samples Funded by English Heritage between 1981 and 1988* (English Heritage, 2012) pp. 225–226.

26 Ibid, p. 315.

27 Cornwall and Scilly HER, reference number 13026.

28 Berridge, Peter and Roberts, Alison, 'The Mesolithic Period in Cornwall'. (*Cornish Archaeology* No. 25, Cornwall Archaeological Society, 1986) p. 27.

29 Schulting, Rick J. and Richards, Michael P., 'Finding the coastal Mesolithic in southwest Britain: AMS dates and stable isotope results on human remains from Caldey Island, South Wales'. (*Antiquity*, Vol. 76, Issue 294) pp. 1011–1025.

30 Eden, Philip, *The Daily Telegraph Book of the Weather* (Continuum, 2003) pp. 13–15.

2 Waves

1   Rackham, Oliver, *The History of the Countryside* (1986).

2   Rackham, Oliver, *The Helford River Woods, a Report on their History, Ecology and Conservation*. (1987) pp. 30.

3   Portable Antiquities Scheme, CORN-852A51.

4   Berridge, Peter, 'A Mesolithic Flint Adze from the Lizard'. *Cornish Archaeology* 21, 1982.

5   Todd, Malcolm, *The South West to 1000 AD*. (Longman, 1987) p. 56.

6   McQuade, M., & O'Donnell, L. (2007). 'Late Mesolithic fish traps from the Liffey estuary, Dublin, Ireland'. *Antiquity*, 81(313) pp. 569–584.

7   Clark, Grahame. *Excavations at Star Carr: An Early Mesolithic site at Seamer near Scarborough, Yorkshire*. CUP Archive, 1954.

8   Strasser, Thomas F. et al., 'Stone Age seafaring in the Mediterranean: evidence from the Plakias region for Lower Palaeolithic and Mesolithic habitation of Crete'. *Hesperia* (2010): pp. 145–190.

9   Jacobi, Roger M., *Aspects of the Mesolithic Age in Great Britain. The Mesolithic in Europe* (1973): pp. 237–265.

10 Pryor, Francis, *The Making of the British Landscape* (Penguin, 2011). p. 27.

11 Childe, Gordon V., *The Prehistory of Scotland* (Kegan Paul, Trench, Trubner and Co., Ltd, 1935) p. 17.

12 Cherry, John F., and Thomas P. Leppard, 'Experimental archaeology and the earliest seagoing: the limitations of inference'. *World Archaeology* 47.5 (2015): pp. 740–755.

13 Spinney, Laura, 'Archaeology: the lost world'. *Nature News* 454.7201 (2008): pp. 151–153.

14 Anderson-Whymark, Hugo, Duncan Garrow, and Fraser Sturt, 'Microliths and maritime mobility: a continental European-style Late Mesolithic flint assemblage from the Isles of Scilly'. *Antiquity* 89.346 (2015): pp. 954–971.

15 Rankine, W., 'Pebbles of Non-Local Rock from Mesolithic Chipping Floors'. *Proceedings of the Prehistoric Society*, *15*, 1949, pp. 193–194. doi:10.1017/S0079497X00019319.

16 Davis, P.R., 'Some navigational considerations of pre-medieval trade between Cornwall and North-West Europe'. (*Cornish Archaeology* 36, 1997) p. 130.

17 Jacobi, Roger M., 'Britain inside and outside Mesolithic Europe'. *Proceedings of the Prehistoric Society*. Vol. 42. Cambridge University Press, 1976.

18 McGrail, Sean, *Early Ships and Seafaring: European Water Transport* (Pen and Sword, 2014) p. 96.

19 Cunliffe, Barry, *Britain Begins*. (Oxford University Press, 2013) p. 59.

20 Roberts, Gordon, Silvia Gonzalez, and David Huddart. 'Intertidal Holocene footprints and their archaeological significance'. *Antiquity* 70.269 (1996): pp. 647–651.

21 Pryor, Francis, *Britain BC. Life in Britain and Ireland before the Romans* (Harper Perennial, 2004) p. 82.

22 Maroo, S., and D.W.Yalden, 'The Mesolithic mammal fauna of Great Britain'. *Mammal Review* 30.3-4 (2000): pp. 243–248.

23 Cristiani, Emanuela, and Dušan Borić, '8500-year-old Late Mesolithic garment embroidery from Vlasac (Serbia): Technological, use-wear and residue analyses'. *Journal of Archaeological Science* 39.11 (2012): pp. 3450–3469.

24 Borlase, William, *Observations on the Antiquities Historical and Monumental of the County of Cornwall*. 1754. p. 166.

25 Letter from 'JGS', *Royal Cornwall Gazette*, 18 March 1869.

26 Daniel, John Jeremiah, *A Compendium of the History of Cornwall*. (Netherton and Worth, 1880) p. 281.

27 Warner, Richard, *A Tour through Cornwall in the Autumn of 1808* (Wilkie and Robinson, 1809) p. 121.

28 Borlase, William Copeland. *Naenia Cornubiae* (Longmans, Green, Reader and Dyer. London. 1872) p. 96.

29 William Borlase, *Antiquities Historical and Monumental of the County of Cornwall*. Bowyer and Nichols, London, 1769.

30 Blight, J.T., *Archaeologica Cambrensis*. Vol.VIII, Third Series (J. Russell Smith). App. 1, p. 40.

31 Hayman, Richard, *Riddles in Stone: Myths, Archaeology, and the Ancient Britons* (Hambledon Press, 1997) p. 21.

32 Henderson, Charles, and Gilbert Hunter Doble, *A History of the Parish of Constantine in Cornwall:* Compiled from Original Sources by Charles Henderson; Edited by the Rev. G.H. Doble. Royal Institution of Cornwall, 1937. p. 10.

33 Portable Antiquities Scheme, Record: 813237.

34 Ibid, record: 813234.

35 Ibid, record: 813238.

36 Chan, Benjamin, Sarah Viner, Mike Parker Pearson, Umberto Albarella, and Rob Ixer, 'Resourcing Stonehenge: patterns of human, animal and goods mobility in the late Neolithic'. Moving on in Neolithic Studies: *Understanding Mobile Lives* [is this journal name – italicise](2016): pp. 28–44.

37 Fox, Aileen, *Ancient Peoples and Places South West England* (Thames and Hudson, London, 1964)

38 Pryor, Francis. Ibid, p. 182.

39 Cornwall and Scilly HER, record number 24470.

40 Ibid, record number 164221.

41 Historic England, *Prehistoric Feld System, Hut Circle and Middens on Southern Annet.* List entry number: 1014997

42 Richards, Michael P., Schulting, Rick J., Hedges, Robert E.M., 'Sharp shift in diet at onset of Neolithic'. *Nature*; London 425.6956 (25 September 2003) p. 366.

43 Bonsall, Clive, et al., 'Climate change and the adoption of agriculture in north-west Europe'. *European Journal of Archaeology* 5.1 (2002) pp. 9–23.

44 Time Team, Channel 4, *Iron Age Market*. Video Text Communications Ltd, 2001.

45 Johns, Charles, *Trevaney Farm, High Cross, Constantine. Field Visit* (Cornwall Archaeological Unit, 1999).

46 Borlase, William Copeland, *Ibid*, pp. 278–280.

47 Cornwall and Scilly HER, record number 10999.

48 *West Briton*, 10 October 1851. Letter.

49 Polwhele, Richard, *The History of Cornwall,* Vol. 1 (Law and Whittaker, 1816) p. 141.

50 Cornwall and Scilly HER, record number 24460.

51 Ibid, record number 51795.

52 Ibid, record number 51802.

53 Henderson, Charles, *Notebooks of Parochial Antiquities, Vol. 4 (unpublished, 1914) p. 429.*

54 Cornwall and Scilly HER, record numbers 24870, 51739, 51732, and 51741.

55 Unlocking Our Coastal Heritage Project, *A Bronze Age Barrow, Godrevy Headland, Godrevy, Cornwall* (2012–13).

56 Jones, A., Marley, J., Quinnell, H., Hartgroves, S., Evershed, R., Lawson-Jones, A., Taylor, R., 'On the Beach: New Discoveries at Harlyn Bay, Cornwall'. *Proceedings of the Prehistoric Society*, 77, 2011, pp. 89–109.

57 Andy Jones (CAU) pers. comm.

58 Haak, W., Balanovsky, O., Sanchez, J.J., Koshel, S., Zaporozhchenko, V., Adler, C.J., Der Sarkissian, C.S., Brandt, G., Schwarz, C., Nicklisch, N. and Dresely, V., 'Ancient DNA from European early Neolithic farmers reveals their near eastern affinities'. *PLoS Biology*, 8(11), 2011, p.e1000536.

59 Care, Verna, 'The collection and distribution of lithic materials during the Mesolithic and Neolithic periods in southern England'. *Oxford Journal of Archaeology* 1, No. 3 (1982): pp. 269–285.

60 Cassidy, Lara M., et al., 'Neolithic and Bronze Age migration to Ireland and establishment of the insular Atlantic genome'. *Proceedings of the National Academy of Sciences* 113.2 (2016): pp. 368–373.

61 Olalde, Iñigo, et al., *The Beaker phenomenon and the genomic transformation of Northwest Europe.* bioRxiv (2017): pp. 1–28.

62 Kristiansen, K., 'The Bronze Age expansion of Indo–European languages: an archaeological model'. *Becoming European. The Transformation of Third Millennium Northern and Western Europe.* Oxbow Books. Oxford (2012): pp. 165–181.

63 Gibbons, Ann, 'Thousands of horsemen may have swept into Bronze Age Europe, transforming the local population'. *Science* (February 2017).

64 Thomas, Charles, *Studies in Cornish Folklore No. 2: The Sacrifice.* Institute of Archaeology, University of London (1952) pp. 52–53.

65 Nowakowski, Jacqueline A., *Leaving home in the Cornish Bronze Age: Insights into Planned Abandonment Processes.* Bronze Age landscapes: tradition and transformation (2001): pp. 139–48.

66 Johns, Charlie and Gossip, James, *Evaluation of a Multi-Period Prehistoric Site and Fogou at Boden Vean, St Anthony-in-Meneage, Cornwall* (2009). Cornwall Council Historic Environment Service.

67 Jones, A., Gossip, J. and Quinnell, H., (2015). *Settlement and Metalworking in the Middle Bronze Age and Beyond: New evidence from Tremough, Cornwall.* Cornwall Council Historic Environment Service.

68 Smith, G. and Harris, D., 'The Excavation of Mesolithic, Neolithic and Bronze Age settlements at Poldowrian, St Keverne, 1980'. *Cornish Archaeology* 21, 1982.

69 Cornwall and Scilly HER, record numbers MCO57025, 24478, 24479, 24598, and 24480.

3 Ancient Mariners

1 Ehser, Anja, Gregor Borg, and Ernst Pernicka, 'Provenance of the gold of the Early Bronze Age Nebra Sky Disk, central Germany: geochemical characterization of natural gold from Cornwall'. *European Journal of Mineralogy* 23.6 (2011): pp. 895–910.

2 Borlase, William, *The Natural History of Cornwall*, 1758. p. 214.

3 De la Beche, Thomas, *Report on the Geology of Cornwall, Devon, and West Somerset* (Longman, Orme, Brown, Green, and Longmans, 1839) p. 613.

4 Morteani, Giulio, and Jeremy P. Northover, eds, *Prehistoric gold in Europe: mines, metallurgy and manufacture.* Vol. 28. Springer Science & Business Media, 2013.

5 *The World's Work*, Vol. 10. (W. Heinemann, 1907) p. 505.

6 Camm, G. Simon, *Gold in the Counties of Cornwall and Devon.* (Cornish Hillside Publ., 1995) pp. 37–42.

7 Standish, Christopher D., et al., 'A non-local source of Irish Chalcolithic and Early Bronze Age gold'. *Proceedings of the Prehistoric Society.* Vol. 81. Cambridge University Press, 2015.

8 'Cornwall was scene of prehistoric gold rush, says new research'. *Independent.* 4 June 2015.

9 *Ling, Johan; Stos-Gale, Zofia; Grandin, Lena; Hjärthner-Holdar, Eva; Persson, Per-Olof (2014), 'Moving metals II provenancing Scandinavian Bronze Age artefacts'. Journal of Archeological Science, 41: pp. 106–132.*

10 Strabo, *Geography.* Book III, Chapter 5.

11 Cunliffe, Barry, 'Ictis: is it here?' *Oxford Journal of Archaeology* 2.1 (1983) pp. 123–126.

12 Caesar, Gaius Julius, *'De Bello Gallico' and Other Commentaries.* Book III, XIII.

13 British Geological Survey.

14 Historic England, list entry number: 1021409. 'Mortar outcrop at Trenear, 9m north east of Poldark Mine entrance'.

15 Reynolds, Ann, *Helford Estuary Historic Audit* (Cornwall Archaeological Unit, 2000) pp. 26–7.

16 Rogers, J. Jope, Romano–British, or Late Celtic, Remains at Trelan Bahow, St Keverne, Cornwall. *Archaeological Journal*, 30, 1873, pp. 267–272.

17 Joy, Jody, *Iron Age Mirrors: a Biographical Approach* (Archaeopress, 2010).

18 Whimster, Rowan Pirrie, *Burial Practices in Iron Age Britain.* Diss. Durham University, 1979.

19 Waldman, Carl and Mason, Catherine. *Encyclopedia of European Peoples* (Facts on File, 2006) p. 181.

20 Rackham, Oliver. *The Helford River Woods: A Report on their History, Ecology, and Conservation* (Botany School, Cambridge, 1987) p. 7.

21 Quinnell, Henrietta, 'Cornwall during the Iron Age and the Roman Period'. *Cornish Archaeology* 25 (1986): pp. 111–131.

22 Cornwall & Scilly HER, record No. 24484.

23 Gossip, James, *The Evaluation of a Multi-Period Prehistoric Site and Fogou at Boden Vean, St Anthony-in-Meneage, Cornwall, 2003.*

24 Amesbury, Matthew J., Dan J. Charman, Ralph M. Fyfe, Peter G. Langdon, and Steve West, 'Bronze Age upland settlement decline in southwest England: testing the climate change hypothesis'. *Journal of Archaeological Science* 35, no. 1 (2008): pp. 87–98.

25 Armit, Ian, Graeme T. Swindles, Katharina Becker, Gill Plunkett, and Maarten Blaauw, 'Rapid climate change did not cause population collapse at the end of the European Bronze Age'. Proceedings of the National Academy of Sciences 111, No. 48 (2014): 17045–17049.

26 Agricultural Land Classification Map South West Region (ALC006). Natural England, 24 August 2010.

27 Wilkes, Eileen, *Iron Age Maritime Nodes on the English Channel Coast: An Investigation into the Location, Nature and Context of Early Ports and Harbours.* Diss. Bournemouth University, 2004.

28 Wood, Imogen, *Changing the Fabric of Life in Post-Roman and Early Nedieval Cornwall: An Investigation into Social Change Through Petrographic Analysis*, 2011.

29 Coleman-Smith, R., 'Experiments in ancient bonfire-fired pottery'. (*Ceramic Review*, 12) 1971, pp. 6–7.

30 Peacock, D.P.S., 'Neolithic pottery production in Cornwall'. *Antiquity* 43.170 (1969): p. 145.

31 Jones, A.M. and Reed, S.J., 'By land, sea and air: an Early Neolithic pit group at Portscatho, Cornwall, and consideration of coastal activity during the Neolithic'. *Cornish Archaeology*, 45, 2006, pp. 1–30.

32 Harrad, L., 'Gabbroic clay sources in Cornwall: a petrographic study of prehistoric pottery and clay samples'. *Oxford Journal of Archaeology*, 23(3), 2004, pp. 271–286.

33 Quinnell, Henrietta, 1987. 'Cornish gabbroic pottery: the development of a hypothesis'. *Cornish Archaeology*, 26, pp. 7–12.

34 Cunliffe, Barry, *Britain Begins* (Oxford University Press, 2013) p. 173

35 Sharples, N.M., *Maiden Castle: Excavations and Field Survey 1985-6.* (English Heritage, 1991).

36 Nowakowski, Jacqueline. 'Appraising the bigger picture – Cornish Iron Age and Romano–British lives and settlements 25 years on'. (*Cornish Archaeology* 50, 2011) pp. 241–261.

37 Harris, Daphne & Johnson, Nicholas, 'Carlidnack Round, Mawnan' (*Cornish Archaeology* 15, 1976) pp. 73–76.

38 Henderson, Jon. *The Atlantic Iron Age: Settlement and Identity in the First Millennium BC.* (Routledge, 2007).

39 Dowson, Edith, 'Medieval Coin Hoard from Mawnan Parish' (*Cornish Archaeology* 10, 1971) pp. 111–2

40 *Book of Mawnan* (Halsgrove, 2002) p. 24.

41 Gover, J.E.B., *The Place Names of Cornwall* (1948) p. 520.

42 *Iron Age Market.* Time Team Series 9, Episode 7. (VideoText Communications, 2001).

43 GSB Prospection. Caer Vallack and Gear Farm: geophysical survey. 2001.

44 Polwhele, Richard. *The History of Cornwall, Civil, Military, Religious* ... Vol. I (Law and Whittaker, London, 1816) p. 125.

45 Ibid.

46 BBC News. 'North Wales Hillfort test of Iron Age communication'. 20 March 2011.

47 Brooks, R.T., 'The Excavation of The Rumps Cliff Castle, St Minver, Cornwall'. *Cornish Archaeology* 13, 1974.

48 Smith, George, 'Excavation of the Iron Age Cliff Promontory Fort and of Mesolithic and Neolithic Flint Working Areas at Penhale Point, Holywell Bay, near Newquay, 1983'. *Cornish Archaeology* 27, 1988.

49 'The Fogou, or Cave at Halligey, Trelowarren, illustrated by the late Sir R.R. Vyvyan, Bart., and Mr J.T. Blight. Edited with introductory accounts and notes by the Rev. W. Iago, B.A'. *Journal of the Royal Institution of Cornwall*, Vol. 8. 1883–1885 (published 1886).

50 Grigson, Jeffrey, *English Excursions* (Country Life, 1960).

51 MacLean, Rachel, 'The fogou: an investigation of function'. *Cornish Archaeology* 31, 1992. pp. 41–64.

52 Ibid.

53 Cathryn Conder, Meneage Archaeology Group. pers. comm.

54 Polwhele, Richard, Ibid, p. 129.

55 Gordon Fielder, Meneage Archaeology Group. pers. comm.

56 Clark, E.V., *Cornish Fogous* (1961) pp. 45–49.

57 Gossip, James, '*The Evaluation of a Multi-Period Prehistoric Site and Fogou at Boden Vean, St Anthony-in-Meneage, Cornwall, 2003*'. *Cornish Archaeology 52* (2013).

58 Gossip, James, pers. comm.

59 Saunders, C., 'The excavations at Grambla, Wendron 1972: interim report'. *Cornish Archaeology* 11 (1972) pp. 50–52.

60 Henderson, Charles, and Gilbert Hunter Doble, *A History of the Parish of Constantine in Cornwall:* Compiled from Original Sources by Charles Henderson; Edited by the Rev. G.H. Doble. Royal Institution of Cornwall, 1937. pp. 133–134.

61 Historic England, list entry number: 1006659. 'Three rectangular defended enclosures 460m north east of Merthen Manor'.

62 David, A.E.U., Ancient Monuments Geophysics Section. Geophysics: Merthen, 1980. (Historic England).

63 Dudley, D., *Sub-Rectangular Earthworks with Rounded Corners.* Proc West Cornwall Fld Club 1.2 (1954): pp. 54–58.

64 Crawford, Osbert Guy Stanhope, *Topography of Roman Scotland: North of the Antonine Wall.* (Cambridge University Press, 2011) p. 2.

65 Historic England, list entry number: 1007273. 'Roman fort called 'Nanstallon Roman fort' 135m south west of Tregear'.

66 Todd, Malcolm (Ed.), *A Companion to Roman Britain* (Blackwell, 2004) p. 55.

67 Jones, Rebecca H., *Roman Camps in Britain* (Amberley Publishing Limited, 2012).

68 Historic England, list entry number: 1017637. 'Roman milestone at Mynheer Farm'.

69 Harvey, D., 'The Double Fort at Merthen, Constantine'. *Cornish Archaeology* 9 (1970): pp. 103–106.

70 Henderson, Charles, and Gilbert Hunter Doble, *A History of the Parish of Constantine in Cornwall:* Compiled from Original Sources by Charles Henderson; Edited by the Rev. G.H. *Doble.* Royal Institution of Cornwall, 1937 p. 14.

71 Historic England, list Entry Number 1004428. Iron Age Defended Settlement 250m north of Higher Trenower.

72 Cornwall & Scilly HER, record No. 51379.

73 Henwood, William Jory, 'Observations on the Detrital Tin-ore of Cornwall' (*Journal of the Royal Institution of Cornwall*, 1873) p. 15.

74 Defoe, Daniel, *A Tour Thro' the Whole Island of Great Britain* (London, 1742) pp. 349–350.

75 Penhallurick, Roger David, *Ancient and Early Medieval Coins from Cornwall & Scilly* (No. 45. Royal Numismatic Society, 2009) p. 36.

76 Polwhele, Richard, *The History of Cornwall, Civil, Military, Religious, Architectural, Agricultural, Commercial, Biographical, and Miscellaneous.* Vol. III. pp. 122–123.

77 Borlase, William, *Antiquities, Historical and Monumental, of the County of Cornwall* (1769) p.312.

78 MacLauchlan, Henry, *Manors of Tybesta and Truro.* (Royal Institution of Cornwall, unknown publication date) p. 15.

79 Fitzpatrick-Matthews, Keith. *Britannia in the Ravenna Cosmography: A Reassessment.* Academia. edu. (2015).

80 Pryce, William, *Archaeologia Cornu-Britannica: Or, an Essay to Preserve the*

Ancient Cornish Language: Containing the Rudiments of that Dialect in a Cornish Grammar and Cornish-English Vocabulary. Cruttwell, 1790.

81 Glendinning, D., *Romano–British Place-Names and River-Names in the Ravenna Cosmography and the Geography of Ptolemy*, 2015.

82 Borlase, William, Ibid, p. 301.

83 Williams, Stephen, *An Attempt to Examine the Barrows in Cornwall. Philosophical Transactions* (Royal Society, 1744) p. 480.

84 Penaluna, William, *An Historical Survey of the County of Cornwall* (1838) p. 57.

85 Cummings, Rev. A.H., *The Churches and Antiquities of Gunwalloe and Cury in the Lizard District* (E. Marlborough & Co., London. W. Lake, Truro. 1875) pp. 98–101.

86 Rogers, J.J., *Archaeological Journal*, Vol. 22 (1865) p. 332.

87 Cornwall & Scilly HER, record numbers: 24857 & 24687.

88 Portable Antiquities Scheme, record No. CORN-3A58B3.

89 Ibid, record No. CORN-D87E79.

90 Unknown author. Meudon document.

91 Hammersen, Lauren Alexandra Michelle, *The Control of Tin in Southwestern Britain from the First Century AD to the Late Third Century AD* (North Carolina State University Thesis, 2007) pp. 71–98.

92 *The Archaeological Journal*, Vol. 22 (London, 1865) p. 333.

93 Borlase, William, *Antiquities, Historical and Monumental, of the County of Cornwall* (1769).

94 Hencken, Hugh O'Neill, *The Archaeology of Cornwall and Scilly*. Methuen & Co. Ltd (1932) p. 201.

95 Collingwood, Robin George, 'Roman milestones in Cornwall'. *The Antiquaries Journal* 4.2 (1924): pp. 101–112.

96 Eutropius, *Abridgment of Roman History.* Translated, with notes, by the Rev. John Selby Watson. London: Henry G. Bohn, York Street, Covent Garden (1853) Book IX. 21.

97 Johnson, Flint F., *The British Heroic Age: A History, 367–664.* (McFarland & Co Inc, 2016) pp. 66–70.

98 Cunliffe, Barry, *Britain Begins*. Oxford University Press, (2013) p. 389.

99 Bromwich, Rachel (editor and translator) (1978), *Trioedd Ynys Prydein: The Welsh Triads*, second ed. Cardiff: University of Wales Press.

100 Royal Cornwall Polytechnic Society, 79th Annual Report (Vol. 2, Part I, 1912) p. 160.

101 Hooke, Della, *Pre-conquest Charter-bounds in Devon and Cornwall* (Boydell, 1994) p. 37.

4 Holy Waters

1   Henderson, Charles, *Original Documents and Personal Investigations*, St Keverne Local History Society.

2   Tangye, Michael, 'Lestowder, St Keverne: a previously unidentified stronghold'. *Cornish Archaeology* 34 (1995).

3   Mothersole, Jessie, *The Isles of Scilly: Their Story, their Folk & their Flowers*, 1911.

4   Henderson, Charles, and Gilbert Hunter Doble, *A History of the Parish of Constantine in Cornwall:* Compiled from Original Sources by Charles Henderson; Edited by the Rev. G.H. Doble. Royal Institution of Cornwall, 1937. pp. 41–43.

5   Thomas, Charles, *The Early Christian Archaeology of North Britain* (Oxford University Press, 1971) pp. 48–68.

6   Cornwall & Scilly Historic Environment Record, HER No. 24556.10.

7   Preston-Jones, A., *Decoding Cornish Churchyards*. In N. Edwards and A. Lane (eds), 1992.

8   Turner, Sam, *Medieval Devon and Cornwall: Shaping an Ancient Countryside* (Windgather Press, 2006) pp. 30–31.

9   Gover, John Eric Bruce, *The Place Names of Cornwall*. (1948) p. 541.

10 Pearce, Susan M., *The Kingdom of Dumnonia: Studies in History and Tradition in Western Britain* (Pad stow, 1978) p. 178,

11 *West Briton and Cornwall Advertiser*, 29 August 1889.

12 Norden, John, *Speculi Britanniae* (Bateman, London, 1728) p. 49.

13 *The Monthly Magazine*, Vol. 26, p. 433.

14 *The Gentleman's Magazine*, Vol. 213, p. 21.

15 Wrenn, C.L., *Saxons and Celts in South West Britain,* Transactions of the Honourable Society of Cymmrodorion, 1959 (Llyfrgell Genedlaethol Cymru – The National Library of Wales) p. 66.

16 Hooke, Della, *Pre-Conquest Charter Bounds of Devon and Cornwall* (Boydell Press, 1994) p. 37.

17 Fletcher, J.R., *Short History of St Michael's Mount Cornwall* (1951).

18 Baring-Gould, S., Fisher, John, *The Lives of British Saints: The Saints of Wales and Cornwall and such Irish Saints as Have Dedications in Britain*. Vol. III (Honourable Society of Cymmrodorion, 1911) pp. 449–453.

19 Ibid. pp. 453–457.

20 Borlase, William Copeland, *The Age of the Saints: a Monograph of Early Christianity in Cornwall* (Joseph Pollard, Truro. 1893) p. 154.

21 Unknown author, Meudon document (undated).

22 Curnow, Frank, *History of St Keverne Church*. St Keverne History Society.

23 Orme, Nicholas, *Cornwall and the Cross: Christianity 500–1560* (Victoria County History, Phillimore and Co. Ltd, 2007) pp. 5–6.

24 Dixon, H.H., St *Anthony in Meneage: The Story of the Parish Church* (1978).

25 Lewis, Samuel., A Topographical Dictionary of England. Vol. I. (S Lewis & Co., London, 1811) p. 55.

26 Sedding, Edmund H., *Norman Architecture in Cornwall: A Handbook to Old Cornish Ecclesiastical Architecture, with Notes on Ancient Manor-Houses* (Ward & Co., London, 1909) pp. 263–264.

27 Cornwall & Scilly Historic Environment Record, HER No. 24704.

28 Hingeston-Randolph, F.C., *The Register of Thomas de Brantyngham, Bishop of Exeter* Vol. II (George Bell & Sons, London, 1906) p. 584.

29 Orme, Nicholas, *The Saints of Cornwall.* (Oxford University Press, 2000) p. 104.

30 Newton, Jill, *The Helford River* (Treleague and Century Litho, 1979) p. 35.

31 Hooke, Della, *Pre-Conquest Charter Bounds of Devon and Cornwall* (Boydell Press, 1994) pp. 47–52.

32 Orme, Nicholas, *The Saints of Cornwall.* (Oxford University Press, 2000) p. 63 & p. 184.

33 Institute Of Cornish Studies, 1987, *Place-Names Index*.

34 Henderson, Charles, *Ecclesiastical Antiquities of the 109 Parishes of West Cornwall & Ecclesiastical History of the 4 Western Hundreds, 1955–1960.*

35 Kirby, Kate, pers. comm.

36 Henderson, Charles, and Gilbert Hunter Doble, *A History of the Parish of Constantine in Cornwall:* Compiled from Original Sources by Charles Henderson; Edited by the Rev. G.H. Doble. Royal Institution of Cornwall, 1937. p. 210.

37 Historic England, list entry no. 1311376. 'Quay and adjoining waterfront walling'.

38 Henderson, Charles & Coates, Henry, *Old Cornish Bridges and Streams* (Bradford Barton, Truro, 1972) p. 96.

39 *Journal of the Royal Institution of Cornwall*, Vol. 10 (1891) p. 435.

40 Hingeston-Randolph, F.C., *The Registers of Walter Bronescombe and Peter Quivil* (George Bell & Sons, London, 1889) pp. 152–153.

41 Taylor, T., St *Michael's Mount* (Cambridge University Press, 1932) pp. 30–31.

42 Hearne, Thomas, *The Itinerary of John Leland the Antiquary.* Vol. III. (Oxford, 1769) p. 25.

43 Lyon, Rod, *Cornwall's Historical Wars: A Brief Introduction* (Cornovia Press, Sheffield, 2012) p. 19.

44 *The Book of Mawnan* (Halsgrove, 2002) p. 90.

45 Hume, David, *The History of England.* Vol. I, Part II. (1826) p. 470.

46 *Philosophical Transactions*, 1770–1776, Vol. 13. pp. 98–100.

47 Pevsner, Nikolaus and Radcliffe, Enid, *The Buildings of England: Cornwall*

(Penguin, 1970) pp. 112–113.

48 Unknown author. Meudon document.

49 Penaluna, W., *An Historical Survey of the County of Cornwall, Etc: In Two Volumes,* Vol. 1. (1838) pp. 125–126.

50 Leland, John, *Itinerary* Vol. III. (Oxford, 1711) p. 12.

51 *Journal of the Royal Institution of Cornwall,* Vol. XVI (1903–1905) p. 395.

52 Lysons, Daniel and Lysons, Samuel, *Magna Britannia,* Vol. III (London, 1814) p. 221.

53 Cornwall & Scilly Historic Environment Record, HER No. 24838.20.

54 Henderson, Charles, and Gilbert Hunter Doble. *A History of the Parish of Constantine in Cornwall:* Compiled from Original Sources by Charles Henderson; Edited by the Rev. G.H. Doble. Royal Institution of Cornwall, 1937. pp. 124–126.

55 Penaluna, W., *An Historical Survey of the County of Cornwall.* Vol. II (1838) p. 69.

56 Historic England, list Entry No. 1159172. 'Trelowarren House'.

57 Cornwall & Scilly Historic Environment Record, HER No. 24696.21.

58 Dowson, Edith, *Parochial Checklist.* Cornish Archaeology No. 5 (1966).

59 Meyrick, J., *A Pilgrim's Guide to the Holy Wells of Cornwall* (1982).

60 Gossip, James, pers. comm.

61 Langdon, Arthur G., *Old Cornish Crosses* (1896) pp. 346–347.

62 Thomas, Charles. *Cornish Archaeology,* Vol. 7 (1968) pp. 81–82.

63 Hitchins, Fortescue and Drew, Samuel (ed.) The History of Cornwall, Vol. II. (Penaluna, 1824) p. 621.

64 Henderson, Charles, and Gilbert Hunter Doble. *A History of the Parish of Constantine in Cornwall:* Compiled from Original Sources by Charles Henderson; Edited by the Rev. G.H. Doble. Royal Institution of Cornwall, 1937. p. 23.

65 Historic England, Monument No. 426946.

66 Ibid, Monument No. 427519.

67 Ibid, Monument Nos. 427295 and 427296.

68 Ibid, Monument No. 427529.

69 Harris, Chris, (Meneage Archaeology Group), pers. comm.

70 Jago, W., 'Mawgan Cross: the Inscribed Stone of the Meneage' (*Journal of the Royal Institution of Cornwall,* Vol. VIII, 1883–1885) pp. 276–284.

71 Brynmore-Jones, David, *The Welsh People* (T. Fisher Unwin, 1900) p. 17

5 Dark Currents

1 Henderson, Charles. *A History of the Parish of Constantine in Cornwall:* Compiled from Original Sources by Charles Henderson; Edited by the Rev. G.H. Doble. (Royal Institution of Cornwall, 1937) p. 210.

2 Henderson, Charles and Coates, Henry, *Old Cornish Bridges and Streams.* (D. Bradford Barton, Truro, 1972) p. 94.

3 Morgan, Rev. Thomas, *Handbook of the Origin of Place Names in Wales and Monmouthshire.* (1887) p. 72.

4 Report and Transactions of the Penzance Natural History and Antiquarian Society, 1887.

5 Wakelin, M.F., *The place-Name Helford.* Neophilologus (1978) 62: 294. [page no?]

6 Ackroyd, Peter, *Thames: Sacred River.* (Chatto & Windus, 2007) p. 23.

7 Toy, H. Spencer, *The History of Helston* (Oxford University Press, 1936) pp. 477–482.

8 Henderson, Charles, Ibid, p. 188.

9 Portable Antiquities Scheme, CORN-91073B.

10 Institute Of Cornish Studies, 1987, *Place-Names Index.*

11 *The Book of Mawnan* (Halsgrove, 2002) p. 13.

12 *The Cornish Telegraph,* 25 January 1865.

13 Jowitt, Clare. *The Culture of Piracy, 1580–1630: English Literature and Seaborne Crime* (2013).

14 Calendar of State Papers, 14 May 1636.

15 Williams, Neville, *Captains Outrageous: Seven Centuries of Piracy* (Barrie & Rockliffe, 1961) pp. 93–94.

16 Johnson, Captain Charles, *A General History of the Robberies & Murders of the Most Notorious Pirates* (Conway Maritime Press, 2002) p. 23.

17 Marsden, Philip. *The Levelling Sea: The Story of a Cornish Haven in the Days of Sail* (Harper Press, 2011) p. 138.

18 National Archives, Ref: HCA 32/2/66.

19 *The Scots Magazine,* 1 December 1780.

20 Morning Chronicle, 2 July 1803.

21 *London Courier and Evening Gazette,* 18 June 1805.

22 *Public Ledger and Daily Advertiser,* 14 May 1808.

23 *Ipswich Journal,* 23 October 1756. Extract of a letter from Falmouth, dated 18 October.

24 *Glasgow Courant,* 10 February 1746.

25 *Derby Mercury,* 3 April 1794.

26 Ibid, 27 March 1740.

27 Calendar of State Papers, Petition 3 October 1640.

28 Calendar of State Papers, 14 July 1636.

29 Ward, R., *The World of the Medieval Shipmaster: Law, Business and the Sea, c.1350–c.1450.* (Boydell & Brewer, 2009) p. 27.

30 Grigson, Geoffrey, 'Some lawless men of Old Cornwall' *Western Morning News,* 8 July 1929.

31 Stephens, William B., *The Seventeenth Century Customs Service Surveyed: William Culliford's Investigation of the Western Ports, 1682–1684.*

32 *Calendar of Treasury Papers*, Vol. 1, 1556–1696. Vol. 7: 1 January 1690–31 March 1690.

33 *Derby Mercury*, 29 March 1754.

34 *Caledonian Mercury*, 1 January 1785. Extract of a letter from Falmouth, 20 December.

35 Carter, Harry, *The Autobiography of a Cornish Smuggler.* Introduction by John B. Cornish (Gibbings & Co., London, 1900) p. 18.

36 *Sherborne Mercury*, Monday, 28 February 1791.

37 *Royal Cornwall Gazette*, Saturday, 2 March 1805.

38 Ibid, Saturday, 7 September 1805.

39 Ibid, Saturday, 29 July 1809.

40 Ibid, Saturday, 10 September 1814.

41 *Lancaster Gazette*, Saturday, 31 January 1807.

42 Polwhele, Richard. *Traditions and Recollections; Domestic, Clerical, and Literary.* Vol. II. (London, 1826) p. 377.

43 Murphy, Peter, *The English Coast: A History and a Prospect* (Continuum, 2009).

44 *Royal Cornwall Gazette*, Saturday, 12 August 1826.

45 Ibid, 13 December 1828.

46 *Western Courier, West of England Conservative, Plymouth and Devonport Advertiser,* Wednesday, 30 September 1840.

47 *Sherborne Mercury*, 11 March 1843.

48 *Exeter and Plymouth Gazette*, Saturday, 24 May 1845.

49 *Royal Cornwall Gazette*, 23 May 1845.

50 Moyle, Terry, *The Mohegan 1898–1998.*

51 *Royal Cornwall Gazette*, 10 November 1898.

52 *The Cornishman*, 20 October 1898.

53 *Royal Cornwall Gazette*, 23 November 1838.

54 Hepper, David J. *British Warship Losses in the Age of Sail, 1650-1859* (Jean Boudriot, 1994) p. 128.

55 Canon W.A. Diggens archive. Digitised by the St Keverne Local History Society.

56 Lettens, Jan. Wrecksite.

57 *The Tablet of Memory; showing every Memorable Event in History, from the Earliest Period to the Year 1817.* Thirteenth Edition, London, 1818.

58 Mark Milburn, Atlantic Scuba, pers. comm.

59 *Royal Cornwall Gazette*, Saturday, 22 December 1804.

60 Lloyd's List (No. 5532). 10 October 1820.

61 Unknown author. *The Blizzard in the West: Being a Record and Story of the Disastrous Storm Which Raged Throughout Devon and Cornwall, and West*

Somerset, on the Night of March 9th, 1891 (Simpkin, Marshall, Hamilton, Kent and Co., London) pp. 76–77.

62 1892, Board of Trade Casualty Returns, Appendix C, Table 1 71 Page(s) 136(662).

63 *Lake's Falmouth Packet and Cornwall Advertiser*, 1 December 1860.

64 *Lloyd's List*, Friday, 23 March 1810.

65 *Lloyd's List*, 12 March 1841.

66 *Royal Cornwall Gazette*, Friday, 7 October 1859.

67 Defoe, Daniel, *The Storm: or, a Collection of the most Remarkable Casualties and Disasters Which Happened in the Late Dreadful Tempest, Both by Sea and Land* (1705) pp. 196–199.

68 *An Essay on Defensive War, and a Constitutional Militia: with an Account of Queen Elizabeth's Arrangements for Resisting the Projected Invasion in the Year 1588: Taken from Authentic Records in the British Museum, and Other Collections.* London, 1782. p. 65.

69 Strype, John, *Annals of the Reformation and Establishment of Religion, and Other Various Occurrences in the Church of England, During Queen Elizabeth's Happy Reign: Together with an Appendix of Original Papers of State, Records, and Letters* (Clarendon Press, Oxford, 1824) p. 309.

70 Polwhele, Richard, *Traditions and Recollections; Domestic, Clerical, and Literary.* Vol. II. (London, 1826) p. 543.

71 Ibid, p. 377.

72 Hyde, Edward (Earl of Clarendon), *Characters of Eminent Men in the Reigns of Charles I and II* (London, Faulder, 1793) p. 122.

73 Burke, John, *A Genealogical and Heraldic History of the Extinct and Dormant Baronetcies of England, Ireland and Scotland* (London, Scott, Webster, and Geary, 1841) p. 489.

74 Vyvyan, C., *Trelowarren Papers* (1910).

75 Cornwall & Scilly Historic Environment Record, Number: 24445.20.

76 *The Cornishman*, 3 June 1909.

77 Polwhele, Richard, *The History of Cornwall, Civil, Military, Religious* ... Vol. 4–7 (Michel & Company, Ptrs., 1816) p. 101.

78 Stoyle, Mark, 'The Gear Rout': The Cornish Rising of 1648 and the Second Civil War'. *Albion: A Quarterly Journal Concerned with British Studies.* Vol. 32, No. 1 (Spring, 2000) pp. 37–58.

79 Chris Hosken (Meneage Archaeological Group), pers. comm.

80 Polsue, Joseph, *A Complete Parochial History of the County of Cornwall,* Vol. 2 (1865) p. 350.

81 Cornwall & Scilly Historic Environment Record, HER No. 24810.

6 Ebb

1 Sylvia King. pers. comm.

2 Pembroke, Barbara (*nee* Rendle). Unpublished autobiography of a girl who lived in Durgan from 1916–36.

3 *Royal Cornwall Gazette*, Thursday, 15 March 1866.

4 Ibid.

5 Ibid.

6 *West Briton and Cornwall Advertiser*, 30 June 1870.

7 *Royal Cornwall Gazette*, 11 January 1839.

8 *Lake's Falmouth Packet and Cornwall Advertiser*, 7 July 1883.

9 *Royal Cornwall Gazette*, 30 October 1846.

10 *Journal of the Bath and West of England Society*, Vol. XII (W. Ridgway, London, 1864) p. 326.

11 *Royal Cornwall Gazette*, 3 April 1846.

12 Ibid. 10 April 1846.

13 Hall, Herbert Byng, *The Oyster: Where, How, and When to Find, Breed, Cook, and Eat it* (Trubner & Co., London, 1861) pp. 47–48

14 Jacobsen, Rowan, *A Geography of Oysters: The Connoisseur's Guide to Oyster Eating in North America* (Bloomsbury, 2008) p. 22,

15 Marzano, Annelisa, *Harvesting the Sea: The Exploitation of Marine Resources in the Roman Mediterranean* (Oxford University Press, 2013) p. 190.

16 Walker, Harlan (ed.) *Food on the Move: Proceedings of the Oxford Symposium on Food and Cookery, 1996* (Prospect Books, 1997) p. 87.

17 Shepperd, Peggy, *The Story of Port Navas* (Second Edition) pp. 54–55.

18 *Royal Cornwall Gazette*, 25 July, 1812.

19 *Belfast News-Letter*, 16 January 1923.

20 Shepherd, Peggy, Ibid, p.30.

21 Lane, F. Cecil, *The Guide to Falmouth and Helford Harbours: Their Rivers, Creeks, and Adjacent Coasts* (Westcott, Plymouth, 1890).

22 Atkinson, B., *Mining Sites in Cornwall*, Vol. 2, Dyllansow Truran (Truro), 1994.

23 *Royal Cornwall Gazette*, 31 December 1814.

24 Covey, Roger and Hocking, Susan. *Helford River Survey Report* (1987) p. 21.

25 Postlethwayt, Malachy. *The Universal Dictionary of Trade and Commerce* (London, 1774).

26 Cornwall Record Office AR/14/18

27 Frank Timmins, Gweek. pers. comm.

28 Henderson, Charles, and Gilbert Hunter Doble. *A History of the Parish of Constantine in Cornwall:* Compiled from Original Sources by Charles Henderson; Edited by the Rev. GH Doble. Royal Institution of Cornwall, 1937. p. 77.

29 Fulton, Robert, *Report on the Proposed Canal Between the Rivers Heyl and Helford* (1796).

30 *Royal Cornwall Gazette*, 18 September, 1890.

31 Cornwall Record Office. RH/7/13/2/2. Harbour dues, Helford harbour.

32 *Newry Telegraph*, Friday, 18 June 1830.

33 Isham, Ken. *Lime Kilns and Limeburners in Cornwall*. (Cornish Hillside Publications, 2000) pp. 165–170.

34 *Public Ledger and Daily Advertiser*, 15 December 1807.

35 *Lloyd's List*, 2 February 1810.

36 *London Courier and Evening Gazette*, Tuesday, 21 November 1826.

37 *Wolverhampton Chronicle and Staffordshire Advertiser*, 21 January 1835.

38 *Hampshire Chronicle*, 25 November 1805.

39 *The Cornishman*, 6 November 1918.

40 Acton, Viv and Carter, Derek. *Operation Cornwall 1940–1944: The Fal, the Helford and D-Day* (Landfall Publications, 1994) p. 22.

41 Ibid, p. 26.

42 Ibid, p. 30.

43 Butler, Nora. *Looking Down the Years: A Memoir 1919–1945* (Butler Beacham, 1996) p. 81.

44 Cornwall & Scilly Historic Environment Record, HER Nos. 167295, 166392, and 51766.

45 Courtenay, Ashley. *Illustrated Dramatic and Sporting News*, 27 December 1940.

46 Butler, Nora, Ibid.

47 *Life Magazine*, Churchill's Memoirs, 28 February 1949.

48 Richards, Brooks, *Secret Flotillas, Vol. I: Clandestine Sea Operations to Brittany 1940–1944* (Frank Cass, London, 2004).

49 Acton, Viv and Carter, Derek, Ibid, pp. 65–68.

50 Ibid, p. 121.

51 Meudon Document. Author unknown.

52 Covey, Roger and Hocking, Susan, Ibid.

53 Tompsett, Pamela E., *Helford River Survey, Monitoring Report No. 6* (Helford Marine Conservation Group, 2011).

INDEX